RUINS

OF

ROME:

A

GUIDE

TO

THE

CLASSICAL

ANTIQUITIES

RUINS OF ROME
A GUIDE TO THE
CLASSICAL ANTIQUITIES

By C. Wade Meade

PALATINE PUBLICATIONS

Ruston , Louisiana

Library of Congress Catalog Number: 80-81128
Copyright © 1980 by Palatine Publications, Inc.
All Rights Reserved
Printed in the United States
ISBN: 0-936638-00-1
        0-936638-01-X (Paperback)

Dedicated to

Don

The Tiger

PREFACE

Ruins of Rome is the culmination of six summers of field work in Rome, along with countless hours spent in university libraries. The idea for such a book came to me while in Rome in the summer of 1970. At that time I discovered that there was no updated archaeological guide for Rome written in the English Language. This work is an attempt to fill this need.

Many have aided me with the field work and in the preparation of this manuscript. As is usually the case, it is not feasible to mention everyone who aided in such an undertaking, but certain ones must be acknowledged.

I am grateful to Dr. John D'Arms, Director of the American Academy in Rome, and his staff, particularly Ms. Christine White and Ms. Bianca Passeri, for all of their aid and assistance;

to Dr. Teressa Dondero-Bricchi of the Department of Antiquities for granting me permits giving me access to places normally closed to the general public;

to Dawn Meade, my daughter, and Gary Joiner, graduate student at Louisiana Tech, for their field assistance;

to Susan Oldroyd, student of architecture at Columbia University, for her architectural assistance;

to Don Meade, my son, for his drafting of the maps and plans;

to my wife, Marie, for being patient;

to Mrs. Nell Hutchins for typing the final draft of the typescript;

to Becky Irwin for helping finalize the layout of the book and preparing the index;

to Morgan Peoples, Professor of History at Louisiana Tech University, for his painstaking editorial services;

and, finally, to Miss Linda Pardue, my secretary, who went far beyond the call of duty in typing the early drafts, including the one taken from my handwriting, plus, being my "Girl Friday" and carrying out countless duties connected with the preparation of this work.

For the aid rendered by the above and those not mentioned, I am deeply appreciative.

Ruston, Louisiana   C. Wade Meade

January, 1980

CONTENTS

ILLUSTRATIONS

INTRODUCTION

This book was written for use of the professional archaeologist to expand his knowledge of ancient Rome. It is also a tool for the student of history and archaeology who wants to follow the development of the "Eternal City." And finally, it is for the tourist desirous of knowing just what it is he is seeing, and how it came to be.

It is not possible to trace the development of the monuments in chronological order, although this would be the approach preferred by historians and archaeologists. This would involve too much skipping around Rome, thoroughly confusing the tourist and student alike. I have, therefore, discussed the monuments on a regional basis, and in each region, insofar as is possible, used the chronological approach. At the end of the book I have appended a list of monuments in the order of their appearance chronologically. This listing is found in Appendix I.

Each significant monument is described and a brief sketch of its history given. Although this work deals only with the structures of Ancient Rome, their history is traced on through medieval time and into the modern period of history. Many of these ancient monuments played a prominent role in political affairs of Medieval Rome.

Dates are usually given for kings, emperors, or popes who are associated with the various antiquities. To place these personalities in their proper perspective, lists are included in the appendices. Appendix II gives a list of the kings and emperors, while Appendix III lists the popes.

Rome has her share of museums that are filled with her own treasures, as well as those of other lands. A list of the more pertinent museums makes up Appendix IV. After the Appendices a glossary is included, making it easier to understand the terms that are unfamiliar to many.

Chapter 1 gives the geographic and prehistoric setting of Rome. Although this material is important for an understanding of the development of Rome, those who are not interested may skip this chapter. To really see and to be able to remember what one has seen, the individual needs about six to eight weeks in Rome. Many are not able to stay this long, therefore, they will have to be selective in what they wish to observe. The reader may then pick out the chapters relevant to his tour of the city.

One thing that should be kept in mind is that the monuments close at different times and on different days. Even when one has the schedule, he may find that it is closed for repairs, and not always with any prior announcement.

Before agreeing to your tour, be sure the travel agent procures for you a tourist card that allows you free access to all state operated museums and monuments. This card costs you about $5.00, and can save you some money. For the professional archaeologist you can receive permits from the

Superintendent of Antiquities. To secure this permit you need a letter from your university or other institution. These permits can give you access to places not open to the general public. There are several offices in Rome, but the best place to start is the Soprintendente alle Antichita di Roma, Foro Romana, Rome.

Although one benefits from walking, it is no disgrace to catch a bus. Transportation in Rome is very economical, bus fare at this writing is only 100 lire (about 12 cents). Before beginning any tour, be sure you have a city map that has all the bus routes marked.

It is important to dress comfortably before beginning a day of sightseeing. Pay particular attention to shoes. Be sure you have a pair of comfortable walking shoes. They should be soft and flexible, but give support. Ladies will be more comfortable in slacks. They must be careful that their shoulders are not bare when entering a church. If you dress comfortably, eat and drink moderately, get sufficient rest, and don't overdo the sightseeing at first, you will find that your stay in Rome will be nothing but pure pleasure.

CHAPTER 1

The Setting

Many different cultural groups inhabited Italy before the Romans united the country under their control. Certain members of these groups exerted more influence on the Romans than did others. Before scrutinizing these early populations, we need to look at the physical features of Italy and the vicinity of Rome.

Rome and Italy

Italy, or the greater portion of it, is a boot-shaped peninsula extending into the Mediterranean Sea. It is bounded on the north by Switzerland and Austria, on the east by Yugoslavia and the Adriatic Sea, on the south by the Ionian Sea, and on the west by the Tyrrhenian and Ligurian Seas and France. Lying off the coast of Italy are the three large islands of Sicily, Sardinia, and Corsica. The latter island is the property of France, while Sicily and Sardinia belong to Italy. The land of Italy is made up of mountains, valleys, and plains. In continental Italy we find a mountain range known as the Italian Alps. The Apennine Mountains start in northwest peninsular Italy as an east-west trending range south of the Po Valley, then abruptly turn southward, forming the backbone of the Italian Peninsula. Major rivers of Italy are the Po, Arno, and Tiber. For political purposes Italy is divided into nineteen regions (regiones), which in turn are subdivided into ninety-two provinces (provincie). Many of the regional names are holdovers from classical times.

Physiographically, earth scientists divide Italy into the three areas of (1) North, (2) Central, and (3) South. The southern boundary of North Italy is the 44° parallel, lying just north of Florence (Firenze). North Italy contains the high-rising Italian Alps, attaining heights of over 15,000 feet. Just to the south of the Alps, lies the Po Valley Plain. This large plain slopes gently on each side toward the river. South of this plain we find the Apennine Mountains that trend southeastward until they reach the center of the peninsula, then they turn in a more southerly direction. Political regions lying wholly within North Italy are Liguria, Piedmont, Valle D'Aosta, Lombardy, Trentino-Alto Adige, Friuli-Venezia Giulia, Venetia, and Emilia-Romagna.

Central Italy encompasses land lying between the 44° and about the 41° latitudes. In this area the Apennines are a land of deep valleys and hills with narrow coastal plains. There is a much wider plain, dotted with hills as we move into the vicinity of Rome. Political regions are Tuscany, Marche, Umbria, Abruzzi-Molise, and Latium (Lazio).

The city of Rome is located at the very edge of Latium (modern Lazio) on the Tiber River. Rome developed on the left bank of the Tiber, spreading later to the right bank. The Tiber separated Latium from Etruria (modern Tuscany).

About forty miles from where the river empties into the sea, the Tiber enters a plain that is dotted with hills. This plain is referred to as Latium. The mountains continue on the left side of the Tiber, trending in a southeasterly direction, referred to as the Sabine Hills. There is a break in the ridge to let the Anio River flow through, after which the highlands are referred to as Monti Prenestini, lying almost due east of Rome. The ridge then trends in a southwesterly direction. South-southeast of Rome another pass creates a gap in the ridge, which then continues on to the sea as the Alban Hills.

Even along the Tiber the plain is dotted with hills. To the north of Rome lies the hills known as the Northern Heights. This highland continues on down into Rome, forming the hills of Rome. According to legend Rome was founded on seven hills, but in reality there are more than seven. Some of the so-called "seven hills" are actually spurs of the same ridge. The original seven hills of Rome were the Palatine, Quirinal, Esquiline, Caelian, Capitoline, Aventine, and Viminal.

The ridge known as the Northern Heights gives off a large southwest trending spur called the Pincian. This ridge continues into ancient Rome where it is called the Esquiline, which in turn gives off four spurs known as the Quirinal, Viminal, Cespian, and Oppian. Isolated from this tableland are the Aventine, Caelian, Palatine, and Capitoline Hills. As the Tiber nears the Pincian it makes a sharp bend to the right before continuing southward. The large plains area formed by this bend of the river is referred to as the Campus Martius. Across the river on the right bank we find the Vatican and Janiculum Hills.

Today the hills of Rome do not have the elevation they did in ancient times, because of erosion and the labors of man. The areas between the hills have been elevated due to the accumulation of detritus and debris over the centuries. The actual street level of ancient Rome is from 5.5m. (18.0 ft.) to 9.0m. (29.5 ft.) below the street level today. These are only average figures and in some areas these numbers are less, while in others they are higher.

Prehistoric Italy

In Italy the Paleolithic age extends from 500,000 B.P. (Before Present) down to about 5,000 B.C. The Lower Paleolithic with chronological limits of 500,000 to about 30,000 B.P. contains two representatives of early man. Neanderthal man (*Homo neandertalensis*) had made his appearance between 125,000 and 100,000 B.P. In Italy his remains have been discovered at Saccopastore and La Ferassie. About 30,000 B.P. *Homo sapiens*, or early modern

5

FIGURE 2

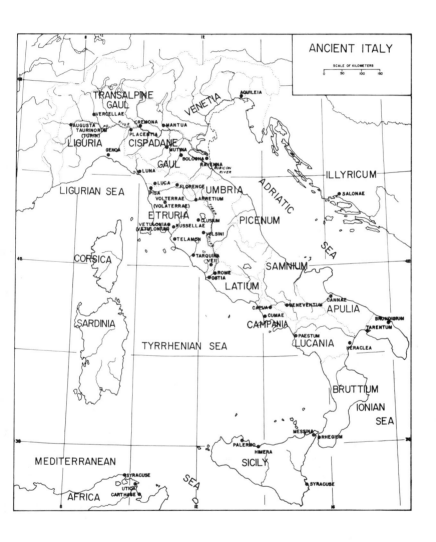

Map of Ancient Italy

man, arrived upon the scene. Two primitive races of early modern man inhabited Italy. These two were Cro-Magnon (named from a French cave) and Grimaldi (from an Italian cave) Men.

About 30,000 years ago the Lower yielded to the Upper Paleolithic. Around 25,000 B.P. Neanderthal Man had departed the scene, becoming extinct for some unknown reason. In this span of time some men began to move out from caves and rock shelters, constructing pit dwellings in the plains. Early traces of religion are revealed by the techniques of burial, as the body was prepared for some type of afterlife. Art was developed in the Upper Paleolithic. Figurines have been found at Grimaldi, while cave paintings have been discovered in Apulia.

In Italy the Neolithic age began around 5,000 B.C. This was the period of time when technology made great advances, and plants and animals were domesticated. It is also an age when Italy began to receive migrants. About 2500 B.C. a cultural group moved into northern Italy from North Africa via Spain. They settled also in southern France and western Switzerland. Owing to their practice of building their houses on stilts in the waters of lakes, they are referred to as the Lake-Dwellers. These Lake-Dwellers were an agricultural people, but still engaged in hunting and fishing on a large scale. They practiced inhumation, or burial of their dead.

Not too long after the arrival of the Lake-Dwellers, another band of migrants from the Iberian Peninsula began settling in the Po Valley. These people were skilled metal workers, who engaged in trade and commerce. One of their most numerous types of pottery was a bell-shaped beer mug. Because so many of these mugs have been uncovered, this group is now referred to as the Bell-Beaker people. They also practiced inhumation in disposing of their dead.

Around the year 2000 B.C. an Indo-European people, warlike in nature, arrived from the Balkan Peninsula. They settled in Central Italy in areas that later came to be called Tuscany and Latium. These people were an agricultural group, who also engaged in much hunting and fishing. Like the other two groups they practiced inhumation.

The use of bronze was widespread in Italy by about 1800 B.C., bringing the Neolithic to a close and introducing the Bronze Age. As the Bronze Age unfolds there seems to be three distinct cultures present in Italy. In the lake regions of the Alpine foothills we find the Lake-Dwellers. The Po Valley is inhabited by the Bell-Beaker people. Throughout most of the remainder of the peninsula the Balkan migrants have established a culture known as the Apennine. This latter culture had begun to produce very beautiful and highly decorated pottery.

About 1700 B.C. a new group of settlers pushed into the Po Valley, probably from Hungary. This group is called the Terremare people, taking their name from the mounds in Emilia. The Terremare people developed advanced techniques of agriculture. They made some of the finest pottery

FIGURE 3

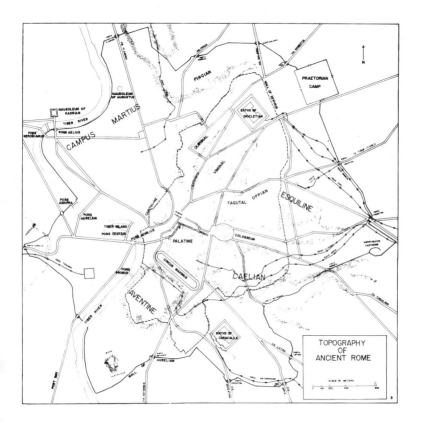

Map of Topography of Rome

found in prehistoric Italy. At first these people seemed to practice inhumation, but toward the close of the Bronze Age began cremation of their dead, burying their ashes in urns.

Another group from the Balkans moved into Central Italy around 1000 B.C. They are referred to as the Villanovans, taking their name from a village near Bologna where their culture was first discovered. The Villanovans settled in Etruria (Tuscany) and Latium. Cremation was practiced by the Villanovans. The ashes of the dead were buried in urns shaped like helmets, or like round and square huts. This group remained in Latium, but most of them were forced out of Etruria, probably by the Etruscans, around 700 B.C. This latter group then settled around Bologna.

More Balkan peoples followed shortly after the Villanovans, settling the west coast of Italy from about Rome southward to Calabria. They are referred to as the Fossa people, because of their practice of inhumation. With the exception of this practice, their culture was very similar to the Villanovans.

Perhaps as early as 1000 B.C. there was settlement on the site of Rome. The first village developed seems to have been on the Palatine Hill. Later Romans called this first village the Roma Quadrata. Of all the hills the steep Palatine was the most defensible. It also overlooked a ford across the Tiber. This village settled by the Latins had easy access to the salt pans to the north. Evidently the Latins were a group of Villanovans.

Shortly after this three other hills were settled. Latin tribes built villages on the Quirinal and Caelian hills. Another group, the Sabines, founded a village on the Esquiline. There is much scholarly debate as to the ancestors of the Sabines. Because they practiced inhumation, some scholars feel they descended from the Fossa people. All that can be stated for certain is that the Sabines, who were closely akin to the Latins, buried their dead while the Latins cremated. The marshy land between the hills was used as a burial ground for all four tribes. As the Iron Age began about 800 B.C., four of the seven hills of Rome had been settled.

An important group of new settlers made their appearance in Italy around 800 B.C. These people, the Etruscans, probably came from Asia Minor, although the place of their origin is much disputed. The Etruscans settled first along the west coast and then penetrated inland. Etruria was the name given to the land they occupied. They would control more than just the area known as Etruria. Their culture was modified both by the Greeks and the Villanovans.

The Etruscans quickly established a flourishing civilization that reached northward to the Po River, bounded on the east by the crest of the Apennines and the Tiber River, and southward their boundary was the Tiber River. Later they would spread their influence into the growing city of Rome and further southward. A series of strong city states was established by the Etruscans, each headed by its own king. Some of the more important

Etruscan cities were Tarquinia, Veii, Orvieto, Volterra, Fiesole, Caere, Vulci, Vetulonia, Rusellae, Clusium, Volsinii, Perugia, and Arretium. Rome would be influenced a great deal by the Etruscan culture.

According to tradition the city of Rome was founded in the year 753 B.C. At least four of the hills were occupied, however, shortly after 1000 B.C. We can deduce that about 753 the three villages of the Palatine united under one king to form the city. In this respect archaeological evidence seems to bear out tradition. From 753 B.C. on we can speak of Rome as a city, although a small one for many years to come.

Shortly after the unification of the three villages, Greek colonists began to settle along the southern coast of Italy. Their settlements along the shores reached from Ostia in the west to Cannae on the Adriatic coast. Hellenic civilization spread into central and southern Italy, and even affected the Etruscans.

As the 8th Century B.C. ended the Greeks occupied the coastal areas of southern Italy, between the Po and the Tiber and west of the Apennines lay the great Etruscan cities, Rome was developing, and native Italic tribes remained unmolested in the remainder of the peninsula. Despite their independence these tribes were influenced by Greeks and Etruscans.

CHAPTER 2

The Palatine Hill

The best site to start an archaeological tour of Rome is the Palatine Hill. For this is where Roman civilization began, a fact the ancient Romans never forgot. While there are several entrances to the Palatine, only one is now open to the public. To gain access to the Palatine, we enter at the entrance to the Forum, located across the street from the intersection of Via de Fori Imperiali and Via Cavour. After entering the Forum we walk down the incline, turn left on the Sacra Via and walk to the Arch of Titus, then turn right at the arch, walk a few steps, turn right and take the steps up to the Farnese Gardens.

Emerging at the top of the second flight of stairs, we find ourselves in the *Farnese Gardens* (*Horti Farnesiani*). These beautiful grounds are actually "hanging gardens," built over the structures of the Palace of Tiberius. At the top of the stairs, we find the loggia of the *Casino Farnese.* It is worth the time to step into the loggia and gaze out upon the eastern end of the Forum, where we are able to see the Basilica of Constantine, the Arch of Titus, the Colosseum, and many other structures. Next we take a walk into the gardens, turn right at the first path, following it all the way to the northwest corner of the hill. Here we have a magnificent view of the northern end of the Forum, the Capitoline Hill, the Victor Emanuele Monument, and other imposing structures.

After enjoying this view, we should then turn to the left and follow the path along the side of the hill southward, arriving at a flight of stairs at the edge of the gardens. Another view confronts us; this one looking off to the Theater of Marcellus, the Tiber River, St. Peter's, etc. Glancing over the edge of the stairs, we see the remains of the large temple dedicated to Cybele. If we descend the stairs and go around to the opposite side of the temple, we will find stairs to take us to the top of the temple to this Near Eastern goddess. Arriving at the top of the temple we find a piece of marble to sit upon in the shade of the ilex trees. Here in the area of the oldest monuments on the hill, we can review the history of the Palatine Hill.

The Palatine Hill rises sharply on three sides, making it easily defensible. It covers an area of about 25 acres, and at the highest point (at the church of S. Bonaventura) reaches about 51.8m. (170 ft.) above sea level. In ancient times the hill was not flat as it appears today, but was divided into three summits with hollows in between. The three peaks or summits are: the Cermalus, which is the area where we are sitting; the Palatium, in the area of S. Bonaventura and the north end of the so-called Stadium of Domitian; and finally, the Velia. This last summit is occupied by the Arch of Titus, and no longer considered a part of the Palatine, but rather of the Forum. The Velia provided the gently sloping side of the hill.

About 1000 B.C., as the Bronze Age was drawing to a close, Latin tribes began to settle on the Palatine. One tribe settled the Cermalus, one the Palatium, and the third took over the Velia. According to tradition these three tribes, the Ramnies, the Tities, and the Luceres united to form the small town of Rome. Tradition tells us that the date was April 21, 753 B.C. The king of the united tribes was Romulus. This new king probably built a wall of tufa around his new city and called it the Roman Quadrata. Later, Sabine tribes were added, and eventually many more hills incorporated.

Romulus probably retained his residence on the Palatine. The second king of Rome, the Sabine Numa Pompilius, evidently moved the royal residence to the Regia in the Forum. Although the Palatine had lost the royal residence after about 715 B.C. it probably had several important temples which made the hill a place of importance. When the Republic began in 509 B.C., the Forum and the Capitoline were the major political and religious areas of Rome.

About 150 B.C., moving into the late Republic, the Palatine became a fashionable residential area. Prominent home owners over the years included Hortensius the Orator, Sulla, Cicero, Crassus, Clodius, Milo, and Antony, to mention a few. Augustus had his residence here when he became emperor in 27 B.C. The Palatine became the seat of the emperors from this time on. Tiberius built the first palace, but the later rulers continued to build so that by the end of Domitian's administration in 96, the imperial palaces almost covered the entire hill. Envoys from the Mediterranean nations paid their homage on what had become the seat of the world.

With the shifting of the capital to Constantinople by Constantine in 330, the structures of the Palatine began to fall into disrepair. The emperors of the West kept an official residence on the hill, although many ruled from northern Italy. Theodoric, the great king of the Ostrogoths (483-526) who ruled Italy in the late 5th and early 6th Centuries, evidently kept the buildings repaired. Narses the Byzantine governor of Rome resided on the hill in 570. He stripped the palaces of much of the art work, which he carried back to Constantinople. The Byzantine emperor, Heraclius, may have had himself crowned on the Palatine in 629 after his recapture of Jerusalem from the Sassanids. This theory, however, is disputed by scholars.

Pope John VII (705-707) moved his residence to the Palace of Tiberius in the 8th Century. In the next century Greek monks built a monastery in the Domus Augustiana. They constructed the Church of S. Caesarius in the so-called Stadium of Domitian. Shortly before 1000, Latin monks established a monastery on the hill. In the 11th Century the Palatine, for the most part, was a jumble of ruins, gardens, and vineyards. From time to time the popes of the 12th Century were forced to seek refuge on the hill. According to reports

FIGURE 4

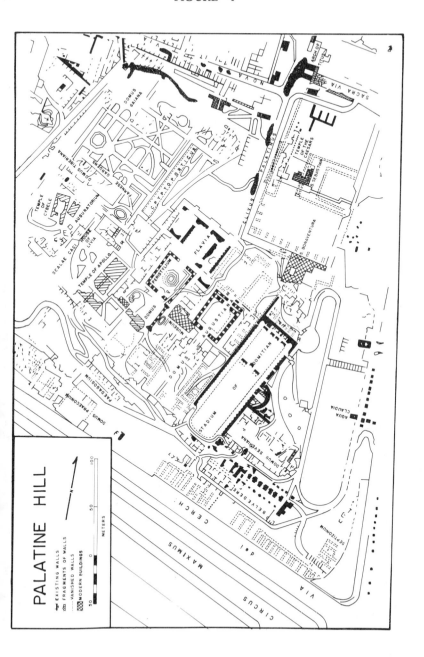

Plan of the Palatine Hill

from travelers in the 15th Century, the Palatine was probably the most desolate hill in Rome.

In the 16th Century Cardinal Alexander Farnese, nephew of Pope Paul III (1534-1549), purchased the central and western portions of the hill and developed the beautiful gardens. After his death the gardens passed into the hands of the Duke of Parma. Between 1720 and 1730 the Farnese Excavations began, but the goal was strictly to obtain art objects. In the 19th Century the first systematic excavations began on the hill. Napoleon III acquired the Farnese Gardens in 1860 and Pietro Rosa began his excavations. The Italian government took over the property in 1870, and at the close of the century such excavators as Boni, Lanciani, and others had revealed much of the mysteries of the imperial residences.

Moving down the stairs from the top of the temple we see slightly to our left an area being excavated. From the evidence uncovered it appears this was an ancient market place. Looking down into the excavation area one can see the site of the *House of Romulus* (*Casa di Romuli*). Actually there are remains of three of the huts, all excavated in 1948, so we can't be absolutely sure which was the House of Romulus. They were elliptical in shape measuring almost 4.88 by 3.35m (16 x 11 ft.). The holes cut into the rock seated the poles that supported the roof. According to classical writers the hut was made of sticks and reeds with a thatched roof. The hut was kept in good repair as late as the days of Augustus. According to Roman legend, this is the hut where Romulus and Remus were brought up. Perhaps, after Romulus became king of a unified Rome in 753 B.C., he continued to live in his thatched hut.

Immediately to the left of the hut area we see a steep roadway ascending the hill from the valley of the Circus Maximus. The lower part is not apparent, as it is covered by buildings from the Imperial period. This path is known as the *Scalae Caci* (*Steps of Cacus*), named after the legendary giant who lived in the vicinity. At the top of the steps the remains of the primitive fortifications and gate can be seen. The walls, or *Murus Romuli*, were made of flat blocks of tufa, part of which can still be seen. The gate posts are made of travertine, but this is probably a restoration from the early Imperial period. There were evidently three gates that gave access to the Roman Quadrata in the Regal period. There was the one just mentioned at the head of the Scalae Caci, the *Porta Romanula*, and the *Porta Mugonia.* The former gate was located on the Clivus Victoriae near the corner of the Domus Tiberiana, while the Porta Mugonia was somewhere between the summits of the Palatium and Velia. Plutarch tells us that Romulus lived beside the Scalae Caci.

At the top of the steps of Cacus there is an archaic cistern. To the left of this one, about 9m (29.5 ft.) away, we observe another cistern. At one time they may have been wells.

Turning our backs to the cisterns and looking toward the Temple of

Cybele, we see between us and the temple a smaller structure. This is the *Auguratorium.* The structure, roughly rectangular, measures approximately 12.20 by 7.32m. (40 x 24 ft.). At the highest corner it attains a height of almost 2.13m. (7.0 ft.). One can see the remains of two rooms. The present substructure dates from the time of Hadrian.

The original structure, however, probably dates back to the time of Romulus. This was supposedly the site where Romulus took the auspices by looking to the south and observing the flight of birds. Later the College of Augurs would look for omens from the flights of the birds, always from the Auguratorium. Before the occurence of any important event, the augurs took the auspices. In the late Regal Period and Early Republic, after the major religious sites had been shifted to the Forum and Capitoline, the Auguratorium retained its importance. It was probably destroyed in the great fire of 3 A.D. For the next century and a quarter the building probably remained in ruins. Finally, about the year 136, the emperor Hadrian had the Auguratorium rebuilt. This is evidenced by a stamped brick found in the structure. It probably never again attained the popularity that it held prior to the fire of 3 A.D.

Walking around the Auguratorium, we find ourselves again at the *Temple of Cybele (Aedes Magnae Deum Matris)*. The temple measures about 33.22 by 17.07m. (109 x 56 ft.), oriented similar to the Auguratorium, but not identical. To reach the podium we climb the recessed stairs. At the top of the stairs there originally stood the statue of Cybele.

In 206 B.C., during the Second Punic War with Hannibal ravaging the Italian Peninsula, the pontifical college consulted the *Sibylline Books.* From this consultation the interpreted signs bade them make a journey to Asia Minor. Envoys were sent to Pessinus where they were given a fragment of a black meteorite. In 203 B.C. the Romans began construction of the temple, complete with the statue of Cybele. The black stone was inserted into the statue, composing the face of the Great Mother. After completion in 191 B.C., the temple was formally dedicated. This sanctuary remained as a symbol of Rome's victory over Hannibal.

A fire partially destroyed the temple in 111 B.C. The consul Q. Caecilius Metellus rebuilt the shrine to the goddess during his consulship in 109 B.C. Another great fire destroyed the structure in 3 A.D. Augustus rebuilt it in this same year. The podium that remains probably dates to the time of Augustus. According to one writer, Elagabalus (218-222) committed sacrilege by removing the meteorite from the face of Cybele to his private chapel. Excavations of the early 19th century uncovered the temple, but it was not identified until 1873, a feat accomplished by Lanciani and Visconti. In 1950 the headless statue of the goddess was discovered in the vicinity, and it now rests in one of the vaults of the Palace of Tiberius.

Turning from the Temple of Cybele and walking past the Auguratorium and the cistern to the left, we find ourselves at a small, but well preserved house. This is the so-called *House of Livia* (*Casa di Livia*). It is called the House of Livia because of an inscription discovered there on a lead pipe. Careful study has revealed that this was the home of Augustus, who resided there with his wife, Livia. Some scholars prefer to call it the *House of Augustus* (*Domus Augusti*).

The house was discovered by Rosa in 1869 and for a period of time after that referred to as the *Domus Germanici* (*House of Germanicus*). An analysis of the masonry dates the building to the middle of the 1st Century B.C. Octavianus probably bought the house in 44 B.C., not long after it had been built, from Hortensius the Orator. After he became the first emperor as Augustus (27 B.C. - 14 A.D.) in 27 B.C. he maintained his residence there. The house was later incorporated into the Domus Tiberiana. Measurements for the structure are approximately 22.9 by 19.8m. (75 x 65 ft.), the long axis trending in a northwest-southeast direction.

Access to the house is gained by the original stairs on the east side. Descending the stairs we find ourselves in a small atrium or courtyard. The doors may be locked, in which case the custodian who stays in the vicinity will let us in. After passing through the door into the atrium, we find straight ahead of us the three rooms of the *Tablinum*, or reception rooms. To the right is the *Triclinium* or dining room. The most fascinating view given us in the House of Livia is of the beautiful wall paintings. While they are somewhat faded, they are still very beautiful to the eye of the art lover. The central theme of the Triclinium is a garden scene. We see trees and fruit depicted through an open window. Of all the paintings the most beautiful are to be found in the central hall of the Tablinum. In this room we see scenes depicting the adventures of the beautiful priestess Io, favorite of Jupiter; a street scene in Rome; and Cyclops Polyphemus in a marine surrounding.

The other twelve rooms, a long hallway, and a courtyard to the south are not open to the general public. They are at a higher level than the area just described, and may have been added by Augustus at a later date. In the southern courtyard there are graves, dating back to the late Bronze or early Iron ages. These other rooms and structures may have been added after the great fire of 3 A.D. that destroyed the house as well as the Auguratorium and Temple of Cybele.

After coming out of the House of Livia, and making a left turn, skirting the building and observing the area of the home not accessible to the public, we then find ourselves at the *Temple of Apollo* (*Aedes Apollo Palatinus*). All that remains today are the podium and a long flight of stairs. The structure is closed to the general public. Many of the 19th Century and early 20th Century archaeologists called it the *Temple of Jupiter Victor*, but recent study confirms it to be the Temple of Apollo. The long axis which measures about 43.90m. (144 ft.) in length is aligned in a northeast-southwest direction; the width is approximately 24.70m. (81 ft.).

Augustus (Octavianus) ordered construction of the temple to begin in 36

B.C. in honor of his victory over Sextus Pompey. Construction was completed in 28 B.C., and the temple was officially dedicated on October 9 of that year. According to the classical writers, the temple contained a large library with one section given to a collection of Greek works and the other to Latin. This library and most of the superstructures of the temple were destroyed by a fire on the night of March 18, 363.

Retracing our steps past the House of Livia, we find ourselves back at the large structure from which we descended to begin our tour of the hill. This large edifice, covered by the Farnese Gardens, is the *Domus Tiberiana* (*House of Tiberius*). When Tiberius (14-37) became emperor in 14, his mother Livia was still living in the House of Augustus (Livia). Tiberius decided to build himself a larger dwelling, that befitted an emperor. This would be the residence of the emperor while in Rome. From 26 till his death in 37, Tiberius resided on the island of Capri. When Caligula (37-41) became emperor in 37, he extended the palace to the edge of the Forum, in fact, he enclosed the Temple of Castor. The two palaces were probably separated by the Clivus Victoriae, which bisected the single unit structure we now see. A great deal of the structure was destroyed by the fire of 80. After Domitian (81-96) came to power in 81, he rebuilt the two palaces, but made them into one structure. From the valley floor he constructed a three tiered facade, facing the Capitoline Hill. Domitian also constructed a balcony along the Forum side. Hadrian (117-138) extended the palace northward into the Forum in the 2nd Century, all the way to the House of the Vestal Virgins.

Before reclimbing the stairs to the Farnese Gardens and the top of the palace, we shall observe the side of the building from the House of Livia to the edge of the hill to the east. The ruins that almost touch the Auguratorium are probably remains of *Guard Rooms* built by Trajan (97-117) and Hadrian in the 2nd century. In one of the alcoves, we see the headless statue of Cybele, that once rested in her temple. After climbing the stairs, we are now in the Gardens and atop the palace. Although hard to detect because of the Farnese Gardens, the palace forms a rectangle that measures about 180 by 120m. (590.5 x 393.7 ft.). The long axis trends in a northeasterly-southwesterly direction.

Near the corner of the palace overlooking the House of Livia, we see the remains of a large fishtank. We are also able to see the remains of an ancient stairway. Moving towards the center of the gardens, we note that we are standing above the Peristyle, which is still full of earth. Further excavations have not been carried out because of the presence of the beautiful gardens.

With permits archaeologists are permitted to descend to a lower level at the northwest corner near the Forum. The custodian will allow us to descend the stairs that are now locked to tourists. This area was open to the public until 1971. Although the entire structure is referred to as the Domus Tiberiana, this area up to the Forum is more properly known as the *Domus Gaiana* (*House of Gaius*), as it was added by Caligula (Gaius). These rooms and passages are built over the Clivus Victoriae, which was one of the principal roads that led to the Palatine. The road supposedly got its name from the *Temple of Victory* (*Templum Victoriae*) built along the road. Remains of the temple have not been identified, but it was probably in the vicinity of where we are standing. The remains were enclosed when Domitian connected the two palaces. A stairway still connects the Domus Tiberiana with the House of the Vestal Virgins.

We can either retrace our steps, or follow the Clivus Victoriae to the base of the Casino Farnese. Either way there is a climb back to the fountain in the gardens. Between the loggia and the fountain is another stairway, which upon descending, puts us in an underground passage. This passageway is the *Cryptoporticus* that runs the entire length of the eastern side of the Domus Tiberiana. At the bottom of the stairs we find the left portion blocked off. We should turn right for a few paces and then make another right turn. At this point we see an opening to the sky overhead and to the east an exit to the outside. To our left we see a long passage that terminates near the House of Livia. Earlier writers felt that the assassination of Caligula occurred here in 41, but this is not possible, as the Cryptoporticus was built by Nero.

After Nero (54-68) became emperor in 54 he built the *Domus Transitoria* that sprawled from the Palatine to the Esquiline, connecting the Domus Tiberiana with the Gardens of Maecenas. The Cryptoporticus connected various sections of the two palaces. Near the end of the long passage way there is another passage to the left that leads to the Domus Flavia. From this point on, the ceiling is very beautifully decorated.

After studying the stucco decorations of the ceiling, we now retrace our steps to the passage on our right and follow it to the surface. This part of the Cryptoporticus probably connected the Domus Tiberiana with the Domus Transitoria. It was probably restored by Domitian to connect his new palace with that of Tiberius. When emerging from the Cryptoporticus into the open air we find ourselves in what was a hallway of the *Domus Flavia* (*Flavian Palace*).

The Domus Transitoria was destroyed by the fire of 64. Nero then built his great Domus Aurea on the Oppian Hill, where he resided after 67. Vespasian (69-79) restored the imperial residence to the Palace of Tiberius in 70. When Domitian succeeded Titus in 81, he had his architect Rabirius draw up plans for a new palace. The ruins of the Domus Transitoria plus some houses of the 1st Century B.C. lay in the hollow between the Cermalus and the Palatium. Using the remains for substructures, the Domus Flavia was built over the area, leveling off the appearance of the hill. The new palace was probably not used as a residence but as a site for official government functions, such as state banquets, receptions, and a place to receive foreign dignitaries.

To our left, after emerging from the Cryptoporticus, the area is off limits, but with our permits we are able with the custodian to explore the

PLATE 1

A. Temple of Cybele

B. Auguratorium

PLATE 2

A. Domus Tiberiana

B. Cryptoporticus of D. Tiberiana

PLATE 3

A. Domus Flavia

B. Domus Augustiana

PLATE 4

A. Stadium of Domitian

B. Domus Severiana

area. The ruins of a large room to our immediate left are the remains of the *Basilica*, where citizens may have pleaded for the emperor to intervene personally in their cases. From the remains we can see that the Basilica was divided into three naves by Corinthian columns.

A most interesting room lies under the Basilica. To get to this room an ordinary permit will not suffice; special permission must be obtained. If this permission is granted the custodian will take us downstairs and through a locked gate. This brings us into a long chamber known as the *Aula Isiaca* (*Hall of Isis*). The walls were originally painted with Egyptian scenes dedicated to the goddess Isis. This goddess from the Nileland was very popular in Rome from the mid-2nd Century B.C. onward. The paintings have been removed to protect them, and to let the public view them. In its present shape the room measures about 13 by 2.6m (40 x 8.5 ft.), but originally it was 13 by 7.6m (40 x 25 ft.). There were no paintings on the right wall, which was made of brick.

Although there have been disputes among scholars, there is general agreement that the decorations of the chamber date to the reign of Caligula. Either in 37 or 38 Caligula established the temple in the open courtyard of one of the private homes. The courtyard was roofed and a hall of worship was created. When Nero began to build his palace after 54, he had a cistern built that cut off about two-thirds of the area of the Aula Isiaca. The right wall of brick is the west wall of the cistern. After construction of the Domus Flavia, Domitian, who was fond of Isis, probably repaired the room. It was he who built the stair that connected the chamber with the Basilica.

Returning to the Basilica, we move on to the next room, the *Aula Regia* (*Throne Room*). Here the emperor sat upon his throne and received foreign dignitaries. This room was decorated with sixteen magnificent columns and twelve black basalt statues resting in wall niches. In 1949 Dr. Vianello discovered the tombs of two unknown children beneath the Aula Regia. They date from the end of the Regal Period or from the early Republic.

Moving to the next room, we find ourselves in the *Lararium*, which was the private chapel for the imperial family. Statues of the deities who protected the household were kept in this chamber. Beneath the Lararium lie two more interesting rooms. With our permit the custodian will take us through the gate and down the stairs. At the bottom of the steps we find ourselves in two rooms of a private mansion dating to the 1st century B.C. Turning left into the second room, we find paintings of griffins on the wall. From these paintings the house takes its name, *Casa dei Grifi* (*House of the Griffins*).

After our return upstairs, we turn our back to the Aula Regia and walk out of the hall into the *Peristylium* (*Peristyle*). In the center of the Peristyle we can still see the large octagonal shaped fountain. This inner court was surrounded by columns, and according to Suetonius the walls were covered with Cappadocian marble. This marble was so shiny that the walls were like mirrors. This was a favorite spot of Domitian, for here no assassin could sneak up behind him. On each side of the Peristyle the remains of rooms can be detected. The six small rooms on the left (facing the Aula Regia) were probably bathrooms and cloak rooms. To the right are the three rooms that made up the *Tablinum.*

From the Peristyle we pass to the *Triclinium* or great banquet hall. Traces of the colored marble that paved the floor can still be seen in places. On both sides of the Triclinium are elliptic fountains. Beneath the western fountain we are able to see a beautiful pavement that was part of Nero's palace. If we get the custodian to take us down the stairs and through the locked gate we can see some of the remains of the Domus Transitoria lying beneath the Peristylium and Triclinium. Here are the remains of the *Nymphaeum* that was destroyed in the fire of 64. We can also see the remains of a servant's latrine, situated to the northeast of the Nymphaeum. Domitian built the Domus Flavia over these structures, using the walls for foundation support.

Returning up the stairs, we move from the Triclinium to the area to the south where a few structures still stand. These rooms probably constituted the library. Domitian may have simply incorporated the libraries of the Temple of Apollo into his great palace.

If we move eastward (Circus Maximus to the right) we come next to the ruins of the Domus Augustiana. Archaeologists refer to the entire grouping of imperial palaces, with the exception of the Domus Tiberiana, as the Domus Augustiana. This all encompassing term includes: (1) the Domus Augustiana proper, (2) the Domus Flavia, (3) the Stadium of Domitian, (4) the Palace or Baths of Septimius Severus, (5) the Paedagogium, and (6) the Domus Praeconum. The Domus Augustiana was a continuation of the Domus Flavia. This latter edifice was for state receptions and banquets, while the former was the private residence of the imperial family. Rabirius may have completed the Domus Augustiana about the year 85. In the 16th century architects and archaeologists began to study the magnificent structure.

We now find ourselves standing on the second floor of the Domus Augustiana, looking down into the *Atrium* or inner courtyard of the palace. This atrium can be viewed from three sides, showing us the remains of a fountain at the lower level. At the north end of the atrium we see the *Palatine Museum (Museo del Palatino).* It is worth the time to take off a half hour and visit the museum. In it can be found artifacts from Palatine excavations, plus plans showing what the hill must have looked like in antiquity. To the east of the museum is the locked room where the paintings from the Aula Isiaca are kept. It is also worth the time to have the custodian allow us to view these paintings.

If we show the custodian our permits, he will escort us to the lower level of the imperial residence. We enter by descending the stairs behind the museum, and passing through the locked gate. After a closer look at the ruins of the fountain in the atrium, we can leisurely wander around the rooms of the palace. Many of these served as bedrooms. On the ceilings are several paintings from as late as the Renaissance period.

After our tour of the first floor rooms, it is best to exit at the southeast corner through a door that leads into the *Stadium of Domitian (Hippodromus Palatii)*. This structure built by Domitian as a part of the Domus Augustiana measures about 160 by 47.2m. (525 x 155 ft.). Scholars have debated whether it was a stadium or a garden. When built by Domitian it was probably used as a garden. From the bases of columns, we can deduce that a colonnaded walk-way encircled the gardens. At each end of the stadium the remains of semicircular fountains can be seen. The two storied portico on the east side was built by Hadrian in the 2nd Century. At the end of the century Septimius Severus built the *Imperial Box (Exedra)*, which could indicate that he was converting the garden into a small arena for private shows. At the southwest end of the stadium we can see the ruins of an elliptical enclosure. From a study of the bricks, it seems likely that this was a small enclosed garden built during the reign of the Ostrogoth Thoedoric (489-526).

At the northeast end of the stadium is a *Nymphaeum,* but is barred off and used as a storage room for fragments of statues and columns. The Imperial Box was built over three rooms at the ground level. In these rooms we can still see the remains of paintings that once decorated them. A passage that led from these rooms to the baths is still filled with earth. To get to the Imperial Box at the upper level we have to exit the stadium at the northeast corner and walk around to the stairs leading up to the structure. Here the emperor could sit and enjoy the view of the arena. We also find a corridor connecting the box with the baths.

Behind the Imperial Box are the structures of the *Palace of Septimius Severus (Domus Severiana)*, which consisted mainly of baths added to the Domus Augustiana. These baths were added by Septimius Severus (193-211) after he became emperor in 193. The substructures were actually built by Domitian, for reasons still not known. Thus, Severus already had a platform to build upon. To the south of the Stadium we see the arcaded structure of the palace. This area, that we are able to climb around, is sometimes referred to as the *Belvedere.* Severus built this great structure up to the edge of the Circus Maximus. From this edifice the emperor could view the events of the Circus without leaving the confines of the imperial palaces.

Leaving the Baths, we descend the hill, walking around to the side of the Circus Maximus. Directly beneath the Libraries of the Domus Flavia, lying almost at street level of the modern Via dei Cerchi, we see the ruins of a small building known as the *Domus Praeconum (House of the Heralds, Domus Gelotiana)*. This structure was built during the administration of Domitian and was a training school for pages who served in the great imperial palaces of the Palatine as government officials and workers. From the ruins it is possible to distinguish an atrium and four rooms. The corner room on the right had a wall painting that has since been detached and placed in the Palatine Museum. In this picture one sees four slaves waiting to receive guests in a banquet hall.

Just behind the Domus Praeconum, up the slope, we see the remains of another structure. This building which is probably a portion of the one we have just examined is called the *Paedagogium*. The remains of a long hall and about eight rooms can still be detected. When this building was excavated at the close of last century, much graffiti was discovered on the walls, left there by the pages. The most famous is now in the National Museum, which shows a boy looking at a donkey hanging on a cross. Many of the Romans thought that the Christians worshipped a deity that was pictured as an ass. One of the rooms to the left was evidently the school detention room, as it was particularly covered with graffiti, relating the miseries of school life.

For the energetic soul a walk around the hill to the corner of the Forum is worth the effort. Leaving the Paedagogium and walking behind the *Church of S. Anastasia* (which is surrounded by a fence), we can see the ruins of a house that probably dates to the 1st Century B.C. Somewhere in this area is the famous *Lupercal,* the ancient cave where the she-wolf is reputed to have found the infants Romulus and Remus. According to Roman writers a statue of the wolf suckling the twins was kept in the cave, and venerated until the fall of the empire. Although the cave was discovered in the 16th Century, we have no knowledge of its exact location today.

In this area we can see the lower end of the Scalae Caci that we examined earlier at the top of the hill. To the left of the Steps of Cacus we see the remains of a small altar. This is the *Altar of Genius Loci (Ara Genii Loci, Ara Aius Locutius)*. According to tradition the voice of a genie who lived here called out in the stillness of the night to warn of the approach of the Gauls in 387 B.C. After the Gauls had withdrawn from the city, an altar to the local genie was built on the spot. From archaeological study we can deduce that the altar has been moved from its original place, because it rests on modern detrital material.

After turning the corner of the hill we see about halfway to the top the remains of the walls of the early Palatine City (Murus Romuli). Passing behind the Church of S. Teodoro, we find ourselves on the ascending path of the Clivus Victoriae. The round church dates from the period between the 6th and 8th Centuries. Skirting the back of the church, we find ourselves at the so-called Temple of Augustus, one of the structures of the Forum. It is time now to retrace our footsteps all the way back to the southeast corner of the hill, to the Baths of Septimius Severus.

Just at the base of the corner of the Palatine, we are able to see the foundation ruins of a structure. This pavement is all that remains of the famous *Septizonium* of Septimius Severus. This great structure, built by the emperor in the 2nd Century, was supposedly constructed to impress travellers approaching Rome by way of the Via Appia. According to the classical writers the building was seven stories tall and contained marble, granite, and travertine as its major components. The edifice was destroyed in 1589 by Domeneco Fontana on orders from Sixtus V (1585-1590). This destruction was perpetrated to obtain building material for the projects of the pope. Building stone from the Septizonium went into the construction of the base of the St. Peter Obelisk, for various tombs, and in many of the churches.

Continuing around the hill and along the fence, as we now move northward, we see the arches of a ruined aqueduct. This is the *Aqueduct of Claudius,* constructed by the emperor in the 1st Century to supply water to the hill. Near the close of the 2nd Century the structure was badly damaged by fire. Septimius Severus restored the aqueduct after he became emperor in 193, using it to give an adequate water supply to his great baths.

Continuing the walk, we can see on the side of the hill the remains of a house dating back to the 2nd Century. To the left of this, at the north end of the Stadium of Domitian, we see the *Church of S. Bonaventura,* which is built over the great cistern fed by the aqueduct of Claudius. The church is separated from the rest of the Palatine by a fence, and to gain entrance to the church, we must go around and ascend the public road that begins behind the Arch of Titus.

Just behind the Church of S. Sebastiano lie the remains of a large temple. This structure is the *Temple of the Caesars (Aedes Caesarum, Temple of Jupiter Ultor).* The temple was built by Livia and dedicated to Augustus. Later the sanctuary was used as a place to worship all the deified emperors, becoming known as the Temple of the Caesars. By the early 3rd Century the temple had fallen into ruins. After he became emperor in 218, Elagabalus (218-222) rebuilt the structure and dedicated it to the Syrian sun god. It was known briefly as the Temple of Sol Invictus Elagabalus. His successor Alexander Severus (222-235) rededicated it to Jupiter Ultor. In the Middle Ages there was a church in the ruins called S. Maria in Pallara. The Church of S. Sebastiano occupies part of the ruins of the sanctuary.

Moving around the gardens of S. Sebastiano we turn left, passing through a tunnel that carries us under the Via di S. Bonaventura, and emerge near the Arch of Titus at the beginning of the Clivus Palatinus. This was one of the access roads to the Palatine in ancient times.

Near the right corner (with our backs to the Forum) of the Arch of Titus, nestled on the edge of the hill, we see the ruins of a building. These are the remains of the *Temple of Jupiter Stator.* Roman legend recounts that this edifice was built by Romulus. These ruins, however, date to the administration of M. Atilius Regulus, consul of 294 B.C., who had the temple constructed during the 3rd Samnite War (298-290 B.C.). The Senate met here in November of 63 B.C. to hear Cicero make his first oration against Catiline, accusing him of conspiracy against the state. A careful study of the architecture indicates that the structure was probably rebuilt during the time of Domitian in the late 1st Century. In medieval times a tower was built over the ruins, called the *Turris Chartularia,* and for a time housed the archives of the Catholic Church. The substructure of the ancient temple was uncovered in the excavations of the 1820's.

If we walk behind the Arch of Titus the custodian will allow us to exit the Forum at the gate (but not enter). Turning right we can now walk on the public street, the Via di S. Bonaventura, up the hill. About half-way up before the road makes a sharp turn to the left, we can see the ruins of a large gateway. This gave access to the Temple of the Caesars. The great entrance was known as the *Pentaphylum* in the *Regionary Catalogue of Rome.* Those who so desire, may go on to the end of the street for a visit to the Church of S. Bonaventura.

Moving down the hill in the soft fading light of the Roman evening, we should reflect on the wonders of the Palatine Hill. It was from here that emperors ruled the Mediterranean Basin. We can truthfully say that the Palatine was the seat of the world.

CHAPTER 3

The Captoline Hill

We should choose the Capitoline Hill as our next area of visitation. From Capitoline comes our words capital and capitol, just as palace, palatial, etc. were derived from Palatine. The Capitoline Hill took over from the Palatine Hill as the religious center of Rome in the late Regal Period, and continued this trend through the Republic. Only in the Empire period did the Palatine regain its previous role of importance. Today, the Capitoline is the seat of the municipal government.

For our purposes the best approach is probably the one directly behind the Forum. Here, with our backs to the Arch of Septimius Severus, we can gaze up the hill and see several important structures. To our extreme right, lying at the base of the Capitoline we also see the Mamertine Prison. Other monuments at the base of the hill from right to left are the Temple of Concord, the Temple of Vespasian, and the Portico of the Twelve Gods. Directly behind the Temples of Vespasian and Concord we also see the Tabularium. These four structures were part of the Forum in antiquity, but today are separated from it by the Via del Foro Romano. For this reason we will treat them in our tour of the Capitoline Hill.

Seated on the low wall overlooking the Forum, we can contemplate the history of the Capitol. This hill is not quite as large as the Palatine, covering an area of almost twenty-one acres. Its long axis is aligned in a northeasterly-southwesterly direction. Although difficult to detect, today, the hill has two summits. The northern summit, known as the *Arx*, is occupied by the Church of S. Maria d'Aracoeli and has an elevation of about 48.5m. (159 ft.) above sea-level. Reaching a height of about 45.7m. (150 ft.) above sea-level, the *Capitolium*, or southern summit, is covered by the Palazzo Caffarelli. The ridge that connects the two summits is called the *Asylum*, and today is completely covered by the Piazza del Campidoglio. Its altitude is about 38.4m. (126 ft.). Until the time of Trajan the Capitoline was connected to the Quirinal Hill by a ridge or saddle. This was cut away by Trajan when he built his forum and market.

Originally the hill was called the *Mons Tarpeius*, but in the Regal Period the name was changed to Capitolium. According to tradition, Romulus included the Capitoline in his city, but to students of the period this fact is doubtful. The hill was probably not annexed until the time of the Etruscan kings. Under the Etruscan kings the Arx was made into a citadel and temples were built on the entire hill. By the end of the Regal Period and the beginning of the Republic, the Capitoline had become the religious center of Rome.

As the Republic began, there were probably three approaches to the hill. The most important was the Clivus Capitolinus, which was the only route for wheeled traffic. This was a continuation of the Sacra Via from the Forum, ending on the Capitoline at the Temple of Jupiter Capitolinus. All Roman triumphs followed this roadway to the temple. The Via del Tempio di Giove follows this route in its upper reaches. Another access route to the summit of the Capitolium was furnished by the *Centum Gradus,* which probably lay to the south of the Clivus Capitolinus, and was a series of steps. Another set of steps to the north gave direct access to the Arx, and was called the *Scalae Gemoniae (Gradus Monetae).*

The importance of the hill in the early Republic is reflected by the fact that the Senate, which had a building in the Forum, held the first meeting of each year on the Capitoline. At the beginning of the 4th Century B.C., many of the private homes were torn down to build public buildings. When the Republic ended the Arx was occupied by at least three temples and a mint, one temple was located on the Asylum, and on the Capitolium there were about seven temples. A few private homes remained, but they were confined to the slopes.

Practically all the emperors from Augustus (27 B.C. - 14A.D.) through Marcus Aurelius (161-180) either repaired or built new structures on the hill. The last monument on the Capitoline was a statue of Claudius Gothicus (268-270), built by the Senate in 270. At the end of the 3rd Century the Capitoline was covered by public buildings. Just as the Palatine did, the Capitoline began to decline with the rule of Diocletian (284-305). Then, in the 4th and 5th Centuries many of its treasures were carried off to Constantinople.

In the early part of the 11th Century a home was built on the top of the Tabularium, but was destroyed later in the century. By this time the Capitol had become the political center for medieval Rome. New buildings were built and the hill was once again a place of importance. During the Schism (1378-1417) the hill was once again neglected, and became known as the Hill of Goats. Not until the late Renaissance was a program of reconstruction begun on the hill.

With this brief sketch of the history of the hill behind us, we can now begin our tour of the Capitoline. Moving to the right, we first examine the *Mamertine Prison (Carcer Mamertinus),* located at the corner of the Forum of Caesar. The cobblestone road that separates the Forum of Caesar from the Capitoline is the *Clivus Argentarius,* that led in antiquity from the Roman Forum to the Campus Martius. It probably entered the Forum between the Temple of Concord and the Arch of Septimius Severus. The street took its name from the shops of the silversmiths that were located along its route.

The term Mamertine comes to us from the medieval period; in earlier

FIGURE 5

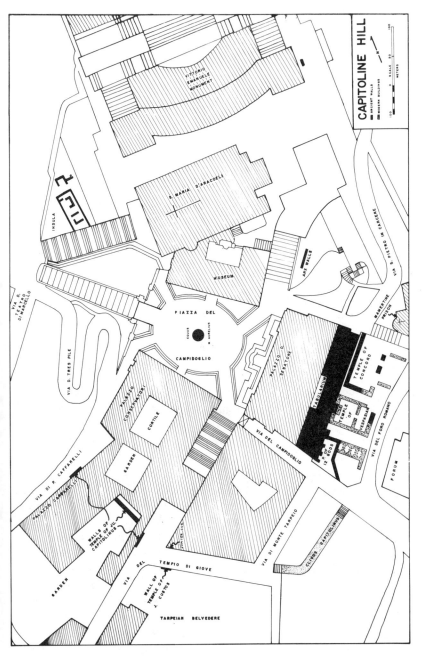

Plan of the Capitoline Hill

times it was known as the *Tullianum*. This term is derived from a Latin word meaning well, and not from the king Servius Tullius. According to Livy the prison was built by the King Ancus Marcius. It may have been a quarry in which there was a spring that flowed, making it into a cistern. In the late Regal Period or early Republic it was probably converted into a dungeon.

This prison is located beneath the modern Church of S. Giuseppe dei Falegnami. We enter by descending a set of stairs under the church, passing through a turnstile that opens after one makes a contribution of 50 lire. Passing on down to the bottom level, we are in the Tullianum proper. Originally, the only opening to the upper level was a hole in the center of the roof. There was also an opening to the Cloaca Maxima to drain off the water from the spring. This was the place where certain prisoners were thrown to be executed. They were either strangled or starved to death. Their bodies were disposed of by throwing them into the Cloaca Maxima. Some of the prisoners who met their death in this lower chamber are reputed to be Q. Pleminius, for his abuses at Locii under Scipio Africanus in 206 B.C.; Perseus, king of Macedonia in 166 B.C.; Jugurtha, king of Numidia in 104 B.C.; Lentulus and Cethegus, members of the Catilinarian Conspiracy of 62 B.C.; and Vercengetorix, a Gallic king, in 49 B.C.

Climbing back up the stairs to the upper cell, we notice the furnishings. Against the wall and opposite the entrance, stands a beautiful altar. Upon the altar there stands four candle holders. To the right of the altar we can see a wall plaque that describes the incarceration of St. Peter. This cell is also called the *S. Pietro in Carcere.* According to Christian legend, Nero imprisoned St. Peter in this upper prison. Prisoners who awaited public execution in ancient Rome were incarcerated in this chamber. Evidently, conditions were much better in the upper cell than they were in the lower chamber.

The exit from this ancient "chamber of horrors" takes us through a souvenir shop onto the steps leading up to the Capitoline Hill. Looking down, we can see that we are directly above the Temple of Concord. We should descend the stairs and walk around to the *Portico of the Twelve Gods* (*Porticus Deorum Consentium*). In this temple there are twelve Corinthian columns of marble dedicated to the twelve Olympic deities.

This structure was probably built at the close of the 3rd Century B.C., during the Second Punic War. None of the material from the early building has survived. Some of the brickwork can be dated to the administration of the Flavians in the latter part of the 1st Century. After the triumph of Christianity it fell into a state of disrepair. The temple was restored by the City Praefect Vettius Praetextatus in 367. Praetextatus wanted to restore paganism to Rome. After his death in 385 the structure was again neglected. The shrine was excavated in 1834. Pope Pius IX (1846-1878) restored some of the columns in 1858. Travertine was used to supplement the marble that had been destroyed. Beneath the structure are the remains of the rooms constructed of brick. Built into the hill we can see the remains of seven small chambers. Originally there were probably twelve of these chambers, each housing a statue of an Olympic deity.

Moving back in the direction of the steps we recently descended, we find ourselves in front of the *Temple of Vespasian* (*Templum Divius Vespasianus*). Not much of this great structure has been preserved. We see three columns that reach a height of about 15.2m. (50 ft.). These are the corner remains of an eight columned pronaos or porch. We can also see the remains of the rear wall abutting the Tabularium. Between the wall and the columns, we can still see the podium and a pedestal that held statues of Vespasian (69-79) and Titus (79-81).

When Titus became emperor in 79 he began to build a temple to his recently deified father, Vespasian. The temple was incomplete at the death of Titus in 81, but his brother and successor, Domitian (81-96), completed it in a short period of time. Statues to both Vespasian and Titus were placed in the temple. By the late 2nd Century the structure had fallen into a sad state of disrepair. It was restored early in the 3rd Century by Septimius Severus (193-211) and his son Caracalla (211-217). By late medieval times all that remained to view were the three surviving columns, and they were buried by the debris up to two-thirds of the height of their shafts. In the Capitoline excavation of 1813 the columns were uncovered, but they were in such a weakened state they had to be taken down, reassembled, and the foundation strengthened. The restoration was carried out by the architects Giuseppe Valadier and Giulio Camporese.

Next to the Temple of Vespasian there is another small structure worthy of note. It is the brick-faced concrete wall that abuts the podium of the temple. This small building, which measures slightly over 2.5m. (8.0 ft.) wide by almost 4.10m (13.5 ft.) in length, is referred to as the *Faustinae Aedicula* or *Shrine of Faustina*. It was built and dedicated to the memory of Faustina the Younger, the wife of Marcus Aurelius, in 175.

Let us now turn our attention to the next monument to our right, the *Temple of Concord* (*Templum Concordia, Aedes Concordiae*). All that remains is the podium of the temple that measures about 45.1 by 24.1m. (148 x 79 ft.). In front we can still see the structure of the pronaos that is about 34.1m (112 ft.) wide. Part of the foundation was covered up by the construction of the Via del Foro Romano.

In 367 B.C. the passage of the Sextian-Licinian Law settled temporarily the armed conflict between the Patricians and Plebeians. This law allowed election of Plebeians to the highest office, the consulship. With peace and harmony restored, the Dictator M. Furrius Camillus began construction of this temple to the goddess Concordia. This deity held the Roman state together in times of turmoil, being derived from the Greek goddess Homonoia. In 211 B.C. the temple was badly damaged by lightning. Lucius Opimius helped restore peace after the death of Gaius Gracchus in 121 B.C., and gratefully restored the temple in thanks to the goddess. The Roman Senate sometimes met in the temple during the years of the late Republic. This is reputed to be the site of the fourth speech of Cicero delivered against Catiline in 62 B.C. By the end of the century the temple was in need of repairs. Tiberius (14-37) began rebuilding the structure as early as 7 B.C. It was finally completed seventeen years later in 10 A.D., and rededicated as the *Aedes Concordiae Augustae* in honor of his adoptive father Augustus. The present structure we see dates from the reconstruction of Tiberius. Writers of 8th Century Rome tell us that the temple was still in good condition at the time; however, it began to crumble and fall in the 15th Century, aided by the lime hunters who began to burn marble for their lime sources. The area was excavated in 1817.

Before beginning our ascent of the hill we should look at the large imposing structure directly behind the Temples of Vespasian and Concord. This structure is the *Tabularium*, which served as the library for the state archives. It is located in the hollow between the two natural summits of the Capitoline Hill. The lower wall, made of rectangular blocks of stone reaches a height of 11m. (36 ft.). This substructure is pierced in the upper reaches by small windows. Between this outer wall, which has a thickness of 3.4m. (11 ft.), and the hill, there is a corridor. Originally the stone was covered by stucco.

The Tabularium was built in 78 B.C. upon orders of Q. Lutatius Catulus, who was serving as consul along with M. Aemilius Lepidus. A great fire, resulting from the struggles for power in 83 B.C., destroyed much of the decor of the Capitoline. After Sulla emerged the victor in 82 B.C., he may have planned the archives, which was then built by his good friend Catulus. This new building probably served not only as the state archives, but also as a treasury building. Originally the main entrance to the building was from the Forum. We can still see a portion of the doorway, but it is blocked by the podium of the Temple of Vespasian.

Above the small windows we can see a second floor which contains three open archways flanked by Doric columns. Originally, there was another floor above this, but today this has been replaced by the lowest story of the Palazzo del Senatore, that dates from the medieval period.

Climbing the stairs beside the Temple Concord, we reach the level of the floor that contains the archways. Looking through the gate we see that the building has an arcaded hall running the width of the Tabularium. If we show our permits to the custodian, he will allow us to enter the gallery. From the hall we can look through the arches and get a good view of the Forum. Only three of the arches are open, originally there were ten. The others can't be opened because of the stress on the building. Behind this hallway we can still see the remains of vaulted rooms partially cut into the side of the hill. There was another floor above this storey, probably similar in nature to the one we are standing upon, but it was replaced by the medieval building.

PLATE 5

A. Tabularium

B. Portico of Twelve Gods

PLATE 6

A. Capitoline Hill

B. Statue of Marcus Aurelius

A stairway that led down to the entrance from the Forum is still excellently preserved. It has sixty-six steps, but the doorway at the bottom is blocked by the Temple of Vespasian. Of all the remains of Republican Rome the Tabularium is the best preserved of structures.

As we continue to the top of the hill, we see to our right the gardens of S. Maria d'Aracoeli. At the edge of the gardens, opposite the north wall of the Tabularium, we see the remains of primitive walls. These primitive fortifications, made of tufa, remind us of the walls we saw on the Palatine. Further into the garden, above the Forum of Caesar, we see a larger segment of these same walls. These structures are the remains of the fortress walls that protected the Arx, which served as a military citadel in the late Regal period and through much of the Republic. They were probably built in the 6th Century B.C.

During the period of the kings, one important structure was built on the Arx. This vanished monument was called the *Auguraculum,* and may have been built similar to the House of Romulus. From this building the augurs took the auspices, just as they did in the Auguratorium on the Palatine. By the end of the Republic the Arx contained a *Temple of Juno Moneta* and the mint where money was coined, a *Temple of Vejovis* and a larger *Temple of Concord.* No traces of these structures remain today, making us dependent upon classical writers for descriptions of them.

Turning our attention to the Church of *S. Maria d'Aracoeli,* we find ourselves looking at what many consider one of the most fascinating churches in Rome. We are not certain when the church was built, however, there was a religious building on the site in 574, and at that time it was considered old. In the 6th Century it was Byzantine property and attached to it was a Greek monastery. In the 10th Century it was given to the Benedictines, and they deeded it to the Franciscans in the 13th Century. Most of the church structure visible today dates from the 13th Century.

A name change probably occurred in the 12th Century. Until that time it was called S. Maria in Capitolio. The legend that comes to us from this century, indicates that the church was built over the remains of the Temple of Juno Moneta, and this is true according to the builder of the Victor Emanuele Monument. The legend goes on to state that a prophet told Emperor Augustus of the coming birth of Christ. Augustus then built an altar on the spot which he named Ara Coeli (Altar of Heaven). Most scholars agree this is not true, but it does account for the name change. A walk through this fascinating church is worth the time spent.

Leaving the charming confines of the church, we now move to the square. Standing in front of the figure of the horseman, we can orient ourselves. To our left and in front of the church we see the building that houses the Capitoline museum. Directly ahead of us is the Palazzo del Senatore, while to our right we see the Palazzo dei Conservatori. Where we stand is the area known as the Asylum and the square is known as the *Piazza del Cam-*

pidoglio. In ancient times the Asylum contained the Tabularium, another temple to Vejovis, an arch to Nero, and private homes.

The horseman in front of us is known as the *Statue of Marcus Aurelius* (*Equus Marci Aurelii*), the Roman emperor from 161 to 180. This large bronze statue of horse and rider dates back to the 2nd Century. In classical times it may have been erected in front of the Lateran Palace although this cannot be documented. There is some evidence that Marcus Aurelius was born in a house on the site of the Lateran. The statue was discovered in the 10th Century, standing in front of the Lateran Palace, where it remained until 1583. It would have met its demise at the hands of Christian vandals had they known it was the statue of a pagan emperor. But, in medieval times it was thought to be the figure of Constantine, the first Christian emperor. Its medieval name was *Caballus Constantini.* Thus, it owes its salvation to a case of mistaken identity. The statue has not completely withstood the ravages of time, as it was repaired twice, once by Pope Paul II in 1466, and again by Pope Sixtus IV in 1473. In the 16th Century Michelangelo began to design the Piazza del Campidoglio, moving the statue to its present spot in 1583.

The *Capitoline Museum* (*Museuo Capitolina, Palazzo Nuova*) to our left is well worth the two or three hours chosen to view its holdings. This antiquarium was completed in 1734 by Pope Clement XII (1730-1740), but many of its collections date back to 1471. There are many sculptures and other art forms collected from all over the city of Rome.

Moving on to the *Palazzo del Senatore* (*Palazzo Senatorio*), we must remember this was built on top of the Tabularium, in fact the upper floor of the state archives was replaced by the first floor of the Palace of the Senator. This building with the great fountain in front was built in 1143, but most of the structure was rebuilt in the 14th and 15th Centuries. In 1538 the pope began to appoint one senator to govern Rome, thus, the name, Palace of the Senator. This building serves today as the city hall for Rome.

Beneath the southwest corner (the corner to our right as we face the front of the building) of the Palace of the Senator there are remains of a temple. With the custodian accompanying us, we descend a stairway to these ruins that constitute the remains of the *Temple of Vejovis* (*Templum Vejovis*). This structure was vowed by the praetor L. Furius Pupurio in 196 B.C. and completed in 192 B.C. A study of the brickwork tells us that the building was repaired in 78 B.C., at the same time the Tabularium was built. The ruins of the Temple of Vejovis were discovered in 1939 during construction of a subterranean passage to connect the three palaces of the Campidoglio. We can still see the remains of the pronaos, bases of columns, and a portion of the podium.

To the right of piazza we see the building referred to as the *Palazzo dei Conservatori.* This structure is actually two buildings since it takes in a wing of the *Palazzo Caffarelli.* The two buildings together are called the *Museo del Palazzo dei Conservatori.* In 1749 the first part of the museum was opened as the *Pinacoteca Capitolina.* The next portion of the museum was dedicated in 1876. Then in 1925 the museum was expanded to take in part of the Palazzo Caffarelli and called the *Museo Nuova Capitolino.* The *Braccio Nuovo* was added in 1950 and *Galleria Lapidaria* in 1957. Two or three hours can be well spent browsing in these museums.

There are remains within the museum confines that serious students of archaeology will wish to view. First, we go to the *Garden of the New Capitoline Museum* (*Giardino del Museo Nuovo Capitolino*), located between the Palazzo Caffarelli and the Palazzo dei Conservatori. Here we see the remains of a primitive wall. We are looking at the sub-structure of the great *Temple of Jupiter Capitolinus* (*Aedes Juppiter Optimus Maximus Capitolinus*). The other side can be viewed by entering the room called the *Sala del Muro Romano.* More remains can be seen outside the Palazzo Caffarelli along the Via di P. Caffarelli, particularly where the street exits the Piazza Palazzo Caffarelli.

This temple gave the Capitoline Hill its important role in Roman history. This area is the summit of the hill called the Capitolium. When Tarquinius Priscus (616-579 B.C.) became the first Etruscan king of Rome about 616 B.C., the Capitoline was probably within the sacred boundaries of Rome. After a war with the Sabines, Priscus vowed a temple to the chief god of the Romans and Etruscans, Jupiter (his Etruscan name was Tinia). Construction of the great temple continued during the rule of Servius Tullius (578-535 B.C.) and through the administration of Tarquinius Superbus (535-509 B.C.). When Superbus was overthrown in 509 B.C. and the monarchy abolished, the temple was on the verge of being completed. The temple was officially dedicated by M. Horatius Pulvillus, one of the consuls of the new republic, on September 13, 509 B.C. This temple made the Capitoline one of the most important hills in Rome.

Evidently, great portions of the interior were built of wood, and a great fire in 83 B.C. destroyed all of the temple but the platform it was built upon. After Sulla had consolidated his power in 82 B.C., he ordered reconstruction to begin. It was rededicated in 69 B.C. by Q. Lutatius Catulus (the builder of the Tabularium). Four years later it was damaged by lightning, which struck it again in 9 B.C. As a result of the fighting between the supporters of Vitellius and those of Vespasian in 69, another fire broke out, and once more the temple was partially destroyed.

After his arrival in Rome in early 70, one of Vespasian's first acts as the new emperor was to rebuild the temple. From coins we know that he not only housed the statues of Jupiter within the temple, but he also included those of Juno (wife of Jupiter) and Minerva (goddess of Wisdom). The edifice was again destroyed in the great fire of 80 that occurred during the administration of Titus. His brother Domitian quickly rebuilt the temple after he succeeded Titus in 81.

The location of the monument was lost in the middle ages. In the early

19th Century there was much debate among scholars as to whether it was located on the Capitolium or the Arx. Excavations of 1865, 1875-76, and 1919 have confirmed that these ruins are those of the temple.

This area of the hill where we are standing is the Capitolium summit. According to the classical historians there were other monuments on this part of the hill. Here on the Capitolium were temples dedicated to *Fides, Jupiter Custos, Jupiter Tonans, Jupiter Feretrius, Mens, Mars Ultor, Ops,* and *Venus Erycina.* There was also another *Casa Romuli* modelled after the original on the Palatine Hill. Hadrian built a great lecture hall, complete with library, which was referred to as the *Athenaeum.* There were also many statues and sanctuaries located on this part of the hill. With the exception of the Temple of Jupiter Custos, no trace of these monuments remain.

If we move to the southeast corner of the hill, we are at the highest point. Here we find a lovely little park and a look-out spot. From here we are afforded a panoramic view of the Forum, the Palatine Hill, and other hills and monuments. The cliff that we are standing upon is referred to as the *Tarpeian Rock (Tarpeius Mons).* Tradition tells us the name comes from Tarpeia, the Roman maiden, who treacherously opened the gates to a Sabine army in the time of Romulus. For this act of treachery, Tarpeia was crushed beneath the invading army. Later this cliff became the execution spot for those convicted of treason.

The street that runs in back of the small park, or *Belvedere Tarpeo,* is known as the Via del Tempio di Giove. This roadway makes an abrupt right turn at the southeast corner of the municipal building. Before making the turn, we should look to the left at the pit abutting the wall of the museum. In the pit we see more remains of the Temple of Jupiter Capitolinus. After we make the turn, we should look to the right, where we see the remains of a structure incorporated into the street wall. Across the street to our left, built into the municipal building, we see more of the same remains. These ruins are the remnants of the *Temple of Jupiter Custos.* In 69 Domitian was forced to hide in a house on this spot, to avoid capture by the troops of Vitellius. After his father, Vespasian, arrived in Rome in 70 as the new emperor, Domitian tore down the house and built a small chapel which he dedicated to Jupiter Conservator. After becoming emperor in 81, he replaced this small sanctuary with a much larger edifice, which he renamed the Temple of Jupiter Custos.

Continuing on down the street we go straight where the road turns left. We now find ourselves on a cobbled roadway. This path is the *Clivus Capitolinus,* which was the major access route to the Capitoline Hill. The great triumphs followed this road from the Forum to the Temple of Jupiter Capitolinus, where they terminated.

Descending the hill by way of the path, we then walk on around to the Mamertine Prison, continue on between the Forum of Caesar and the Capitoline, finally coming to a street that ascends the hill. To the right of the entrance of the *Museo del Risorgimento* we see in the pavement more remains of walls. This is an extension of the walls of the citadel of the Arx that we examined in the gardens above earlier.

As we continue to skirt the hill, we see to our left the gigantic *Victor Emanuele Monument* (*Vittoriano*) and its Tomb of the Unknown Soldier from WWI. This structure, begun in 1885 and completed in 1911, was dedicated to the unification of Italy by King Vittorio Emanuele II in 1870. Just to the left of the edifice, looking very lonely amidst the grass, we see a small structure made of white stone. This is the remains of the Tomb of *Publius Bibulus* (*Sepulcrum Bibuli*) built in the 1st Century B.C. The opening is probably the niche where a statue of Bibulus stood. This tomb which lay outside the Servian Walls, was located at the beginning of the Via Flaminia.

To the right of the monument and just to the left of the 122 steps leading up to S. Maria d'Aracoeli, we see the ruins of a magnificent building. This structure, called the *Insula*, shows the remains of a six-storied building. Such a building is an example of a typical tenement of the Roman empire. The structure dates back to the middle of the 2nd Century, when Rome was crowded with these buildings. Below the street level we see the first floor which was occupied by shops. The top five floors were family residences. We are able to see only the remains of four of the floor levels. The building was excavated in 1928-29.

Moving past the steps that lead up to S. Maria D'Aracoeli and the more gentle ones leading up to the Piazza del Campidoglio and just across the street from the Theater of Marcellus we see along the side of the hill some yellowish-gray tufa blocks. They have an appearance similar to the walls of the Arx citadel. These are the remains of the Servian Wall that ran along the western flank of the Capitoline. We will have more to say about these walls later.

At the corner of Via di Teatro Marcello and Vicus Jugarius we can see a portico with three arcades. These are probably the remains of the *Porticus Minucia* that helped enclose the Forum Holitorium (more will be said of this later). According to some scholars this structure was built about 110 B.C. by the Consul M. Minucius Rufus.

It is hoped that our tour of the Capitoline has been productive for student, archaeologist, and tourist alike. There are not nearly so many ruins as we found on the Palatine, but the Capitoline was an important hill to the ancient Romans.

CHAPTER 4

The Forum

Our itinerary should direct us next to the *Roman Forum* (*Forum Romanum*). Although there are more ruins here, the Forum is not as confusing as the Palatine Hill. It is best to align ourselves by standing at the base of the Capitoline Hill with our backs to the Tabularium. Looking down into the Forum, which lies about 5.5 m. (18 ft.) below the modern level, we are able to pick out several conspicuous landmarks. Immediately in front of us we see the Arch of Septimius Severus. In ancient times the Tabularium and everything to the base of the Capitoline Hill was included in the Forum. For our purposes we will consider the more confined and modern fenced-in area.

In the distance we can see the Arch of Titus, which marks the other end of the Forum. Looking from the Arch of Septimius Severus to the Arch of Titus we find that this gives us the long axis of the Forum, aligned in a north-westerly-southeasterly direction. It is bounded on the right by the Palatine Hill and on the left by the Via de Fori Imperiali.

Here at the northwestern end of the Forum we can seat outselves on the low wall and dwell briefly upon the history of the area. This spot located between the Palatine, Capitoline, Quirinal, and Esquiline Hills was once a marshy area, containing springs, as well as collecting runoff from the hills. Shortly after 1000 B.C., with the settling of the Palatine, Quirinal, and Esquiline, the Forum became a burial place for these Latin and Sabine settlers. Both inhumation (Sabine) and cremation (Latin) type burials were practiced.

After 753 B.C. and the founding of Rome, the Forum began to take on some religious significance. On the Velia, the gentle sloping side of the Palatine, now occupied by the Arch of Titus, a hut shrine was probably dedicated to Vesta. In this primitive temple the sacred fires of Rome were kept burning. The second king of Rome, Numa Pompilius (715-673 B.C.), evidently moved his residence from the Palatine to the Forum at the close of the 8th Century B.C. To do this the king probably had to begin a program of drainage, which was accomplished by deepening the stream called the Spinon that ran through the area. The new royal residence, called the Regia, did not remain here alone, other settlers began to move into the Forum after the turn of the century. Before his death in 673 B.C., Numa, according to tradition, turned his house over to the Pontifex Maximus (high priest). The Regia would remain the seat of this religious official; thus, at that time the

Forum was becoming an important religious center.

During the latter part of the 7th Century B.C. with all kinds of shops being built, the Forum also became a market place. After Rome passed under Etruscan control in 616 B.C., drainage of the Forum was given top priority. Tarquinius Priscus (616-579 B.C.) probably paved the bed and sides of the Spinon, converting it into a drainage ditch. With the Forum now properly drained, the kings could now begin to pave the market place. About 575 B.C., under Servius Tullius (578-535 B.C.), the first pebble pavement was laid down.

With the advent of the Republic in 509 B.C., the Forum became the political center of Rome. The Senate and the assemblies met in what was called the Forum Romanum or simply the Forum, to distinguish it from the other fora that evolved. A second pebble pavement was laid down around 500 B.C., and a third about 490 B.C. By the close of the 3rd Century B.C. there were many religious and political structures in the Forum. Around 200 B.C. it was necessary to lay down another pebble pavement, followed by a fifth about 100 B.C. During the time of Caesar, about 50 B.C., a 6th floor of pebbles was laid. Caesar began to rearrange and to realign some of the monuments in the 40's B.C.

Augustus (27 B.C. - 14 A.D.), after the beginning of the imperial age, paved the area with slabs of travertine. This surface lasted through the empire, and is what is visible today. In all there were seven layers of pavement in the Forum. Under Caesar and Augustus the Forum became the political center of the world.

After Constantine (310-337) shifted the capital to Constantinople in 330, the Forum began to fall into a state of disrepair. Constantius II (337-360) closed the buildings of the Forum to the public in 346, but the structures were recognized as historic monuments. By the end of the century they were neglected again. These monuments suffered drastically at the hands of Alaric and the Visigoths in 410, an earthquake in 422, and Gaiseric and the Vandals in 455. The Ostrogothic king Theodoric tried to repair the monuments at the close of the 5th Century. Narses, the Byzantine general, celebrated the last triumph in the Forum in 554.

In the 6th Century the popes began to build churches in the monumental structures. Early in the century the library of the Forum of Peace was converted into the Church of SS. Cosmas and Damian. Near mid-century a church to the Virgin was built in the library of the Temple of Caesar. The Senate was converted into the churches of S. Martina and S. Adriano. A portion of the guard room of the Domus Tiberiana, at Forum level, was made into S. Maria Antiqua.

Another earthquake in the 9th Century that destroyed much of the Basilica of Constantine and made S. Maria Antiqua unsafe for worship services, caused the Forum to be fairly well abandoned. Monuments began to fall and to be covered by detrital material. By the end of the century it was

FIGURE 6

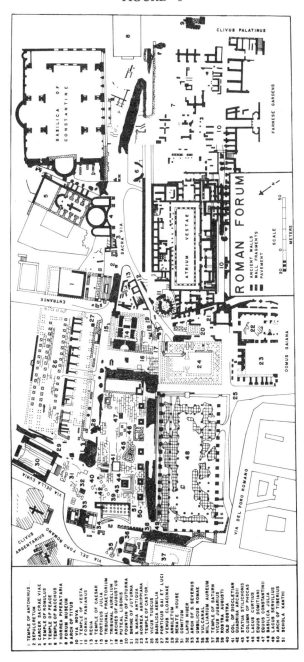

Plan of the Forum

referred to as the "Campo Vaccino (Cow Field)". Near the end of the 14th Century the popes began to use the area as a quarry for securing building stone for their churches.

In 1848 the first systematic excavations of the Forum began. This initial phase lasted until 1853. Between 1870 and 1884 Rosa, Fiorelli, and Lanciani conducted excavations. In 1898 Boni and Bartoli took over, continuing to dig until 1922. By the end of the first quarter of the 20th Century, most of the major monuments had been exposed. Since then there have been excavations on a small scale.

Now after our brief glimpse of the history of the Forum, we can now descend to tour the monuments. We enter at the place where we entered to begin our tour of the Palatine, at the intersection of Via Cavour and Via de Fori Imperiali. As we walk down the incline we become aware of the great structure to our left with steps leading to the entrance. This is the *Temple of Antoninus and Faustina* (*Templum Antoninis et Faustinae, Aedes Divae Pii et Divae Faustinae*). Emperor Antoninus Pius (138-161) erected this building in 141 to honor the memory of his dead wife Faustina. After the death of Pius in 161, the Senate voted to dedicate it also in his honor.

This well preserved structure is made of peperino which was originally covered with marble. Twenty-one steps lead to a porch or pronaos with ten columns of marble that are 19.8m. (65 ft.) tall. In the middle of the steps about halfway up, we can see the remains of an altar. Six columns are located along the front of the porch and there are two along each side. Originally there were colonnaded porches running along each side of the temple, but these have long since disappeared. On the pronaos there were statues, presumably of the deified couple. Fragments of these statues were discovered on the porch. Along the top of the porch is a frieze showing griffins in pairs facing each other. Between each pair of griffin is a candelabrum.

In the 10th or 11th Century the temple was converted to the Church of S. Lorenzo in Miranda. This was one of the reasons that it is one of the best preserved structures in the Forum. By this time due to detrital deposits the level of the Forum had risen near the height of the floor level of the temple. Today the floor level is almost 12.2m (40 ft.) above the level of the Imperial Forum. In the late 14th Century Urban V (1362-1370) began to use its stone to rebuild the Lateran. The twenty-one steps were not uncovered until the excavations of 1811. This excavation also uncovered the crypt below the stairs.

Descending the stairs that led up to the temple, we find ourselves standing on a paved street. This street is the famous *Sacra Via* or *Sacred Way*. The slabs of travertine upon which we are standing date back to the close of the 1st Century B.C., during the administration of Augustus. It began in the valley where later the Colosseum would be built, crossed the Velia north of the Arch of Titus and entered the Forum. That portion near the Arch is referred to as the *Clivus Sacer* (*Sacred Rise*). There is some evidence that the street was built over the course of an ancient stream that headed up on the Velia. Later the stream was covered over.

The earliest pavement (pebble) of the Sacra Via probably dates back to the 6th or 7th Century B.C. As it neared the Regia, the roadway splits into two forks. One branch (the one we are standing on) passes between the Regia and the Temple of Antoninus and Faustina. The other fork passes between the Temple of Vesta and the Regia. After passing the Temple of Caesar, the two branches of the Sacra Via unite, turn southwesterly near the Arch of Septimius Severus and finally joins the Clivus Capitolinus. The great Roman Triumphs of the Late Republic and Empire followed the Sacra Via to the Clivus Capitolinus, then on to the Temple of Jupiter on the Capitoline.

Walking up the Sacra Via toward the Arch of Titus, we see to our left, just past the Temple of Antoninus and Faustina, an archaic cemetery referred to as the *Sepulcretum* (*Sepolcretum*). The discovery was made by Giancomo Boni in 1902, and it contained both rectangular and circular graves. Further study indicated that the round graves were the cremation burials of the Latins, while the rectangular ones were the inhumation pits of the Sabines. In all a total of 41 graves were found dating from the 9th to the 6th Centuries B.C. Excavations of the 1950's indicate that the cemetery extended all the way to the Temple of Caesar.

Just past the cemetery, and on the same side of the Sacra Via, we can see the remains of some rooms, lying below the street level. These are the so-called *Carcer Sacrae Viae,* a name given to them by G. Boni after he had excavated them at the turn of this century. It is doubtful, however, that this was a jail as the name implies, but probably nothing more than the lower rooms of a private house, dating to the 1st Century B.C. There is a corridor extending perpendicularly from the Sacra Via, and there are three rooms on each side of this hall. The ones on the right side are partially destroyed.

Moving on past the cemetery, we find to our left a round shaped building with a bronze door. This structure has been identified as the *Temple of Romulus* (*Templum Divi Romuli, Heroon Romuli*). After the death of his young son Romulus in 309, Maxentius (310-312) decided to dedicate the building to his memory. Pope Felix IV (526-530) converted it into a vestibule connecting the Forum and the Church of SS Cosma e Damiano in the early 6th Century.

This circular edifice made of brick and covered with marble, once had two side rooms built like halls flanking it. On the front of these halls were porches with two rows of marble columns. The columns on the right side have survived. Framing the doors, are two columns of porphyry. The roof is not original, the marble covering for the building is gone, but the bronze doors are original. Even the ancient lock is still in working order.

The area behind the temple is usually referred to as the *Forum Pacis* (*Forum of Peace*). It was built by Vespasian (69-79) in 71, commemorating the end of the 1st Jewish War. Actually, Vespasian built only the church we see, calling it the *Templum Pacis* (*Temple of Peace*). The area was not converted into a forum until about the beginning of the 5th Century. Only the remains of the temple have survived. A great portion of Vespasian's Forum of Peace lies underneath the Via Cavour and Via dei Fori Imperiali.

This church, SS. Cosmas and Damian, the former Temple of Peace, had a marble plan of the city attached to the outside wall of the library. Septimius Severus (193-211) was responsible for adding this plan at the beginning of the 3rd Century. This plan is the famous *Forma Urbis*, of which fragments can be seen in the Capitoline Museum. Severus rebuilt the temple after it was partially destroyed by fire in 191. After the reconstruction the structure was probably referred to as the *Templum Sacrae Urbis* or *Archives of the Cadastre*. The dowel holes for the pegs that held up the Forma Urbis can still be seen in the side of the church building.

Just past the Forum of Peace stands the magnificent edifice of a great building. This is called the *Basilica of Constantine* (*Basilica Constantini*) or *Basilica Nova*. The back of the basilica borders on the sidewalks along the Via dei Fori Imperiali. Maxentius began construction of the building between 306 and 310, thus, it is also referred to as the *Basilica of Maxentius*. It was enlarged and completed by Constantine shortly after 313.

The two-storied building had its long axis aligned along a line running in a northwesterly-southeasterly direction. Maxentius provided for the apse on the long axis in the northwest wall. Constantine then added an apse on the short axis, facing the Sacra Via. After completion, the basilica was 91.44m. (300 ft.) long by 60.96m (200 ft.) wide. Along both axes it had a central nave and flanking aisles. Each nave terminated in an apse. Four large piers divided the aisles from the naves. In front of each pier was a marble column of the Corinthian style.

Maxentius intended for the long nave, which at the time was the only one, to be the dominant feature, with the roof standing 35.05m (115 ft.) above the floor. Constantine made the shorter nave the major one. The three arches that marked the terminal end of the shorter naves and aisles still stand today. They are 20.42m (67 ft.) wide and 24.38m. (80 ft.) high. This basilica was studied very carefully by the architects who constructed the world famous Basilica of St. Peter. The northwest corner cut off access between the Forum and the Esquiline Hill, so a pedestrian tunnel was built under the corner. In the Middle Ages it was a hangout for thieves and robbers and became known as the *Arcus Latonae* or *Arco di Latrone*. The tunnel is still there, but has been sealed off since 1566.

Crossing the street directly in front of the northern arch of the basilica, we see the remains of a rounded podium. This is the ruins of the *Temple of Bacchus* (*Sanctuary of Bacchus, Sacellum Bacchi*), that was in existence by mid-2nd Century. Other fragments from the temple have been found in the vicinity. The other ruins date from medieval times.

Near the opposite end of the Basilica of Constantine and on this side of the Sacra Via, we see the foundation ruins of a series of buildings. These are the remains of shops and warehouses that date back at least to the early 1st Century. Later Nero (54-68) built his *Domus Transitoria* over these shops, connecting the Palatine with the Esquiline. After Domitian (81-96) became emperor in 81, he built over the remains of the Neronian Palace that had been constructed after the fire of 64. Most of these ruins date to the time of Domitian, and are called the *Horrea Piperataria* or *Spice Warehouses.* The complex was built to store and sell oriental spices.

In 191 a fire destroyed the complex, it was rebuilt, and damaged by another fire in 284, after which it was never rebuilt. Maxentius and Constantine then constructed their basilica over the ruins. The Horrea Piperataria extended over to the Forum Pacis, but most of it is now covered by the Basilica of Constantine. Excavations in 1899 and 1935 helped establish the extent of the area of these shops and warehouses.

Directly in front of us in the left corner of the Forum complex we see the *Forum Museum* or *Forum Antiquarium* (*Antiquarium del Foro*). Many of the marbles from the Forum, plus material from the Sepulcretum can be found here. It is well worth a half hour or so to browse through the building. Here one can also obtain archaeological permits. The museum is housed in what was the Convent of the Church of S. Francesco Romana, built into the ruins of the Temple of Venus and Rome, of which more will be said later.

Now, we turn our attention to the *Arch of Titus* (*Arcus Titi*). This marble arch was built to honor Titus (79-81) after his death in 81. The edifice commemorated his destruction of Jerusalem in 70. In 66 the Jewish Rebellion had broken out and the Roman legions had been expelled from Jerusalem and all of Judaea. Nero sent Vespasian to quell the revolution. He was making slow progress when he heard of the suicide of the emperor late in 68. Vespasian then waited to see what would happen in Rome. In December of 69 Vespasian was proclaimed emperor. He then sent his son Titus to put down the rebellion, which was accomplished by the complete destruction of Jerusalem the following year.

The arch has a single opening through which the triumphal processions passed in their course along the Sacra Via. There are many reliefs and inscriptions depicting the conquest of Jerusalem. One relief shows the Romans carrying off the famous seven-branched candlestick from the Temple of Solomon. It was brought to Rome, but unfortunately, it has long since disappeared. In the Middle Ages the arch was built into the Frangipani fortifications. When Giuseppe Valadier cleared it in 1822, he had to take it down and reassemble it. Some of the parts were replaced by travertine.

In front of the Arch of Titus are the remains of what appears to be a large building, reaching from the Sacra Via almost to the Palatine Hill. These are the ruins of the *Porticus Margaritaria* (*Porticus Neronis, Horrea Margaritaria*), discovered by Lanciani in 1879. Later scholars have determined that these ruins formed part of the vestibule of Nero's Domus Aurea.

In the latter part of the second century the ruins were broken up into shops for the sale of jewelry, becoming known as the Porticus Margaritaria.

Between the building we just examined and the Palatine Hill, actually on the side of the hill, runs a roadway. This is called the *Via Nova* or *New Way,* but in reality is the second oldest street in Rome, only the Sacra Via is older. The road ran along the base of the hill and eventually into the lower portion of the Domus Tiberiana, where it became the Clivus Victoriae. With our permits we will be allowed to walk down the road, if we didn't do so in our visit to the Palatine Hill.

Crossing back in front of the Arch of Titus, we now retrace our footsteps down the Sacra Via. Just past the ruins of the Porticus Margaritaria and across the street from the Temple of Romulus, stand more imposing ruins. These are the remains of the *Atrium Vestae* or *House of the Vestals.* This building which housed the Vestal Virgins was one of the most sacred and important precincts of the Forum.

Six Vestal Virgins resided in the Atrium Vestae, their job to tend the sacred fires of Rome under the protection of Vesta, goddess of the hearth and protector of the household. Keeping alive the sacred flames was a tradition dating back to the Regal Period when fires were not easily kindled. If the flame went out the Virgin responsible was given a public whipping by the Pontifex Maximus.

As previously stated, there were six Vestal Virgins or priestesses enrolled in the sacred order of the Vestal Virgins. Two young girls were selected between the ages of six and ten. They then spent the next ten years learning their duties as Vestals, being tutored during this decade by the oldest pair of Vestals. The remaining two were the ones who actually carried out the functions of priestesses of Vesta. Thus, there were always two in training, two practicing, and two acting as teachers. After serving for thirty years they could retire into private life. Their punishment for losing their virginity during their tenure was to be entombed alive in a brick wall. During the period of the Republic they were the most respected women in Rome, and in the Empire they were second only to the empresses. Wills, sacred vows, and other important documents were deposited with the Vestal Virgins for safe keeping.

The building was named for its atrium or courtyard that took up about one-fourth of the area of the structure. At some time in the Regal Period the House of the Vestals and the Temple of Vesta were moved from the Palatine to the Forum, perhaps when Numa shifted the royal residence. The remains that we see today date from the time of Nero and later. Beneath the imperial pavement, there are, in places, the remains of the Republican flooring. In pre-Neronian times the building had a different alignment than is shown today. After the fire of 64, the house was rebuilt and enlarged by Domitian, Trajan (97-117), and Septimius Severus.

From the ruins we can see that the building was 115m. (377.29 ft.) long by

53m. (173.88 ft.) in width. The courtyard or atrium was 67m. (219.82 ft.) in length by 24m. (78.74 ft.) wide. Three cisterns in the atrium have survived, we can see gold fish flitting around in the waters. This courtyard had a great colonnade of forty-eight columns. The statues of the Vestal Virgins were housed under the colonnaded roof. These figures still stand today, most of them headless, having suffered the wrath of medieval Christians. The building had at least two stories, with the priestesses occupying the second floor as their living quarters. As can be seen, the house was built up against the Palatine, in fact, it formed the outside boundary of the Nova Via. Various traces of rooms can be detected, but today, their functions are not clearly understood. At the northwestern end of the atrium (toward the Temple of Vesta) we can detect the remains of a kitchen, a triclinium or dining room, and a vestibule. At the opposite end of the atrium we can see a reception hall or tablinum. There are three rooms on each side of the hall, which were probably the offices of the six Vestals.

Near the remains of the Atrium Vestae in the northeast corner are the ruins of a rounded temple with six columns still standing. This is the *Temple of Vesta* (*Aedes Vestae*) where the Vestals kept the sacred fires burning. According to tradition, the temple was built by Numa Pompilius, the second king of Rome. Because of their obligations to keep the sacred fires burning perpetually, the priestesses from time to time were negligent, and the temple was burned many times.

Fire destroyed the temple in 241 B.C. and again in 210 B.C. Then in the 1st Century B.C. it was damaged by flood waters. Augustus quickly repaired it, thus, the present foundation dates to the rule of Augustus. The great fire of 64 destroyed it, and again it burned in 191. A couple of years later Julia Domna, wife of Septimius Severus, restored it for the last time. Most of the remaining parts of the temple date to this reconstruction in the late 2nd Century. It was closed by Theodosius the Great (378-395) in 394, and the sacred fires that had burned for over a thousand years were permanently extinguished.

The temple was in good shape in 1549 when the scavenging lime hunters began to burn its marble for the lime. It was again discovered in 1883 and completely excavated in 1899-1900. In 1930 it was partially restored, the missing marble replaced with travertine.

Across the street from the Atrium Vestae, at the beginning of the fork in the Sacra Via, are some piers made of tufa. This foundation marks the site of a triumphal arch known as the *Fornix Fabianus.* It was made up of a single span, and was not an arch in the true sense of the word. Fragments of the structure were found in 1543 and 1899. Excavations in 1953 uncovered the foundation.

Quintus Fabius Maximus Allobrogicus, consul for 121 B.C., erected it to commemorate his victory over the Gauls. This was the year that Transalpine Gaul (Gallia Transalpina) was made a province, although the area was not controlled by Rome until Caesar's time. A grandson of the Allobrogici, with the same name, restored it in 57 B.C.

Behind the ruins of the Fornix Fabianus are located the remains of a brick building with a marble door sill. This structure is the *Regia,* the former home of the second king of Rome. According to tradition Numa Pompilius transferred the royal residence from the Palatine to the Forum, which was still marshy in places in the late 8th Century B.C. Numa, who concerned himself with religion, turned over the residence to the Pontifex Maximus or chief high priest. Until the imperial period it remained the residence of the Pontifex Maximus.

Like most of the other structures in Rome it was damaged or destroyed several times by fire. The Regia was burned in 210 B.C., 148 B.C., 36 B.C., and 64 A.D. In 36 B.C. it was rebuilt on a smaller scale by the general Gnaeus Comitius Calvinus, who also realigned it to its present orientation. Some of the remains of the substructure date back to about 575 B.C. Remains of several rooms can be detected, which probably included sleeping quarters, a chapel, a room where sacred objects were stored, and an area to deposit the sacred records. There was also a courtyard, partly covered by a roof.

Behind the Regia, the remains of another monument can be seen. If we walk around to the front (the side opposite the Regia), we find that we are looking at the remains of the *Temple of Caesar (Templum Divi Julii, Aedes Divi Julii).* In the center is a recessed area that once contained an altar, marking the spot where Julius Caesar was cremated on March 17, 44 B.C. Only the lower portion of the altar can still be seen. After the cremation a rabble rouser named Amatius erected an altar there and dedicated it to the "Father of His Country." Fearing riots and mob hysteria, Antony, though a loyal follower of Caesar, had the 6.1m. (20 ft.) high column of marble torn down and the builder executed.

In 42 B.C. with the situation under control, the Second Triumvirate, composed of Antony, Octavianus, and Lepidus, vowed to build a temple on the same spot to the deified Caesar. Construction began in 33 B.C. The temple was completed and dedicated by Octavianus on August 18, 29 B.C. In the niche in the front side of the temple, the new altar stood on the site of the one that had been torn down. About five courses of building stone that make up the rostra have survived today. Octavianus decorated it with prows of captured ships from the Battle of Actium in 31 B.C. This platform is called the *Rostra Aedes Divi Julii.* The core that remains is made of brick and concrete. On this altar Tiberius (14-37) gave the funeral oration for Augustus (Octavianus) in 14 A.D. The great fire of 191 destroyed most of the building, but it was rebuilt by Septimius Severus in 193 or 194.

On each side of the temple the remains of walls and foundations can be noted. These are the ruins of the *Porticus Julia* that enclosed the Temple of Caesar on three sides. On the back side it connected the temple with the Regia by means of a cryptoporticus.

PLATE 7

A. Forum (from Capitoline)

B. Forum (from Palatine)

PLATE 8

A. Arch of Septimius Severus

B. Arch of Titus

PLATE 9

A. Basilica Aemilia

B. Temple of Vesta

PLATE 10

A. Temple of Romulus

B. Senate House

In front of Caesar's Temple and to the extreme right toward the Temple of Castor, we see four steps and a short column. These and the pavement in front of the Temple of Caesar are the remains of the *Tribunal Praetorium*. This was the place where the urban praetor heard cases and dispensed justice.

At the southwest corner of Caesar's Temple, extending out from the ruins of the Porticus Julia, several large tufa blocks can be seen. This constitutes the remains of the *Tribunal Aurelium*. On this platform or podium, the defendants and witnesses of the trials conducted by the urban praetors were sequestered. This structure dates back to about 75 B.C., at which time it was probably built by the Consul C. Aurelius Cotta.

To the right of the temple, note the brick and masonry foundation protruding from the pavement. What we see are the remains of two *Arches of Augustus (Arci Augustorum)*. The rear foundation is the oldest, built in 29 B.C. to support the single arch commemorating the victory of Octavianus at Actium. After he successfully obtained the return of the Roman Eagles captured by the Parthians from Crassus at Carrhae in 53 B.C., Augustus built another arch in 19 B.C. in honor of this momentous event. Augustus converted the single arch into a triple arch. This later addition is shown by the ruins in the foreground. The remains of the Parthian arch was discovered in 1888, but the Actium arch not uncovered until 1950.

Beside the Actium arch can be seen some travertine and tufa remains. These ruins have been identified as the *Puteal Libonis (Scribonianum, Well-Head of Libo)*. Puteal originally meant a curbstone around a well, but in later ages it was used to designate a sacred spot. It probably marked a spot where lightning had struck, since remaining fragments indicate lightning probably did strike here. It took its name from Lucius Scribonius Libo, who depicted it on a coin around 60 B.C. When it was built, we have no way of knowing, the date of its construction has not yet been established.

Moving on to our right, we see, behind the large temple, a bricked-in sunken fountain. This is the *Fountain of Juturna (Lacus Juturnae, Spring of Juturna)*. It was originally a spring where travellers watered themselves and their horses upon entering Rome. Roman legend recounts the story that the Dioscuri stopped to water their horses here in 496 B.C., as they brought back news of the Roman victory at Lake Regillus. The fountain was probably the earliest meeting place in the Forum. After 496 B.C. the basin was probably lined with brick, and in the time of Augustus faced with marble.

Located behind and diagonally across from the fountain, is a shrine. This is the *Shrine of Juturna (Aedicula Juturnae)* that housed a statue of the deity. Juturna, a water goddess, became popular in Rome after the 1st Punic War. This shrine was built sometime near the middle of the 3rd Century B.C. The small pronaos with its two Corinthian columns was restored between 1953 and 1955. Behind the shrine are rooms that abut the Palatine Hill. These rooms were built in the 4th Century when the city water department (Statio Aquarum) established its headquarters here.

Behind the shrine and built into the sides of the Palatine we notice a very large structure. This was a part of the Domus Gaiana of the Palatine which was Caligula's (37-41) addition to the Domus Tiberiana. In the late 1st Century Domitian made it into a guardroom. It had a sloping ramp leading up to the top of the hill, which is still present. Several scholars feel that Domitian may have constructed a shrine to Minerva in the portion nearest to the Shrine of Juturna. In the 7th Century it may have been converted into a shrine to the Virgin Mary. John VII (705-707) made it into the *Church of S. Maria Antiqua* around 705. After an earthquake made the building unsafe in the 9th Century, Leo IV (848-856) abandoned it, building a new church, S. Maria Nova, in part of the ruins of the Temple of Venus and Rome. Later this church was called S. Francesca Romano, which now houses the Forum Museum that we have already visited.

Several beautiful Byzantine frescoes can still be seen on the walls. There were more, but since the excavation of the building in 1900, several of the paintings have disappeared. The portion of the building that housed the city water works has been called the *Oratory of the Forty Martyrs*, dedicated to forty Christian soldiers who were frozen to death in Armenia during the persecutions of Diocletian (284-305) in the late 3rd Century.

The ruins of this structure that lies to the northwest of the church have mistakenly been labelled the *Temple of Augustus* (*Templum Divi Augusti*) by early archaeologists. While the temple lay somewhere in this vicinity, the site has not yet been discovered. The portion of the ruins lying next to the hill have been correctly identified as the *Horrea Agrippiana*, a warehouse that was probably erected by Agrippa, the capable right-hand man of Augustus. Remains of the altar dedicated to the Genius Horreorum Agrippianorum can still be seen against the brick wall. The building evidently dates back to the late 1st Century B.C.

Turning our backs to the Church of S. Maria Antiqua, we see three Corinthian columns standing 12.50m. (41 ft.) high on a podium of brick. These are the remains of the *Temple of Castor and Pollux* (*Aedes Castorum*). The temple was dedicated to the divine Dioscuri brothers, Castor and Pollux, shortly after they had watered their horses at the Fountain of Juturna while bringing news of the Roman victory at Lake Regillus in 496 B.C. Completed some twelve years later, the structure was officially dedicated in 484 B.C. This large temple was enclosed by a colonnaded porch or pronaos. The three surviving columns with the entablature at the top are the remains of this colonnade.

Toward the close of the 2nd Century B.C. it had fallen into a sad state of disrepair. L. Caecilius Metellus in 117 B.C., flushed with success from his victories over the pirates of Dalmatia, rebuilt the shrine. Tiberius restored the building again in 6 A.D. The columns and podium probably date to the restoration of Tiberius. Under Domitian, Trajan, and Hadrian major repairs were carried out. Each year two great anniversary celebrations were held.

They were the anniversary of the dedication, which was January 27, and July 15, the anniversary of the Battle of Lake Regillus. Although excavations began as early as the end of the 14th Century, the temple was not completely uncovered until 1871.

In front of the temple are the remains of an ancient street. Looking carefully, we can detect traces of an ancient pavement. This street was first known as the *Vicus Tuscus* (*Street of the Etruscans*). Its purpose was to connect the Forum with the Forum Boarium and the Circus Maximus. The name was probably given due to the large number of Etruscans who lived along it. They were probably brought into Rome by the Tarquins to build the Capitoline Temple of Jupiter. During the Republic many spice shops were built along its way; and later, it became known as the *Vicus Turarius* or *Street of the Spice Merchants.* The pavement we are standing upon dates from the 1st Century B.C., and was probably built by Augustus. An earlier pavement of brick, lying beneath the present one, could well be the original. In 1549 a statue of the Etruscan god Vortumnus, the god of plant life was found along the street. He was apparently an important god to the Etruscans, known to them as Voltumna. In Rome he was never adopted by the Latins.

The street continues to the junction with the Sacra Via near the opposite side of the Temple of Castor and Pollux. We should then walk on in front of the Temple of Caesar to the large paved area with the bases of columns still present. These ruins lying between the Temple of Antoninus and Faustina and the Senate House are the remains of th *Basilica Aemilia* (*Basilica of Fulvia and Aemilia*). The large structure, 93.88m. (308 ft.) long by 26.07m. (79 ft.) wide, was built in 179 B.C. by the Censors M. Aemilius Lepidus and M. Fulvius Nobilior. It consisted of a nave with an aisle on each side. The roof of the nave was higher than that of the aisles. Remains of the columns can still be seen lying around. In 159 B.C. a water clock was placed in the basilica.

After Sulla came to power he began, in 80 B.C., to rebuild the basilica, which was in bad need of repair. By 78 B.C. the repairs had been finished, complete with a two storied colonnaded porch added on all sides of the building. L. Aemilius Paullus completely rebuilt the structure in 55-54 B.C. at the expense of Julius Caesar. Shops were later added on the south side of the building. After a fire partially destroyed the basilica in 14 B.C., it was rebuilt by Augustus. More restoration was carried out by his successor Tiberius. The basilica suffered its final destruction in August of 410 at the hands of Alaric and the Visigoths. It became common practice for the money changers to set up shop and ply their trade in the basilica in the mornings. Alaric took their gold and silver coins on this summer day of 410, but disdained those of copper. In the ensuing fire the copper coins melted and fused to the pavement. If you look closely enough you can still see the green copper stains on the pavement.

At the southeast corner of the Basilica Aemilia, near the ramp leading to the Forum entrance, we see a large block of marble bearing inscriptions. This block and the pavement and columns in the area belong to the *Porticus Gai et Luci (Porticus of Gaius and Lucius)*. Augustus added this porticus to the basilica in the first decade of the 1st Century to honor his deceased grandsons Gaius and Lucius. An arch spanning the street was anchored here with the other base attached to the Porticus Julia.

Toward the northwest corner of the Basilica Aemilia a circular foundation of marble can be seen. These are the remains of the *Shrine of Venus Cloacina (Sacrum Cloacinae)*. The marble ring rests upon a travertine block. Underneath the travertine are blocks of tufa. This shrine was placed at the spot where the drain from the Basilica Aemilia emptied into the Cloaca Maxima. A coin dating from about 40 B.C. shows the elevated podium with a metal fence, complete with two statues of Venus. It is somewhat strange that the goddess of love was also the protector of the great drain.

As was stated earlier, one of the streams that drained the Forum area was the Spinon that entered on the northeast from the Esquiline and exited on the west to the north of the Palatine, eventually emptying into the Tiber. King Numa Pompilius deepened the stream around 700 B.C. to aid in the drainage of the Forum. Toward the close of the 7th Century B.C. the Etruscan king Tarquinius Priscus paved the bed and sides of the stream to better drain the area. After this it became known as the *Cloaca Maxima*. The drain was not covered until the middle of the 2nd Century B.C.

Before it was covered, a portion of its length was diverted in order to avoid passing under the Basilica Aemilia. It passed on the north side of the basilica under the street called the Argiletum, turned abruptly along side the building to the site of the Venus Cloacina. Here it made almost a right angle turn passing under the southeastern end of the Basilica Julia and exiting the Forum. The main purpose of the drain, and all Roman cloacae, was to handle rain water. Sewage from public buildings was allowed to drain into the Cloaca, but private homeowners could not use the drain. At lower levels in certain buildings the rushing water of the Cloaca Maxima can still be heard.

Between the Basilica Aemilia and the Senate, the remains of another paved street can still be detected. This is called the *Argiletum*. It connected the Forum with the noisy eastern quarters of the city named the Subura. Julius Caesar was supposedly born in the Subura. From the Via Sacra the roadway passed between the Esquiline and the Viminal and finally terminated at the Clivus Suburanus.

The well preserved building we see standing before us is none other than the famous *Senate House*. It is also referred to as the *Curia Julia* or *Senatus*. The greater portion of the building dates from the 3rd Century. Originally, the building was called the *Curia Hostilia*, perhaps dating back to the 7th Century B.C. to the reign of *Tullus Hostilius* (673-642 B.C.).

With the advent of the Republic in 509 B.C., the Senate became the ruling body of Rome. Kings and ambassadors met this august body of patricians as Rome became the dominant power in the Mediterranean Basin.

By the beginning of the 1st Century B.C. the building was in need of repair. Large scale repairs were carried out by Sulla in 80 B.C. Later, in the middle of the century, the building suffered a major disaster. With Caesar in Gaul, the followers of Pompey and Crassus began to drift apart. Milo led the followers of Crassus, who was now dead, and Clodius had the support of Pompey. One day in 52 B.C. there was a confrontation between the two groups that led to a gang fight. Clodius was killed in this street fighting. His beautiful wife, the red-haired and violent tempered Fulvia, had his body carried to the Senate where she cremated it. While carrying out this cremation, she also burned the building down.

Faustus the son of Sulla was commissioned to rebuild it, but the task was never completed. Julius Caesar began to restore it to its original shape and size in 44 B.C., but his subsequent death brought the project to an abrupt halt. The job was completed by Octavianus in 29 B.C., at which time it was renamed the Curia Julia in honor of Caesar. It was damaged severely in Nero's fire of 64, and suffered again in the fire of 80. After coming to power in 81, Domitian had the Senate building rebuilt, although by this time the body had lost most of its power to the emperors.

A fire in 283 completely destroyed the structure. Diocletian rebuilt it a few years later. Most of the edifice that we see today, dates from the restoration of Diocletian. In the 7th Century the building became the Church of S. Adriano and was kept in excellent condition by the Christians. The bronze doors were removed to S. John in Lateran in the 17th Century. Between 1935 and 1938 the building was restored to its ancient form, just as we see it today.

The building measures about 51.3m. by 27.5m. (168 x 90 ft.). From the mid-1st Century B.C. the brick that we see was covered in marble. It also possessed ornamented gables. Inside we can detect its simplicity. The leaders of the world met in austerity. The feature that stands out is the beautifully ornamented marble and tile floor that is remarkably well preserved. Until the emperors, the fate of much of the world was decided in this building.

Before leaving the building we should take note of the two large marble panels in relief that are "temporarily" stored here. These reliefs are the *Plutei Trajani* or *Anaglypha Trajani*. Among the various scenes shown on these panels, the most important shows Hadrian remitting taxes, an event that took place in 118, probably the year the reliefs were completed. It is called the Plutei Trajani rather than Plutei Hadriani, because one of the emperors depicted is Trajan. Originally, the reliefs stood near where the Column of Phocas stands today. For protection from the elements the two reliefs were placed in the Senate House in 1949.

In front of the door of the Senate remains of travertine can still be seen. This marks the spot of the *Comitium,* an area where the assemblies met. In the late Regal Period and much of the Republic it reached up onto the slope of the Capitoline Hill. After Caesar's reorganization of the Forum, the

Comitium was limited to the area in front of the Curia. In the early years only the Assembly of Curies met here, but after 218 B.C. it also became the meeting place of the Assembly of Tribes. The Assembly of Centuries met in the Campus Martius. By the middle of the 3rd Century B.C. the Assembly of Tribes rivalled the Senate as the guiding body in Roman politics.

Lying in front of the Comitium is an area that arouses a lot of curiosity. It is a paved area covered with black marble called the *Lapis Niger* or *Black Stone.* The pavement was discovered in January of 1899. A few months later, about 1.5 meters below the surface of the pavement, a truncated rectangular tufa column was discovered with writing on all four sides. These Latin inscriptions are among the oldest to be found in Rome, dating back to the 6th Century B.C. Steps allow sightseers to go down into the hole to look at the monument. The stele located there is a copy, the original is housed in the Forum Museum.

Its inscription can not be completely deciphered since the column is badly damaged. From what can be read, it appears to be a text warning against the violation of this sacred area. Some early writers alluded to it being the tomb of Romulus. Excavations in 1955 revealed no tomb, however, there is no question that the early Romans did consider the site a sacred spot.

Turning away from the Black Stone, we find ourselves confronted with the Arch of *Septimius Severus* (*Arcus Septimii Severi*). This arch is much larger than that of Titus at the other end of the Forum. The Arch of Severus measures about 22.86m. high by 25m. wide (75 x 82 ft.). It was built of marble in honor of Septimius Severus in 203 by his two sons Caracalla and Geta. After the murder of Geta in 212, all references to him were chiselled away. The Arch of Titus had only one opening, but this one has three.

Built upon a base, the Arch of Septimius Severus stood much higher than the pavement of the Forum, thus the great triumphs could never pass under this arch, but instead paraded to the south of the structure. A small door on the south side leads to a staircase that ascends to several small rooms above the arches. Even with permits we will not be allowed to enter these chambers.

The middle archway is 7.0m. wide (23 ft.) and 12.29m. high (40.25 ft.). At the sides the lateral archways are 3.0m. wide (ca. 10 ft.) and 12.29m. in height. Many reliefs can be detected on the arch, but the most important are those of the Capitoline side showing the conquests of Seleucia and Ctesiphon by Septimius Severus in his eastern campaigns against the Parthians. The reliefs and the arch itself served as models for many Renaissance works.

In the Middle Ages the Church of SS. Sergius and Bacchus enclosed the south side, while the north side had fortifications built against it. This aided in the preservation of the arch. In the 18th Century the two lateral archways were rented out to merchants to use as shops. This was certainly a come down from its elegance in Imperial Rome.

To the left and behind the arch (facing the Capitoline), we see the remains of a cone-shaped structure made of brick. These are the ruins of the *Umbilicus Romae*, which supposedly marked the center of Rome. As it turns out, the monument marks the designated center, but not the geographical one. Fragments of travertine indicate that there must have been a small shrine connected with the cone. The Umbilicus Romae dates from the first quarter of the 4th Century. It was discovered in 1803, while the base of the Arch of Septimius Severus was being cleared.

Beside the Umbilicus Romae, an altar made of tufa is situated. This is the *Vulcanal (Volcanal)* or *Shrine of Vulcan.* Shrines or temples to the Roman fire god had to be constructed outside the limits of the city, thus, this must date back to the days of Romulus. After the city annexed the area the shrine was permitted to stay. According to tradition it marks the spot where the Latin Romulus and the Sabine Tatius concluded a peace treaty. Remains of the altar, a tufa pavement, and a drainage channel are still visible. Until the Rostra was built, the Vulcanal probably served as a speaker's platform.

Moving on past the Rostra, which we will examine later, we see, just before we get to the Basilica Julia, the ruins of a concrete foundation. This marks the site of the *Milliarium Aureum* or *Golden Milestone.* Its foundation was discovered in 1959. Part of the marble base and shaft lie in front of the Temple of Saturn. These fragments were uncovered in 1835 and 1852. The structure, which was a marble shaft gilded with bronze, was erected by Augustus in 20 B.C. Recorded upon it were the mileages from Rome to all the great cities of the Empire.

Looking up from the fragments of the Milliarium Aureum, we see the stately ruins of the *Temple of Saturn (Templum Saturni, Aedes Saturni).* Eight unfluted granite columns stand upon a rather high travertine base. Most of the lintel, frieze, and cornice are still present atop the columns, along with a portion of the gable. Looking west from the Arch of Septimius Severus we see the six gray columns that formed the front of the temple, while the two red ones on the north and south sides are the remains of the pronaos or porch.

According to legend construction began under the Etruscan king Tarquinius Priscus in the early 6th Century B.C. It was finally completed and dedicated on December 17, 497 B.C. In the early Republic the temple was also used as the state treasury. Remains of this *Aerarium Saturni* or *Aerarium Populi Romani* can still be detected as the ruins of the room can be seen on the southeast corner. If one looks closely at the marble sill, the holes for the door lock can still be seen.

By mid-1st Century B.C. the temple was in a sad state of repair. Extensive restoration was carried out by L. Munatius Plancus in 42 B.C. The travertine veneer of the base dates to the time of these repairs. In 283 a fire severely damaged the building. It was finally repaired in the early 4th Century. The granite columns which stand almost 11m. (36 ft.) high, date back to this reconstruction.

As we stand on the south side and look up at the temple, we should take note of the pavement we are standing upon. This is the *Vicus Jugarius*, also known as the *Street of the Yoke Makers*. It is the continuation of an ancient trade route from the land of the Sabines to the Tiber ford at Rome. The portion from the Porta Carmentalis in the Servian Wall to the Forum became known as the Vicus Jugarius. Where it entered the Forum there was an arch, the remains of which can still be seen at the corner of the Temple of Saturn located across the street. The pavement was discovered in 1882, along with a large drain or cloaca lying beneath the pavement.

If we retrace our path to the vicinity of the Golden Milestone, we are confronted by a large rectangular structure on the right. These ruins with a straight front and a concave back are the remains of the *Rostra* or *Rostra Augusti*. The original Rostra stood to the side of the Lapis Niger. Behind the Black Stone we can see the tufa walls of the *Old Rostra (Rostra Vetera, Rostri Cesarei)*. This is the spot where the Roman orators delivered their speeches. Cicero was probably one of the best known of these speakers. It was built sometimes in the 5th Century B.C. In 338 B.C. it was decorated with the beaks (rostra) of warships captured at Antium from the Latin League by C. Maenius. Most of the structure was destroyed when Caesar realigned the Forum.

Moving back to the *"New Rostra"* that was observed earlier we should now examine it in more detail. As Caesar was constructing new buildings and redesigning the Forum, he decided to relocate the Rostra. The Old Rostra was duplicated completely in the new location. Caesar began work on the platform in 44 B.C., but his untimely death halted construction. Augustus completed the task fifteen or twenty years later. The Rostra is about 23.77m. (78 ft.) long, 12.19m. (40 ft.) wide, and 3.05m. (10 ft.) high. On the concave back side six marble steps lead to the top of the platform. The front, complete with holes for the beaks of the ships, was reconstructed in 1904 by archaeologists.

Just past the northeast corner of the Rostra, are the remains of the base of a marble column, all that remains of a monument of five columns erected by Diocletian in 304 or 305. This *Column of Diocletian* was to commemorate his 10th anniversary as Rome's imperial leader.

In front of the Rostra we can see three large marble fragments. These belong to the concrete foundation located at the north end of the Rostra and near the Arch of Septimius Severus. Built at the close of the 4th Century, it was a tablet commemorating a victory over Gildo, a rebellious governor in North Africa. It is referred to as the *Quadriga Arcadii et Honorii*, honoring Arcadius the victorious general and the emperor Honorius.

Further out in front of the Rostra, and not too far from the Column of Phocas, there is a large engraved block of marble seated upon a travertine base. This is the base of the *Statua Stilichonis* that originally supported an Equestrian statue of Flavius Stilicho, another general serving under

Honorius. After Stilicho was murdered in 408, his name was chiselled off the block.

Near the southeast corner of the Rostra we see a large standing column. This Corinthian column on a marble base is the *Column of Phocas* (*Columna Phocae*), supposedly the last monument to be erected in the Forum. The column, standing 14m. (45.93 ft.) tall, with a diameter of 1.39m. (4.56 ft.), dates from the 1st Century B.C. or A.D. Its base comes from the 4th Century. These purloined parts were placed on a brick pedestal in 608 and dedicated to the Byzantine Emperor Phocas by Zmargdus, Exarch of Italy. Marble steps lead up on all sides, concealing the pedestal. The steps on two sides were removed in 1903. A statue of Phocas originally topped off the column.

Southeast of the column we see a sign designating the area as the *Lacus Curtius* (*Pond of Curtius*), lying below pavement level. This was evidently a marshy area of the early Forum. Various stories recount how the area got its name. Some say it was named for the Sabine Mettius Curtius. Others say it was named for the Roman Marcus Curtius who sacrificed himself to the gods by having his horse leap with him into a chasm that opened before him. A third version states that it was named for the Consul of 445 B.C., C. Curtius, who put a pluteal there to mark the spot where lightning struck. Most of the tufa slabs date from the time of Sulla.

East of the Lacus Curtius we can see an area that lies lower than the surrounding pavement. Here can be seen a concrete foundation measuring 18.80m. (61.67 ft.) by 5.90m. (19.36 ft.) that supported the *Statue of Domitian* (*Equus Domitiani*). Looking at the foundation, we see three travertine blocks which supported the horse's feet (one was held in the air). After the assassination of Domitian in 96, the statue was torn down, not to be rediscovered until 1903.

Just a few steps away stands the base of another equestrian statue. This was the support for the *Equus Constantini* (*Statue of Constantine, Caballus Constantini*) erected in 334. Between the Arch of Septimius Severus and the Senate, we can see a marble base on a brick pedestal. It supported another equestrian statue of Constantine, erected about 352.

Retracing our steps to the foundation of the first Equus Constantini, we see to our right the remains of a large structure. The pavement and the stumps of columns are the ruins of the *Basilica Julia.* It is the second largest structure of the Forum, ranking close behind the Basilica of Constantine. The Basilica Julia measures about 97.54m. (320 ft.) by 48.16m. (158 ft.). After completion the two-storied building displayed arcaded galleries both internally and externally. The great inner hall and nave had their ceilings just under the roof. In the time of Caligula in the 1st Century, a bridge was built from the basilica roof to the Domus Tiberiana on the Palatine. Caligula could then stroll safely from his palace to the flat roof of the Basilica Julia where he observed the crowds, and at times he threw them money, watching them scramble for the coins.

Julius Caesar began the edifice in 54 B.C., building it over the ruins of the *Basilica Sempronia.* Although it was not completed, Caesar dedicated it in 46 B.C. At the death of the dictator two years later, it was still unfinished. Augustus completed it fifteen or twenty years later. In 12 Augustus rebuilt portions of it. Unlike the Basilica Aemilia, which served as a business house, the Basilica Julia was the seat of justice in Rome. The Centumviri, a special board of 180 members who tried civil suits, had their headquarters here. In 284 the building was damaged badly again by fire, but Diocletian rebuilt it at the end of the 3rd Century. About 377 the structure underwent another restoration. Beginning in the 15th Century the popes and other collectors began to cart off its artwork and building stone.

The building of the Basilica Julia cut into the area of the Old Roman Forum. While we refer to the entire area as the Forum, the Romans considered only the area that was bounded by the Temple of Caesar, the Basilica Julia, the Rostra, and the Basilica Aemilia as the true Forum, called the *Forum Romanum Magnum.* As new buildings were built, the area of the Forum was reduced. The remains of the area that we have been calling the Forum, was designated by the Romans as the *Forum Adiectum.* It is convenient to refer to the entire area as the Forum.

At the northwest corner of the Basilica Julia, near the Vicus Jugarius, there is a cavity in the pavement. This was once a small fountain known as the *Lacus Servilius.* It measured about 6.70 by 2.50m. (22 x 8.2 ft.), and became famous during the proscriptions of Sulla as the place where the heads of the victims were exhibited. The fountain was fed from the Aqua Marcia and drained into the Cloaca Maxima.

Slightly to the right of the fountain (looking at the Temple of Saturn), about 1.52m. (5 ft.) below the pavement, there is the concrete foundation of another monument — all that remains of the *Arch of Tiberius* (*Arcus Tiberii*). It was dedicated in 16 to honor the recovery of the Roman Standards by Germanicus, son of Tiberius, from the Germans. The standards or eagles had been lost by Varus at the Battle of Teutoburg Forest in 9. It was only a single arch, nothing to compare with the Arch of Septimius Severus. Fragments of the arch were found in 1833 and 1852. The foundation itself was uncovered in 1900.

Between the Arch of Tiberius and the Rostra, the marble floor of a small room is detected. This is the *Schola Xantha* (*Schola Xanthi*) or *Office for the Clerk of the Curule Aediles.* Here the clerks of these magistrates carried out their duties. The date that it was originally built is not known, but it was restored by Tiberius in the 1st Century, and by Caracalla in the 3rd Century. It received its name from one of the men who helped dedicate it during the rule of Tiberius, Aulius Fabius Xanthus.

With our survey of the Forum completed, we are able to realize why it was such an important place to the Romans. It lost much of its political importance to the Palatine under the emperors. The Campus Martius rivalled it as a monumental center. It shared its religious importance with the Capitoline. Despite all of this, the Forum remained the most important place to the people who ruled the Mediterranean world for several centuries.

CHAPTER 5

The Imperial Fora

By the time of Julius Caesar, the Forum Romanum had become a crowded area. Caesar and several of his successors built new fora, that actually were an extension of the Great Forum. We should begin our tour of these imperial fora by leaving the corner of the Forum where the Senate House is located, crossing the Via di Tulliano, at the corner of this street and Via dei Fori Imperiali, we find ourselves at the Forum of Caesar. In front of the forum along the street we see a statue of the great dictator.

Toward the close of the 1st Century B.C., Augustus (27 B.C. - 14 A.D.) built his forum, which now sits directly across the Via dei Fori Imperiali. It is also identified by a bronze statue situated in the front. Toward the close of the 1st Century A.D. Vespasian (69-79) built his Forum of Peace, a part of which we examined in our visit to the Forum. Most of this forum lies beneath the Via dei Fori Imperiali and Via Cavour. Several years after this Nerva (96-98) built his forum which now stands between the Forum of Augustus and the Via Cavour. A statue of Nerva stands in front of his forum. Then in the next century Trajan (97-117) built his forum, the greatest of the imperial fora, across from the Victor Emanuele Monument, with the gigantic column rising from it.

The *Forum of Caesar* or *Forum Julium* is open the same hours as the Forum and closed on Tuesday. Sometimes weeks will pass without it being opened, however, in which case go to the Forum Museum and secure permission to enter. The entrance is at the southwest corner not far from the Mamertine Prison. While still busy conquering Gaul in 54 B.C., Caesar conceived the idea of building the forum, actually an extension of the Forum Romanum or main forum. He had Cicero and other agents to begin the purchase of land. Compared to today's prices the land was reputed to have cost about two million dollars, which is probably an exaggeration. By 51 B.C. all necessary land had been acquired and construction began. Its main axis was aligned northwest-southeast, measuring about 115m. (337.30 ft.) by 30m. (98.43 ft.).

After Caesar's victory over the Republicans at Pharsalus in 46 B.C., he vowed a temple to his mythical ancestress Venus Genetrix. Even though not completed, the forum and temple were dedicated on September 26, 46 B.C. at Caesar's great triumphal procession. These projects were still unfinished at Caesar's death in 44 B.C. Augustus completed the temple and forum after he

FIGURE 7

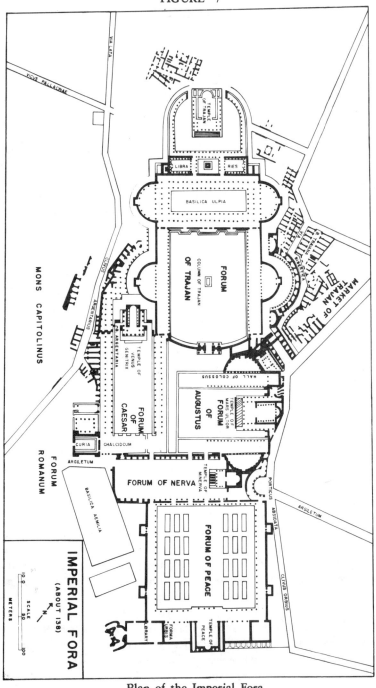

Plan of the Imperial Fora

came to power in the 20's B.C. An equestrian statue of Caesar was placed in the forum. The forum was originally surrounded by a wall and a colonnade. All that now remains of the enclosure is a part of the wall at the southwest corner, measuring 12m. (39.37 ft.) high and 3.7m. (12.14 ft.) thick. The area was excavated in 1932-33.

Entering the forum and turning left we view the *Porticus* with quite a few columns (re-erected) still standing. To the left of the portico we see row after row of cubicles, now barred to all visitors. These are the *Tabernae* or shops that lined this side of the forum. Shops were always an important part of all the early fora. The Clivus Argentarius runs behind and above the tabernae.

Past the tabernae rises a large structure, almost even with the modern street level. This is the podium of the *Temple of Venus Genetrix*. Three of the columns have been re-erected and stand on the edge of the podium. Pieces of the entablature of the temple can be seen lying on the pavement below. A statue of the goddess was formerly set up in the temple. This statue can now be seen in the National Museum (Museo della Terme). Caesar allegedly also placed a statue of Cleopatra in the temple. Some say Augustus had a statue of Caesar installed in the structure.

On the side of the podium near the open end of the forum, foundations can be seen jutting out from the temple, probably the remains of the fountain that was surrounded by water nymphs or appiades. We do know that there was a *Fountain of Appiades* in front of the temple.

Past the temple are steps leading up to another level of the forum. These lead to the structure with the archways. The edifice is known as the *Basilica Argentaria*, perhaps taking its name from the street behind it on the slope of the Capitoline. This portion of the forum and the basilica were built by Trajan in 113. In this same year he rededicated the Temple of Venus Genetrix.

If we exit the forum and walk up along the Clivus Argentarius behind the forum, we can see an interesting sight. Just above the shops or tabernae are the remains of a large latrine.

Moving across the street we arrive at the *Forum of Augustus* (*Forum Augustum, Forum Augusti*) which was an extension added perpendicularly to the Forum of Caesar. To enter the Forum of Augustus we have to go down the street and pass through the entrance into the Forum of Trajan. After entering we walk under the street and then to our right, where we pass through an opening in the wall. It is open every day except Monday, however, you may find it closed days at a time with no explanation. In which case it may necessitate a trip to the office of the superintendent in the Forum Museum.

Shortly after the death of Caesar, Octavianus began to make plans to build his forum. After the Battle of Philippi in 42 B.C., he vowed to build the forum and temple, just as his great-uncle had before him. Octavianus had his agents to begin purchasing the necessary land. After he became the first Roman emperor as Augustus in 27 B.C., he set about completing the Forum of Caesar, before starting his own. Augustus completed and dedicated his own forum in 2 B.C. After completion the forum was 125m. (410.10 ft.) by 90m. (295.28 ft.) wide. Part of this forum and that of Caesar lies under the Via dei Fori Imperiali.

Upon entering the forum, we immediately see the ruins of the *Temple of Mars Ultor*, vowed after Philippi and completed and dedicated in 2 B.C. Because the temple is the dominant feature, the square was also called *Forum Martis* or *Forum of Mars*. It was built against the rear enclosure walls of the forum. These walls stood 36m. high (118.11 ft.) and were constructed of perperino and travertine. They were built high to shut off the view of the houses on the slope of the Quirinal. The back enclosure was not in a straight line because Augustus could not buy all the land that was needed. After completion the inner surface of the perimeter walls were covered with stucco and marble.

Climbing the steps of the podium, we now find ourselves within the confines of the temple. There are 16 steps in the stairway leading to the podium. The marble covering of the temple is still visible in places. On the right-hand side, to the rear, we see three white marble columns still standing. These columns stand about 15.3m. (50.20 ft.) high. This is the only evidence left of the *Portici* that ran the length of both sides of the temple. Some of the steps leading up to the Portici are still visible. Within the temple was a central nave with flanking aisles.

To the left of the temple, in the corner, is a paved area called the *Hall of the Colossus*. It was evidently a colonnaded hall extending out from the temple to the perimeter walls. Against the perimeter wall we see a pedestal that probably was the base for a large statue of Augustus.

Looking carefully along the steps leading up to the Porticus, we see a foundation cut into the steps. An *Arch of Drusus* (*Arcus Drusi*) stood on this spot. It was built by Tiberius in 19 to honor his son, Drusus, for his victories in Germany. Walking around to the other side of the temple, we see the foundation of another arch cut into steps. This was the site of the *Arch of Germanicus* (*Arcus Germanici*) built also in 19 to honor the emperor's nephew for his German victories.

If we turn and look behind us, we can see in the enclosure walls a large semicircular indentation called an *exedra* or *apse*. On the opposite side of the temple is a duplicate. Statues were placed in these exedrae, in fact the niches to house them can still be seen.

To the right of the three standing columns of the Temple of Mars Ultor, an arched opening can be seen, although it is closed up to the modern street level. It was one of the arched entrances to the Forum of Augustus, known as the *Arco dei Pantani*. This name dates from medieval times.

Southeast of the Forum Augustum there is a smaller one. This is the

Forum Nervae or *Forum of Nerva.* This square is not open to the public, so we will have to call upon our archaeological permits to gain admission. After Vespasian had built his Temple of Peace there existed a gap between the Forum Romanum and the Forum of Augustus. Most of this area was occupied by the street called the Argiletum (See Chapter 4). Vespasian had plans drawn up to block off a portion of the street and convert it into a forum. His second son Domitian (81-96) began construction on it, but was assassinated in 96 before he could complete it. Nerva completed and dedicated it in 97. Because it was a connecting forum between the others, and because it enclosed a portion of a street. it was also known as the *Forum Transitorium.*

After completion the forum was about 120m. (393.70 ft.) long by 40m. (131.23 ft.) in width. The walls were 36m. high (same height as the Forum Augustum walls) and was made of large sized stones. Like the Forum of Peace, about two-thirds of the Forum Nervae is covered by the Via dei Fori Imperiali. Inside the enclosure walls there was a colonnade extending all around the perimeter. Two of these columns can still be seen on the south side. Originally an archway gave entrance to the square from the Main Forum. This opening was between the Basilica Aemilia and the Senate along the Argiletum.

The elevated area is the ruins of the *Temple of Minerva* (*Templum Minervae*). About all that stands out are the remains of the podium uncovered in 1932 and 1933. Evidently Domitian had completed the temple before his death, even though the rest of the forum was left unfinished. A statue of Janus Quadrifrons was erected outside the temple by Domitian. In the 3rd Century Alexander Severus (222-235) set up statues of all the deified Roman emperors in the temple.

Later, various popes appropriated the building stone of the temple and the forum for their various building projects. Clement VIII (1592-1605) used some of the marble for the high altar in the Basilica of S. Peter in 1594. The rest of the temple stones were used in 1606 to build the Aqua Paolo, the fountain of Paul V (1605-1621), on the Janiculum.

Behind the temple there was a gateway that opened onto the Argiletum. In medieval times this was called the *Arcus Aureus.* In this area we can also see the foundation of a semicircular building. This structure that was excavated in 1940 is the ruins of the *Porticus Absidata.* It enclosed the rear of the forum and connected the Forum of Augustus and the Forum of Peace.

Retracing our steps back through the Forum of Augustus, we return to the great square where we originally entered the *Forum of Trajan* or *Forum Trajani.* The Via Alessandrina (Via Foro Traiano) along with the Via dei Fori Imperiali cover up a large portion of what was the greatest of all the imperial fora.

Some say that Domitian had actually planned to build this forum, but was killed before he could get started. It was probably designed by the great architect, Apollodorus of Damascus, and completed by Trajan between 112 and 114. After the administration of Hadrian the forum consisted of (1) a propylaia with a great arch, (2) the square itself with an equestrian statue of Trajan, (3) the Basilica Ulpia, (4) a great column, (5) Bibliotheca Ulpia, and (6) the Temple of Trajan. The entire area of the forum was about 310m. (1017 ft.) by approximately 185m. (607 ft.) or covered about 14.2 acres. To fit it into the area to the northwest of the Fora of Caesar and Augustus, a portion of the Quirinal had to be cut away.

The square or forum proper measured about 116m. (381 ft.) long and 95m. (312 ft.) in width. Due to the modern streets only about one-third of this area remains today. In the center of the perimeter wall and connecting with the Forum of Augustus was a great propylaia or arched gateway, erected by the Senate in 116 to commemorate Trajan's victories in Dacia. Neither this nor the base of the equestrian statue can be detected today. On each side of the forum, centered and opposite from each other, were two large exedrae or hemicycles. The northeast one in front of the Market of Trajan can still be detected.

Passing under the Via Alessandrina, we arrive back to the area we first entered, the place with all the columns. These are the ruins of the *Basilica Ulpia.* The floor of the basilica is about 1m. higher than the forum pavement. Not counting the apses or exedrae at each end of the nave, the building was about 130m. (426.5 ft.) in length and approximately 35m. (114.8 ft.) wide. According to some scholars, the roof was 36.58m. (120 ft.) above the pavement. A double row of 96 columns provided for a double aisle on all sides of the nave. There was a large monumental entrance on the side facing the forum.

Behind the basilica, towering into the sky, we take note of the *Column of Trajan* (*Columna Trajani*). This edifice was erected by Trajan in 113 to honor his victory over the Dacians in 101-102 and again in 105-106. It stands upon a square pedestal, 5.18m. (17 ft.) that covers an area of 26.83 sq. m. (289 sq. ft.) There is a door in the side of the pedestal that faces the basilica. Although there is a dispute about it, most scholars agree that the ashes of Trajan were placed in this chamber in a golden urn. But, the urn has long since been missing.

The column is over 30m. (100 ft.) high, composed of 17 marble drums. There are more than 2,500 figures on the reliefs depicting the Dacian campaign. Originally, a statue of Trajan stood at the top, but was lost in the Middle Ages. In 1588 Pope Sixtus V (1585-1590) had the statue of St. Peter placed at the top. An ordinary permit will not allow us to enter, but with special permission and a custodian to guide us, we can enter the door and climb the 185 steps to the top. Forty-three windows light the way for us up the winding stairway. No more than three or four are allowed to climb to the top at one time.

Northwest of the basilica were *Libraries* or *Bibliothecae* (*Bibliotheca Ulpia, Bibliotheca Templi Trajani*). One wing contained works of Latin and

PLATE 11

A. Forum of Caesar

B. Temple of Venus Genetrix

PLATE   12

A.   Clivus Argentarius

B.   Forum of Trajan

PLATE 13

A. Column of Trajan

B. Market of Trajan

PLATE 14

A. Forum of Augustus

B. Forum of Nerva

the other was for Greek works. Besides the bookshelves, each wing contained a reading room. According to pictures on reliefs, the libraries were two-stories tall. Southwest of the column, under the street, some library ruins can still be seen.

After Hadrian (117-138) succeeded Trajan in 117 he began to construct a temple in the northwest end of the forum centered in a line from the columns. After completion it was known as the *Temple of Trajan* or *Templum Trajani*. He dedicated it to the memory of Trajan and his wife Plotina. The remains of this building cannot be seen, as they lie beneath the modern day pavements.

Retracing our steps to the area of the exedra in the forum proper, we see behind the hemicycle a large area of ruins that seem to be fairly well preserved. This is the *Market of Trajan* (*Mercatus Trajani*) that contained about 150 shops or tabernae. Trajan probably had construction in a semicircle like the exedra behind which it sits. Some of the remains of the wall that separated the forum from the market can still be seen.

We can count six-stories of shops. Not only did these contain the shops but there were also administrative offices. Streets running at the three different levels gave access to these tabernae and offices. The street at the forum level ran right along behind the partition wall separating the forum from the market. This street gave access to the first two floors. On the slope of the Quirinal at the third floor level was the second street, giving access to the third and fourth levels. Here, we should take our time and stroll leisurely through this ancient, but well preserved market place.

As we move up the second street, we see a great hall and evidence of the offices. This street is still known by its medieval name *Via Bibertica*. From here we get an excellent view of the Forum of Trajan.

The top level street runs even with the fifth level and lies between the shops and the Quirinal. From this street there was easy access to the shops of the fifth and sixth levels. These shops fronted the opposite way from the shops of the first four levels. After looking at these upper levels, we can then exit at the entrance that leads us out onto the Via IV Novembre.

These imperial fora from Julius Caesar to Trajan are most impressive. Even though they are the personal work of one dictator and several emperors, they are actually only an extension of the main forum or Forum Romanum Magnum.

CHAPTER 6

The Colosseum And Circus Maximus

Our next sightseeing tour will take us to the area that contains both the Colosseum and the Circus Maximus. We will not be limited to these two monuments, but will examine other antiquities that lie in proximity to these two historic structures.

We should begin by walking down the Via Fori dei Imperiali to its entrance into the Piazza Colosseo. To our right, on the Velia, we see the imposing ruins of the *Temple of Venus and Rome* (*Templum Veneris et Romae, Aedes Veneris Romae*). It was considered a part of the Forum in ancient Rome, but is not within the fenced area surrounding the Forum, today. At this point, turn to the right and take the stairs to the top of the podium. Here, at this level, we are slightly above the Sacra Via as it begins its ascent to the Arch of Titus.

This great temple, dedicated to Venus, the legendary ancestress of Rome, and to Roma, the genius of the city, was built by Hadrian (117-138) upon the site of the vestibule of the Domus Aurea. Construction probably began on April 21, 121 and was completed and the building dedicated in 137. The temple was constructed with concrete, faced with travertine. Granite was used to form the beautiful columns. More decorations were added in the 140's by Antoninus Pius. After its completion the temple was 145m. (475.72 ft.) long and 100m. (328.08 ft.) wide. The apses or exedrae were built back to back.

The temple was well preserved until the fire of 307, at which time it was badly damaged. Shortly after this disaster, it was rebuilt by Maxentius (310-312). Only the podium dates from the time of Hadrian, everything else is from the restorations of Maxentius, including the marble floors on the Roma side. This temple was closed along with many other pagan temples in 394. Unlike some of the other temples, it was not looted nor stripped, remaining in good condition until the second quarter of the 7th Century. Shortly after becoming pope in 625, Honorius I (625-638) began to remove the tiles of the temple roof to the Church of S. Peter.

In the 8th Century a church was built in the vestibule, on the Forum side, called the Church of SS. Peter and Paul. This church gave way in the 9th Century to S. Maria Nova. The new church was to replace the earthquake damaged S. Maria Antiqua in the Forum. In 1612 Pope Paul V (1605-1621) rebuilt the Church of S. Francesca Romana. We have already visited it, as it is

FIGURE 8

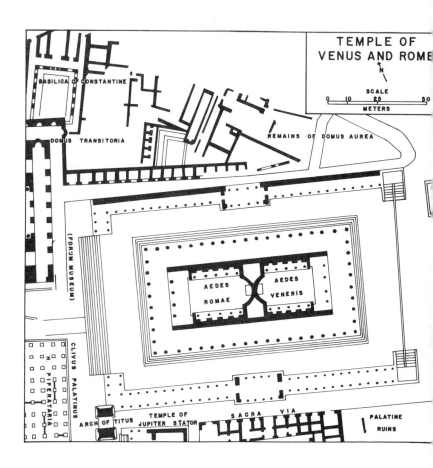

Temple of Venus and Rome

now the Forum Museum. The temple was excavated in 1810-1814 and again in 1827-1829.

With our backs to the Colosseum, we see the apse of the cella of Venus. By looking carefully, we can also see the stumps of many columns. To our right we are able to see 12 columns of varying sizes and to our left there are 10 more. These columns were re-erected in 1934-1935. Going around to the opposite side we see the cella of Roma, with the beautiful marble pavement still preserved. Descending the stairs to the Piazza Colosseo, we see rooms built into the side of the podium. These rooms were used to store equipment from the Colosseum.

If we dare to venture into the hazardous Roman traffic, we can see at the corner where the Via dei Fori Imperiali runs into the Piazza Colosseo, a 7.5m. (24.6 ft.) paved square. This marks the site of the *Colossus of Nero* (*Colossus Neronis*). Originally it stood on the Velia in the vestibule of the Domus Aurea. The statue made of bronze, and cast in the likeness of Nero, stood 40m. (131.23 ft.) high. After the death of Nero in 68, the face was probably altered so that it no longer resembled the unpopular emperor.

When Hadrian began construction of the Temple of Venus and Rome in 121, the statue was moved to the spot where we are now standing (or looking for those less brave). In 354 it was still standing. According to some scholars, it was still standing as late as 972. The concrete base, faced with brick, was uncovered in 1828. Finally, in 1936 Mussolini had the base removed.

At the opposite corner of the Temple of Venus and Rome, and about halfway to the Arch of Constantine, we see a circular mark in the pavement. This marks the site of the *Meta Sudans,* which was a large fountain. Domitian (81-96) built this fountain in the late 80's. The term *meta* in Latin means boundary marker, and could mean a meeting point of four regions (II, III, IV, and X). *Sudans* probably means spray of water. Discovery of the fountain was made in April of 1743. It was completely excavated and studied in detail in 1936, before being demolished along with the Neronic base.

Moving away from the circular spot, we now find ourselves at the *Arch of Constantine (Arcus Constantini)*. This is probably the best known of all the arches of Rome. Constantine (310-337) started building it in 312 to honor his victory over Maxentius in this year. It was completed and dedicated in 315 or 316. Made of white marble, the monument stands 21m. (68.90 ft.) high, 25.7m. (84.32 ft.) wide, and is 7.4m. (24.28 ft.) in depth.

As was the case with the Arch of Septimus Severus, the roadway did not pass through this arch. The base of the arch stood higher than the roadway. Of the three archways, the central one is by far the largest. It is 11.5m. (37.73 ft.) high and 6.5m. (21.33 ft.) in width. The lateral archways stand 7.4m. (24.28 ft.) high and 3.36m. (11.02 ft.) wide. Around and in the archways, the area was paved with travertine. The arch is covered with beautiful friezes and reliefs.

Because Constantine is considered a Christian emperor, the arch was spared destruction in the Middle Ages. A little church was built around it in the 12th Century. In 1536 Pope Paul III (1534-1549) removed the debris that had collected around it, preparing for the triumphant entry into Rome of Charles V, the Holy Roman Emperor. Pope Clement XII (1730-1740) began a complete restoration of the Arch in 1731. There are three small rooms in the upper part of the arch, but it is doubtful that we will be permitted to visit them.

Leaving the arch, we now turn out attention to the dominant feature in the area, the *Colosseum.* This term originates from the early Middle Ages when the Colossus of Nero stood nearby. To the Romans it was the *Amphitheatrum Flavium (Flavian Amphitheater).* Lying in a low area between the Palatine, Velian, Oppian, and Caelian Hills, the area was a marshy place. After Nero had built his great Golden House, the region was turned into a lake for his fabulous gardens.

Shortly after becoming emperor in December of 69, Vespasian (69-79), the first of the Flavian rulers, began to entertain thoughts of building a permanent arena for the gladiatorial games. Up to this point, the gladiators had performed their bloody feats in the Circus Maximus, the Forum, or various other sites in the Campus Martius. Neither the Forum nor the locations in the Campus Martius were satisfactory, and the Circus Maximus was designed mainly for chariot racing. Construction of the amphitheater probably began about 72. The major obstacle the builders faced was to drain the area and to make the earth firm enough to hold an enormous amount of weight. To accomplish this a large area was excavated, drained, and then covered with tremendous amounts of concrete.

At the death of Vespasian in 79 the arena had not been completed. Titus (79-81) succeeded his father as Roman emperor, and dedicated the amphitheater, although it still had not been completed. At the death of Titus in 81 it was still not finished. His younger brother Domitian, who succeeded him, finally completed the Colosseum between 85 and 86. The edifice was elliptical in shape, measuring 188m. (616.8 ft.) by 156m. (511.8 ft.). Although figures as high as 87,000 have been tossed about, it is doubtful that the Colosseum could seat more than 50,000 spectators.

The Colosseum had four stories with corridors running around the building, between the seats and the outer wall. There were corridors for each floor. It was built mainly of travertine with a veneer casing of marble in many places. Concrete and brick were also used in many places. The top of the amphitheater reached about 45.72m. (150 ft.), and the oval arena itself was about 87.48m. (287 ft.) by 54.86m. (180 ft.). Access to the stadium was by 80 arched openings located all around the structure. Seventy-six of these were for the general public, two were for the imperial party, and two for the gladiators. Of the last two mentioned, one known as the *Porta Libitinaria,* was used to remove the dead gladiators.

PLATE 15

A. Exedra of Temple of Venus

B. Colosseum

PLATE 16

A. Interior of Colosseum

B. Arch of Constantine

PLATE 17

A. Circus Maximus

B. Stands of Circus Maximus

PLATE 18

A. Temple of Mater Matuta

B. Temple of Fortune

PLATE 19

A. Theater of Marcellus

B. Arch of Janus

PLATE 20

A. Temple of Juno Sospita

B. Temple of Spes

Above the entrance arches there were the same number of arches on the second and third floors, which housed statues. The fourth floor was pierced by small square windows placed above every other arch on the third floor. To protect the spectators from sun and rain, an awning was drawn across the opening in the roof. A stone fence to regulate the crowds about the entrances was built around the Colosseum.

We enter now in the center, almost directly across the street from the Temple of Venus and Rome (open from 9:00 a.m. to 7:00 p.m.). Great portions are now blocked off to the public, however, if we show our permits we will be given access to the upper floors. We can still climb to the third level on the Palatine side of the Colosseum. Descending to the first floor again we can look out over the arena and see where the floor has been removed, revealing the basement where the gladiators and the wild beasts awaited their turn to perform in the arena. The stone floor above this basement was covered by sand to absorb the blood of combat. With special permission we can descend into the basement. The architect or engineer can quickly determine that the arena could never be flooded for naval battles as some scholars would have us believe.

Over the centuries many of the emperors made repairs to the edifice. This included Nerva (96-98), Trajan (97-117), and Antoninus Pius (138-161). In 217 the amphitheater was badly damaged by lightning. Six years later Alexander Severus (222-235) completed the repair job. In 247 Philippus (244-249) celebrated the 1,000th anniversary of the founding of the city with an elaborate program of games in the Colosseum. Gladiatorial combat was abolished in Rome in 404, but they continued to use the arena to stage wild beast hunts. The great earthquake of 422 and another in 508 wrought extensive damage upon the structure. Forty-seven years after the fall of Rome, one of Theodoric's son-in-laws staged a wild animal hunt in the arena. This spectacle of 523 was the last recorded hunt in the Colosseum.

In the middle of the 8th Century the Flavian Amphitheater began to be called the Colosseum. More earthquake damage occurred in 847. Then in 1144 the new owners of the Colosseum, the Frangipani family, converted it into a personal stronghold. Earthquakes in 1231 and 1349 caused so much damage, that much of the outer wall and great portions of the western side came tumbling down. These fallen stones were used to help build the Vatican, to rebuild the Aurelian Walls, and to build or to repair hundreds of other buildings in Rome.

Excavations in the arena began in 1811. In this century several of the popes — Pius VII in 1805, Leo XII in 1828, Gregory XVI in 1845, and Pius IX in 1852 — helped shore up the building. More excavations were carried out between 1874 and 1875. The excavations of the arena were finally completed in 1940.

This is no place to go into a detailed account of the history of the Colosseum. There are several books that do this quite well. Of all the monuments in Rome, the Colosseum is the best known. If he sees nothing else, every tourist manages to visit the Colosseum. In the 8th Century the English writer, the Venerable Bede, wrote, "While stands the Coliseum, Rome shall stand, When falls the Coliseum, Rome shall fall, and when Rome falls — the World." The Colosseum still stands, but the heavy traffic of passing automobiles each day endangers it. As the pyramids are to Egypt, so is the Colosseum to Rome.

After leaving the Colosseum we now walk by the Arch of Constantine and on along the base of the Palatine Hill. With the hill to our right, we are walking along the Via di S. Gregorio, noticing a branch of the Aqua Claudia that we examined in our tour of the Palatine. The first street we enter is the Via dei Cerchi. We take a right turn on it and immediately to our left we see the *Circus Maximus*. It takes a few minutes to completely walk around it. Along the spina of the Circus, shrubs and flowers have been planted. The best area to view the large arena is from the side opposite the Palatine Hill, or the Via di Circo Massimo which is much higher than the Via dei Cerchi.

Built in the Valley Murcia between the Palatine and Aventine, tradition tells us that the Circus dates back to the days of Romulus (753-716 B.C.). According to legend horse racing took place here under the rule of Romulus, and supposedly this is also the site of the rape of the Sabine women. No permanent structures, however, were built until 329 B.C. These first permanent features were probably chariot stalls built of wood. By the middle of the 1st Century B.C., there were three tiers of stands. The bottom two were of stone and the top one of wood.

According to some scholars, Julius Caesar built a moat 3.05m. (10 ft.) wide and 3.05m. deep to separate the arena from the stands. At the end of the 1st Century B.C. the Circus Maximus was 600m. (1,968.50 ft.) long and 150m. (492.13 ft.) wide. The arena was 550m. (1,804 ft.) by 80m. (262.47 ft.), with the stands having an average width of 35m. (114.83 ft.). Figures as high as 385,000 have been given as a seating capacity, but the more probable figure is about 150,000. Under the stands on the first two tiers attractive shops opened toward the outside of the arena.

The Circus Maximus was built primarily for horse and chariot racing, although until the Colosseum was built, authorities occasionally staged gladitorial shows here. In 80 the center gate on the eastern side was replaced with an arch honoring Titus for his conquest of Jeruselem. This was called the *Arcus Vespasiani et Titi* (*Arch of Vespasian and Titus*). The spina was decorated with several monuments. From contemporary coins we learn there was a statue of the Magna Mater riding a lion, located on the northeast end of the spina. It was called the *Magna Mater in Circo Maximo* (*Aedes Matrix Deum*). Today, no trace of it remains. Two obelisks that became known as the Obelisks of Augustus and Constantine also decorated the spina, however, we will have more to say about them when we arrive at their new locations.

In 549 Totila the Ostrogoth conducted the last events in the Circus

Maximus, a wild beast hunt. The stones from this giant stadium went to build a great portion of medieval Rome. A few remains of the stands with their shops can still be seen on the southeast corner of the Circus. These remains date to the end of the 1st Century B.C. This giant Circus must have been a sight to behold.

At the north end of the Circus, just across the Via dell'Ara Massima di Ercole are the ruins of an ancient building, discovered in 1931, but hidden today by a modern building. From the size of the structure it has been decided that it was a public building, probably connected in some way with the affairs of the Circus Maximus. In the latter part of the 3rd Century the floor at ground level was made into a Mithraeum or temple for worhip of the Persian god Mithra. The vaulted hall has niches for statues, presumably of the god. Marble covers the floor, and originally it covered the benches, although much has been stripped from the latter.⌉

Leaving the north end of the Circus Maximus, we immediately enter the area that was known in ancient Rome as the *Forum Boarium (Cattle Market)*. This cattle market also became an area where religious temples were built. The forum was bounded on the north by the Vicus Jugarius, on the east by the Palatine Hill, on the south by the Circus Maximus, and by the Tiber to the west.

If we stay along the flank of the Palatine Hill we will then find ourselves on the Via di S. Teodoro. Turning left at the first street, we find that we are now on the Via del Velabro, and almost immediately arrive at the *Church of S. Giorgio in Velabro*. Here we see an arch with one side now built into the church. This is the *Arcus Argentariorum (Arch of the Silversmith)*, built in 204 by the silver merchants of the Forum Boarium to honor Septimus Severus (193-211), his wife Julia Domna, and his sons, Geta (211-212) and Caracalla (211-217), and Caracalla's wife, Fulvia Plautilla. In 212 after he had murdered Geta and Plautilla, Caracalla had their figures removed. The empty spaces where their figures were located can be seen on the inside of the piers.

. An iron fence surrounds the arch, it is the property of the church. Actually, it is not a true arch, but a flat lintel resting upon two piers. The opening is 6.15m. (20.18 ft.) high and 3.30m. (10.83 ft.) wide. Only the base is travertine, the remainder is made of marble.

The church itself is worthy of an inspection, as it dates back to ancient Rome. A small basilica was built in the 4th Century, perhaps during the rule of Constantine the Great. The larger church was built by Pope Leo II about 682, and restorations made in the 13th Century. A portion of the skull of St. George, the famous English saint, is said to be contained in the altar, supposedly brought here from the Lateran in the 8th Century.

Continuing down the Via del Velabro, we find in the middle of the street a four-sided arch. This is known as the *Arch of Janus* or *Janus Quadrifrons*. It is made of marble and stands directly over the Cloaca Maxima. The structure is 12m. (39.37 ft.) square and 16m. (52.49 ft.) high. Each archway is 10.6m.

(34.78 ft.) high and 5.7m. (18.70 ft.) wide. There are 48 niches to hold statues, twelve on each side. Sixteen of these niches are unfinished.

The builder of this peculiar arch is unknown. From the architectural style, we can surmise that it was built in the early 4th Century, perhaps in the time of Constantine. In the 13th Century a fortress was built on top of the arch by the Frangipani family. This tower was removed in 1830.

At the southwest corner of the Arch of Janus, lying 3.25m. (10.66 ft.) below the ancient pavement and connected to the Cloaca Maxima, are the remains of six rooms. Twenty-two m. (72.18 ft.) to the west are more of those subterranean chambers. Both sets of rooms have been identified as the *Doliola*. This is the place where the Vestal Virgins supposedly hid their sacred relics and implements during the Gallic invasion of 387 B.C. The rooms were discovered in 1900 and 1901 and have since been covered by the pavement.

After leaving the Doliola, we walk down the street to the square (Piazza della Boca della Verita), turn slightly to the left, and we are at the Church of S. Maria in Cosmedin. The western portion of this church is built over the *Statio Annonae*. This ancient structure was the headquarters for the Praefectus Annonae, the official responsible for keeping the Roman people supplied with food. Throughout the western part of the church some of the remains can be seen. One example is an arch at the front entrance, just inside the front wall and along the northeast side of the church. Exactly when the Statio Annonae was built is not known, but a porticus was added in the 4th Century.

The east side of the church is built over the *Temple of Ceres, Liber, and Libera (Templum Cereis Liberi Liberaeque)*. It was started by the Dictator A. Postumius in 496 B.C. Three years later it was dedicated to the three gods by the Consul Spurius Cassius. The temple was the headquarters of the plebian aediles — a state house for their treasury and records. Hadrian I (772-795) destroyed all but a portion of the podium. These remains, made of tufa and travertine, can still be seen in the eastern portion of the church. Two sites that furnish a good glimpse of the podium are the courtyard and in the crypt. The crypt is actually cut into the podium.

After stepping out of the church, we see ahead of us a circular temple. Because of its shape it has often been called a Temple of Vesta. It is, however, the *Temple of Mater Matuta (Templum Matris Matutae)*. Named after the dawn goddess, the temple was supposedly built by King Servius Tullius (578-535 B.C.) in the 6th Century B.C. After the fall of Veii in 396 B.C. it was rebuilt by the Dictator Camillus. In 215 B.C. it was badly damaged by fire, but completely restored the next year. More restorations were carried out by Augustus (27 B.C. - 14 A.D.) in the 1st Century B.C. The podium of tufa dates to the Republic, while the rest of the marble structure dates from the time of Augustus.

In the 16th Century it was made into a church and a wall was built between the columns. Its name was changed to S. Maria del Sole. At the beginning of the 19th Century the temple was restored to its ancient form. We can see a round peristyle with 20 Corinthian columns. In the center is a cella with a diameter of 10m. (32.81 ft.). This little temple near the Tiber is a unique looking monument.

North of the Mater Matuta we sight a rectangular structure. This is the *Temple of Fortune* (*Templum Fortunae, Aedes Fortunae*). Its style is Ionic. It is made of stone covered by stucco. Like the round temple, this one supposedly dates back to Servius Tullius. It was also damaged in the fire of 215 B.C. and restored in 214 B.C. Augustus probably repaired it in the 1st Century B.C.

The temple is on a podium that stands 2.5m. (8.2 ft.) above the ground and is 26m. (85.30 ft.) long and 12m. (39.37 ft.) wide. In front there is a 6m. (19.69 ft.) pronaos. In 872 it was converted into a church and the columns were walled in. In the 16th Century Pope Pius V (1566-1572) gave it to the Armenian church and it became known as S. Maria Egiziacs. At the beginning of the 19th Century it was restored to its original form.

Walking from the Temple of Fortuna to the Tiber, we arrive at the bridge called the Ponte Palatino. If we look up the Tiber we are able to see a lone arch standing in the middle of the river. This is the remains of the *Pons Aemilius,* called today, by the Italians, the *Ponte Rotto,* The Pons Aemilius was the first stone bridge to span the Tiber. It was constructed in 179 B.C. by the Consuls M. Fulvius Nobilior and M. Aemilius Lepidus. The bridge was built on piers, the arches were not added until 142 B.C. A flooded Tiber washed it away in 280, but it was quickly rebuilt. In the Middle Ages it became known as the *Pons Senatorum* and also the *Pons S. Mariae.*

Another heavy flood in 1230 caused great damage, but it was again rebuilt. In 1557 another deluge of water caused it to collapse. Gregory XIII (1572-1585) had it rebuilt for the Holy Year in 1575. This time it lasted until the great flood of December 1598 destroyed the eastern portion. Three arches remained anchored to the west bank. An iron bridge was built in 1853, using the arches for support. This bridge was torn down in 1885, along with two of the arches, leaving only the one we see today, a lone sentinel of a historic structure.

We now walk up the Via del Teatro di Marcello to the intersection of Vico Jugario, the ancient Vicus Jugarius. There on the right corner we spot an area of fenced in ruins. This is the *Area Sacra of S. Omobono.* In this area the remains of two temples are located. The two podia are made of tufa. Scholars are not certain just to whom these temples were dedicated. Some speculate that it may have been a temple to Carmentis.

This completes the list of monuments to be found in the Forum Boarium. The small area to the left and up to the Theater of Marcellus is the *Forum Holitorium* (*Vegetable Market*). It was not nearly as large as the Forum

Boarium. As buildings were built in the region, the area of the forum was diminished, until it was only about 125m. (410.10 ft.) by 50m. (164.04 ft.).

On the west side of the street near the theater is the Church of S. Nicolo in Carcere. This church covers all or part of three temples of the Forum Holitorium. The first one on the south side is the *Temple of Juno Sospita* (*Templum Junonis Sospitae, Aedes Junonis Sospitae*). It was vowed in 197 B.C. by the Consul C. Cornelius Cethegus during the wars in Spain. This Doric temple was completed and dedicated on February 1, 194 B.C. Six of the columns can be seen built into the south wall of the church.

The middle temple, almost hidden under the church, is the *Temple of Pietas* (*Templum Pietatis, Aedes Pietatis*). Remains can be seen in front of the church. Construction was started on it in 191 B.C. Manius Acilius Glabrio began it to honor his victory at Thermopylae. His son completed and dedicated it in 181 B.C.

In the crypt of the church some remains of the south side of the northern temple can be seen. On the north side of the church four columns can be spotted built into the side of the wall. These are the remains of the *Temple of Spes* (*Templum Spei, Aedes Spei*) or *Temple of Hope.* A little away from the north church wall is a podium and two columns that were not incorporated into the church of S. Nicola in Carcere. This Ionic temple was built by M. Atilius Calatinus in 254 B.C., during the 1st Punic War.

Lightning damaged it in 218 B.C., and fire caused more harm in 213 B.C. It was completely rebuilt in 212 B.C. at the height of the 2nd Punic War. Fire damaged it again more severely in 31 B.C. After 27 B.C. Augustus began to restore it, but the task was not completed until Tiberius (14-37) did it in 17. After completion it was about 30m. (98.43 ft.) long and 10m. (32.81 ft.) in width.

At the corner of the Via del Teatro di Marcello and the Vicus Jugarius, on the Capitoline corner, we see three archways built of peperino and some travertine walls. As was stated earlier in the chapter on the Capitol, this is probably the *Porticus Minucia* that helped enclose the Forum Holitorium. Some scholars, however, dispute this claim. The porticus was built by M. Minucius Rufus in 110 B.C. Beginning with the rule of Claudius (41-54) in the 1st Century, this became the site of the regular Roman grain dole.

For the moment we will skip the Theater, as it was not considered one of the buildings of the Forum Holitorium, although right in the middle of it, and continue on to the two on the north side that were. In actuality the Theater and Forum Holitorium are considered by many to be within the Campus Martius, but we will treat them in this chapter for the sake of continuity.

On the north side of the Theater of Marcellus there are three columns from the southeast corner of the temple, and a podium surrounded by a pavement. This is the *Temple of Apollo,* (*Templum Apollonis*) the first to be built in Rome to this sun god. It was vowed in 433 B.C. as a deadly plague held a tight grip upon Rome. The temple was completed and dedicated in 431 B.C. The remains here date from the reconstruction of C. Sosius in 33 B.C. It was not until 1940 that the three standing columns were re-erected.

To the right of the Temple of Apollo are the ruins of another ancient monument. These are the remains of the *Temple of Janus* (*Templum Jani, Aedes Jani*). About all that remains is the podium, built of masonry. The temple was built by C. Dulius in 260 B.C. to honor his victory over the Carthaginians at Mylae. It was restored by Tiberius about 17. These remains date to this restoration.

Let us now turn our attention to the dominant structure of the area, the *Theater of Marcellus* (*Theatrum Marcelli*). Julius Caesar planned this building, and began to acquire property and demolish buildings on the site. Work on it had barely begun at his death in 44 B.C. Augustus completed it and dedicated it to his nephew and son-in-law, Marcellus, who had died in 23 B.C. The year of dedication was about 11 B.C.

After completion the diameter of the theater was about 150m. (492.13 ft.) and the stage was about 90m. (295.28 ft.) wide and 20m. (65.62 ft.) deep. The seating capacity was about 14,000. It was constructed of travertine and then covered with stucco and marble. The first floor arcade has Doric columns while the second floor arcade is Ionic. Above the second floor was an attic pierced with windows. The theater served somewhat as a model for the Colosseum.

Evidently, by the end of the 4th Century it was in ruins, as material from it was used to repair the Pons Cestius. Several powerful families used it as a home and fortress in the Middle Ages. Finally, it was cleared and restored between 1926 and 1933.

After the tour of the theater, we now walk behind it to the bridge that connects to the Tiber Island. This is the *Pons Fabricius* commonly called *Ponte Fabricio*. It was built in 62 B.C. by L. Fabricius. There is some evidence that there had been a wooden bridge at the site as early as 192 B.C. Repairs were made on the bridge in 21 B.C. by the consuls M. Lollius and Q. Lepidus.

Most of the material in the bridge is the original. It is built of tufa, travertine, and peperino. The bridge has two arches with a very small one in the middle. Pope Innocent XI (1676-1689) added the parapet in 1679.

CHAPTER 7

Campus Martius

Our next visit into Roman Antiquity covers a large and famous area, known as the *Campus Martius* (*Field of Mars*). Generally speaking, this region encompasses the peninsular area where the Tiber makes a great bend, with the Tomb of Hadrian lying on the opposite bank. The ancient Romans looked upon the Capitoline, Quirinal, and Pincian Hills as forming the eastern boundary. On the south the boundary was the southern side of the Forum Holitorium, including the Theater of Marcellus. We have already visited the Forum Holitorium and the Theatrum Marcellae, therefore, the boundary of our visitation area will be a line extending from the Theater of Marcellus to the Capitoline and then up the Via del Corso to the east side of the Piazza del Popolo. Our line then extends westward from the Porta del Popolo to the river. The Tiber forms our western boundary.

Eventually, the Campus Martius became one of Rome's monumental centers, rivalling the Forum and Capitoline. At the beginning of the Republic, however, it was a swampy plain that tended to be flooded by the Tiber at times. The first major structure to be built in the region about 221 B.C. was the Circus of Flaminius. By this time the Forum Holitorium was beginning to develop on the southern fringes of the plain. Then, in the middle of the 1st Century B.C. Pompey and Caesar began to convert the swampy land into a great monumental area. Many of the emperors, beginning with Augustus (27 B.C. - 14 A.D.) added more structures to the region.

Our tour should begin at the Theater of Marcellus. The street running from the river northward along the west side of the theater is the Via del Portico d'Ottavia. After a couple of blocks the street then turns in a northwesterly direction. Before it makes this turn we will walk upon it for a block and then turn left on the Via Catalana. As we stroll along this street for a couple of blocks, the area to our right is where the *Circus Flaminius* was once located. Some of the earlier scholars thought it lay further to the north, but it has now been established that it was in this region. No archaeological remains have been discovered, thus, scholars have to rely upon a fragment of the marble Severan plan (Forma Urbis).

C. Flaminius Nepos constructed it in 221 B.C. He held the censorship that year, but was later killed at the Battle of Lake Trasimene in 217 B.C. against Hannibal. Its long axis was oriented in a northwest-southeast direction. To the best of our knowledge it was about 260m. (853 ft.) long by

100m. (328 ft.) wide. The tribunes sometimes met here to discuss problems with their constituents. Augustus reportedly flooded it upon one occasion in 6 B.C. and held an alligator hunt. Much later in imperial times it seems to have been neglected and fallen into disrepair. Nevertheless, it seems that parts of it were still standing in the 4th Century.

Now let us turn and go back down the Via del Portico d'Ottavia to the Via di S. Angelo in Peschevia, where Portico d'Ottavia turns left. This street takes its name from the fish markets located here during ancient and medieval times. At the corner of the two streets lie the ruins of a classical structure that has been identified as the *Porticus Octaviae* (*Porticus of Octavia*). On the south side we see the main entrance with two columns to the left of the archway. Inside the arched opening is another row of three columns. Walking around the structure we see more columns and stumps of columns. The rectangular porticus was 136m. (466.2 ft.) by 118m. (387.1 ft.).

It was built in 147 B.C. by Q. Caecilius Metellus to enclose the already existing temples of *Jupiter Stator* and *Juno Regina*. In 23 B.C. Augustus rebuilt the structure and renamed it for his sister Octavia. Behind the temples were a meeting hall and a library with two wings, one for works in Greek and the other for Latin. The structure was badly damaged by the fire of 80, and not completely restored until 203 by Septimius Severus (193-211). Most of the remains on the site today date back to this Severan reconstruction.

Moving north from the Porticus of Octavia we walk along the Peschevia which becomes Via Michelangelo Caetani after a block. We see at No. 23 a brick archway built into the building. It is flanked by two travertine columns and has been identified as part of the remains of the *Crypta Balbi*. Some scholars of Roman Archaeology feel that the Crypta Balbi was nothing more than the outer corridor around the east side of a theater of the same name.

Walking two blocks west to the Piazza Mettei, we find ourselves in the vicinity of the *Theater of Balbus* or *Theatrum Balbi*. All visible remains of the theater are underground and it will be necessary to get the various owners' permission to view them. Under the house at No. 19 in the Piazza Mattei are the remains of a reticulate wall. Across the street there are more remains lying beneath the Palazzo Mattei. Here we can see reticulate walls and large travertine blocks. Moving north of the palace to No. 19 Via delle Botteghe Oscure there are travertine walls beneath the building. These walls are part of the north walls of the theater.

The theater was started by L. Cornelius Balbus in 19 B.C., and completed and dedicated in 13 B.C. It could hold about 7,700 spectators. It is uncertain when the theater fell into disuse, but it probably enjoyed a very short life since the more magnificent Theater of Marcellus was completed about the same time.

We should then stroll eastward (turn right) on the Via Botteghe Oscure to a point near the intersection with Via Celsa. On the left can be seen two fluted peperino columns on a travertine base flanked by brick walls. These are the remains of the *Temple of Bellona* (*Templum Bellonae, Aedes Bellonae*). The temple, dedicated to Bellona, goddess of war, was vowed by Appius Claudius Caecus in 296 B.C. and it was probably completed around 291 or 290 B.C. From time to time the Senate gathered here to greet victorious generals and foreign ambassadors.

Next we walk back westward on the Via Botteghe Oscure until we arrive at the southwest corner of a rectangular area that lies about 4.5m. (14.76 ft.) below the modern street level. This is the *Area Sacra del Largo Argentina.* It gained its name from a 15th Century tower built in the vicinity called the Argentoratum. With our permits we may descend, but it is better to do that later, as we can orient ourselves better from the street level at this time.

Standing at the intersection of Via Florida (at this corner it becomes Via Botteghe Oscure) and Via S. Nicola de Cesarini, we are at the southeast corner of the excavated area. Looking into the area we see the remains of four republican temples. At the extreme left hand side we can see the partial remains of a temple. Most of it still lies beneath the Via Florida. Only about one-fourth of this temple is uncovered, showing a brick podium with a set of stairs of nine steps that ascend on the east side.

To the right stands the remains of another temple, whose length is not quite as long as its comrade on the left. There is a short flight of stairs leading up to the first landing and then an excavated area. A combination of brick and travertine has been used in the construction of this building. Directly behind this temple lies what looks like a peristyle, but most of it still lies buried under the Via di Torre Argentina, and its identity is uncertain.

In the middle of the sunken area are the ruins of a round temple. Besides the pronaos and podium, there are the remains of an altar with six columns forming a semicircular background. The podium behind the temple and slightly to the left probably is the remains of the front of the *Curia Pompei.* This was the place where the Senate met after the Senate House burned down in 52 B.C. If this is indeed the Curia Pompei, then, upon this spot Julius Caesar was assassinated in 44 B.C.!

Between the round temple and the temple on the right we can see the remains of several buildings. The right hand temple seems to be the largest temple of the group. It also contains the stumps of many columns on the north and south sides. The apse of the medieval Church of S. Nicola de Calcarario which was built into the temple can also be seen. In the northwest corner of the sunken area a large latrine can still be detected. The functions of these temples are not clearly understood, and scholars still can't determine the exact date of their construction. It may be as early as the 4th Century B.C.

Leaving the Argentina area behind us, we proceed south on Via Arenula to Via del Portico d'Ottavia (first street to the right), turn right on it and after a block it becomes Via de Giubbonari. The street taking off to the right, the Via de Chiavari, forms the boundary of the front of the *Theater of*

Pompey (Theatrum Pompei). The remainder of the theater was semicircular, with the center located about where the Via de Giubbonari intersects the Piazza Campo di Fiori. Ruins of this theater can be seen beneath several houses in the area, on Via Grotta Pinta and Via del Biscione.

This theater, also called *Theatrum Magnum*, was the first in Rome to be constructed of stone. It was built by Pompey and completed in 55 B.C. The diameter of the auditorium was about 150m. (454.63 ft.), while the width of the scaena (stage) was 95m. (311.68 ft.). Within the theater at the top of the cavea, Pompey built the Temple of Venus Victrix. Remains of this temple can be seen beneath the Palazzo Pio-Righetti. It is worth our time to get permission to look at the ruins of the tufa foundation. As late as 357 the theater was still in use. It could comfortably seat between 10 and 13,000 spectators.

After completing our visit to the theater, we walk north on Chiavara to Corso Vittorio Emanuele, turn left, and very shortly we find ourselves at the northeast corner of the Palazzo della Cancelleria (at the corner of Emanuele, Via dei Baullari, and Vicolo dell' Aquila). This part of the building stands over the *Tomb of A. Hirtius (Sepulcrum A. Hirtii)*, and a portion of it can still be seen in the basement of the building. Parts of the east, north, and south brick perimeter walls are preserved. This is the Tomb of A. Hirtius, one of the consuls killed at Mutina in 43 B.C. The sepulcher was discovered in 1938.

Leaving the vicinity of the Palazzo de la Cancellaria, we walk east on the Corso Vittorio Emanuele to the Via dei Cestari (northeast corner of Largo Argentina) and turn left and walk for one block. We are now at the Via Arco della Ciambella where we turn left again. On the north side of this street (to our right) we can see the remains of a semicircular wall. These are the ruins of the circular hall of the *Baths of Agrippa (Thermae Agrippae)*.

Arco della Ciambella is the local name given to these remains. The baths were begun by Agrippa in 25 B.C., but probably were not completed until 19 B.C. Fires severely damaged the structure on many occasions. It was restored by Domitian (81-96), Hadrian (117-138), Alexander Severus (222-235), and Constantius II (337-360) and Constans (340-350). The brick remains of the circular hall that we see dates back to the restoration by Alexander Severus between 222 and 235.

Next we should walk north on the Via dei Cestari for about a block to the Piazza della Minerva. Upon entering the square we see an Egyptian obelisk standing upon the back of an elephant. This *Obelisk of the Piazza della Minerva (Obeliscus Isei Campense-Piazza della Minerva)* is made of red granite. According to the inscribed hieroglyphics it was erected at Sais in the Egyptian delta by the Pharaoh Apries (589-570 B.C.) of the XXVI Dynasty. No information is available to determine who brought it to Rome or when. It was erected in the Iseum Campense, but we have no record of when it fell.

PLATE 21

A. Porticus Octaviae

B. Temple of Bellona

PLATE 22

A. Largo Argentina Area

B. Probable Site of Caesar's Murder

PLATE 23

A. Pantheon and Obelisk

B. Roof of Pantheon

PLATE 24

A. Basilica Neptuni

B. Tomb of Augustus

PLATE 25

A. Tomb of Augustus

B. Porta Flaminia

PLATE 26

A. Column of Marcus Aurelius

B. Hadrianeum

The obelisk was uncovered in 1655 as Dominican friars discovered it while making excavations. Bernini, working for Pope Alexander VII (1655-1667), erected it upon the back of the elephant in the Piazza della Minerva. Unfortunately, Alexander died before it was dedicated, but the task was completed by Pope Clement IX (1667-1669) in 1667.

North of the Church of S. Maria sopra Minerva is the area that was occupied by the *Iseum Campense.* Evidence given to us by the discovery of columns, obelisks, and the Severan marble plan, indicate that this great temple to the Egyptian goddess was located in the region bounded on the north by the Via del Seminario, on the east by Via di S. Ignacio, on the south by Via Pie' di Marmo and Via S. Stefano del Cacco, and on the west by S. Maria sopra Minerva. The main axis of the temple ran north-south, with entrances on the eastern and western sides. Just south of this temple, sharing the same courtyard, was a large temple to Serapis (Serapeum), an Egyptian god.

This Iseum was the largest and best known in Rome. It was probably built in the late 2nd Century B.C. After a scandal in the year 19, Tiberius had the temple destroyed, the priests crucified, and the statues of Isis thrown into the Tiber. Caligula rebuilt it and the Iseum flourished until destroyed by the fire of 80. Domitian rebuilt the temple shortly after 81. The Iseum was probably maintained until the sack of Rome by Alaric and the Visigoths in August of 410. After this it was probably never rebuilt.

We now walk east on Via della Minerva and immediately find ourselves at the *Pantheon.* After the Colosseum and St. Peter's Basilica, the Pantheon is probably the most visited tourist site in Rome. On this spot Agrippa, the right hand man of Augustus, built a temple between 27 and 25 B.C. It was dedicated to the ancestral gods of the Julian family, Venus and Mars. This large temple faced south. The fire of 80 almost completely destroyed it. Domitian restored the structure in the 90's. It was badly damaged by lightning in 122, and was completely rebuilt by Hadrian, who finished it by 126. The new building faced north with a pronaos built on the front.

Septimius Severus and Caracalla (211-217) made some repairs to the building at the start of the 3rd Century. In 608 Phocas, the Byzantine emperor, presented it to Pope Boniface IV (608-615), who turned it into the Church of S. Maria ad Martyres. Even though it was now a church, it still became a source of building material in Rome. Byzantine emperor Constantine II removed the bronze roofing tiles in 663. Pope Urban VIII (1623-1644) took the bronze beams from the pronaos in the 17th Century and made 80 cannons for the Castel S. Angelo.

Passing through the ancient bronze doors, we enter the Pantheon. Prior to the building of the Houston Astrodome and the New Orleans Superdome, this was the largest domed structure in the world. The walls are 6.20m. (20.34 ft.) thick. From the floor to the opening in the dome the height is 43.20m. (141.73 ft.), and the opening has a diameter of 9m. (29.53 ft.). The pronaos that we passed through is 34m. (111.55 ft.) wide and 13.60m. (44.62 ft.) deep. It also has three rows of Corinthian columns.

Words cannot describe the interior beauty of the Pantheon. One gets the picture by walking slowly and drinking in its majestic beauty. Victor Emmanuel II, the unifier of Italy is buried here. Another king to have the Pantheon as a mausoleum is Umberto I. The great painter Raphael (Raffaello Santi da Urbino) is also interred here. Other artists whose remains are buried here are: Annibale Carracci, Taddeo Zuccharo, Baldassare Peruzzi, Perin del Vaga, and Giovanni da Udine.

Passing back through the bronze doors and the pronaos, we find ourselves in the Piazza della Rotunda. In front of us is another obelisk on top of a fountain. This is the *Obelisk of the Piazza della Rotunda* (*Obeliscus Isei Campensia di S. Macuto*). It is made of red granite. The hieroglyphs inscribed upon it date the monolith to the reign of Ramses II (1290-1224 B.C.) of the XIX Dynasty in the first half of the 13th Century B.C. It was erected at Heliopolis, and no one knows when it departed Egypt for Rome.

When it arrived in Rome it was erected within the walls of the Iseum Campense. There are no accounts depicting its fall in the Middle Ages. Early in the 15th Century it was discovered and toward the middle of the century it was reerected in the Piazza S. Macuto. By this time part of the shaft had been lost, and it is still missing today. In the latter part of the century a legend developed that indicated it was the tomb of the Bruti. Finally, between 1710 and 1711, Pope Clement XI (1700-1721) had it erected at its present site.

Walking around to the east side of the Pantheon, we see below street level, and against the Pantheon, some brick ruins. These are the remains of the *Porticus Argonautarum,* one of the two portici of the *Saepta Julia.* The Saepta Julia was the voting place for the elections of tribunes. Begun by Caesar prior to his death, continued under Lepidus, and it was finally completed by Agrippa in 26 B.C. It was about 300m. (984.25 ft.) in length and 95m. (311.68 ft.) wide. The Porticus Argonautarum bounded it on the west and to the east was the *Porticus Meleagri.*

On the south end was another structure called the *Diribitorium* where the votes were counted. Ruins of this building were discovered in 1884 while workers were excavating for a new sewer. The only evidence to be seen today of any of these structures is this little stretch of the wall of the Porticus Argonautarum lying next to the Pantheon.

Behind the Pantheon along the Via della Palombella, situated below the street level are more ruins. These are the remains of the *Basilica Neptuni.* This structure was built and dedicated by Agrippa in 25 B.C. to the sea god Neptune in honor of the naval victories of Agrippa. Not only can we see the north wall of the basilica, but parts of a few columns remain. Across the street the south wall is built into a building.

The basilica measured about 45m. (147.64 ft.) by 19m. (62.34 ft.). It connected with the Porticus Argonautarum of the Saepta Julia. It, too, was seriously damaged in the fire of 80, and was probably rebuilt by Hadrian when he restored the Pantheon.

One block to the west is the Piazza S. Eustachio. North of this plaza and up the Via di S. Eustachio we see the remains of two columns against a building on the west (left) side of the street. The columns were transported here from the *Baths of Nero (Thermae Neronianae)*. These baths, the second public ones to be built in Rome, were roughly bounded on the south by the modern Via S. Giovanni d'Arco and Via del Piazza delle Cornacchia, on the east by the Piazza della Rotunda, on the south by Via d. Crescenzi, and on the west by the Corso del Rinascimento.

Nero (54-68) built the baths in 62. They faced north and were about 190m. (623.36 ft.) long by 120m. (393.70 ft.) wide. Alexander Severus repaired them in 227. In the 18th and 19th Centuries parts of the baths were uncovered every time excavations were undertaken for construction of new buildings. The two columns we see were uncovered under the Piazza S. Luigi Francesi in 1934, and were then set up along the Via Giovanni d'Arco. They were moved to their present location in 1950.

Going west one block from the Corso del Rinascimento we find ourselves suddenly in the very large Piazza Navona. This plaza occupies the area of the former *Stadium of Domitian (Stadium Domitiani)*. The stadium was built by Domitian between 92 and 96 and reportedly seated around 15,000 spectators. It was repaired by Alexander Severus in 228, and in the Middle Ages it was referred to as the *Theatrum Alexandri*. The length of the stadium was about 250m. (820.21 ft.) and the width about 100m. (328.08 ft.).

Excavations in 1842 confirmed that this was the Stadium of Domitian. Beneath the houses on the west side of the Via Agonale ruins of the north end of the stadium can be seen.

Resting upon Bernini's Fountain of Four Rivers in the center of the plaza is the *Piazza Navona Obelisk (Obeliscus Pamphilius)*. The monolith was probably hewn from stone in Egypt, but the hieroglypics were not inscribed upon it until it arrived in Rome. These inscriptions indicated that it was dedicated to the sun god. The obelisk was erected in the Iseum Campense by Domitian shortly after he became emperor in 81. In 309 Maxentius (310-312) moved it to his circus along the Appian Way. It fell or was knocked down some time in the Middle Ages.

In the 16th Century the obelisk was found broken into five pieces in the Circus Maxentius. Pope Innocent X (1644-1655) moved it to the family palace, the Pamphili in 1648. This palace lay in the Piazza Navona. In 1649 the pope had it erected upon the Fontana dei Fiumi of Bernini. Not all the original fragments of the obelisk were included, in its restoration new material was added. Some of the fragments remained in the Circus Maxentius.

Leaving the Piazza Navona behind us, we now walk south to the Corso Vittorio Emanuele, take a right turn and continue walking west to the Tiber. Reaching the river, we find ourselves at the bridge called the Ponte

Vittorio Emanuele. South of the bridge, lying on both sides of the river, remains of travertine piers can still be seen just above water level. These are the remains of the *Pons Neronianus* built during the administration of Nero. In the 16th Century they were called the ruins of the *Pons Triumphalis*. By the beginning of the 4th Century the bridge had already been destroyed.

Moving upriver to the next bridge, we find ourselves at the Ponte S. Angelo. This modern bridge is built upon the more ancient *Pons Aelius*. It was built in 134 by Hadrian to enable people to cross the river to his tomb. Sometimes it was referred to as the *Pons Hadriani*. In the Middle Ages it was often called the *Pons Sancti Petri* or *Pons Sancti Angeli*. The balustrade that we see today was built by Pope Nicholas V (1447-1455) in 1450.

About 160m. (524.93 ft.) upriver from the Pons Aelius we can see on the east bank some debris reaching into the river. This marks the spot where a mole or pier projected into the Tiber, marking the site of the *Navalia*. The Navalia made up the shipyards and arsenal of the Roman navy. It was evidently built early in the 4th Century B.C. When the Pons Aelius was completed in 134, the Navalia was abandoned. Identification of the shipyards and arsenal was made by the excavations of 1890-91.

After a short walk up the bank of the Tiber, we come to the Ponte Cavour (second bridge) and just beyond that we see a structure enclosed in glass. Within the glassed area lies the *Ara Pacis Augustae* (*Altar of Augustan Peace*). It is open every day except Mondays from 9 a.m. to 1 p.m. and from 3:00 p.m. to 6:00 p.m. After Augustus had pacified Spain and Gaul in 13 B.C., the Senate honored him by decreeing that a monument honoring this peace be constructed. The monument was built near the Via Flaminia; construction officially began on January 30, 9 B.C.

When excavations were made near the Church of S. Lorenzo in Lucina in 1568 the first marble reliefs of the altar came to light, although at first the archaeologists didn't realize what they had uncovered. This original site lies to the southwest of us at the east end of the Piazza Borghese. In 1894 Italian and foreign archaeologists finally discovered the identity of these marble reliefs. Excavations of 1903 revealed a great portion of the altar, but flooding groundwater halted the work. Finally in 1937 the water problem was solved, and by the end of 1938 the altar had been completely excavated. It was then moved to its present site and put together, using casts for the missing parts. Originally the long axis ran east-west, but today it is oriented north-south.

The altar is enclosed by a wall of white marble 6m. (19.69 ft.) in height, 11.63m. (38.16 ft.) long, and 10.55m. (34.61 ft.) wide. A student of art can certainly appreciate the beautiful reliefs on the altar and on the perimeter walls. A description of the various reliefs is outside the scope of this book, but many articles and monographs describing them in detail are available to those interested in the topic.

To the east of the altar we see a round structure. This is the *Tomb of Augustus* or *Mausoleum of Augustus* (*Mausolem Augusti*). In 28 B.C. before he became emperor and before he had the title Augustus, Octavianus began to build a tomb for himself and his family. At that time the mausoleum lay outside the boundaries of the city, since Roman law forbade the construction of tombs within municipal limits.

The first to have his ashes placed in the tomb was Marcellus, son-in-law and nephew of Augustus, in 23 B.C., followed by Agrippa, faithful lieutenant and also the son-in-law of Augustus, in 12 B.C. The remains of a stepson, Drusus, followed in 9 B.C., then the two grandsons Lucius and Gaius were buried here in 2 and 4 respectively. The ashes of Augustus, himself, were placed here in 14, almost forty years after he had started the mausoleum. Others to have their ashes interred here were Germanicus, son of Tiberius in 19, Livia, wife of Augustus in 29, Tiberius (14-37) in 37, and then three of Caligula's (37-41) family. Included were: his mother Agrippina; and Nero and Drusus, his brothers. Claudius (41-54) and his son Britannicus had their ashes laid to rest in the mausoleum. Vespasian (69-79) found his way here after his death in 79. The last person to be buried in the mausoleum was Nerva (96-98) in 98.

On the south side we find the entrance. Although it is supposed to be open with regularity, it rarely is. In which case we must make arrangements to be admitted. The diameter of the base is 87m. (285.43 ft.). After passing through the passageway we come to the burial chamber which sits in the center of the enclosed area. In ancient times there was a roof with a garden planted on its top. Also, there was a statue of the emperor towering above the trees. On each side of the entrance were located two Egyptian obelisks, that have long since been removed.

In medieval times it became a stronghold for the Colonna family, until the converted fortress was destroyed in 1167. In the 18th and 19th Centuries it was used as a bull ring. Then in 1907 it was converted into a concert theater. Although some attempts at excavations had been made in 1519 and 1793, it was not until 1926 that serious archaeological work began. By 1938 the excavation and restoration had been completed.

If we walk north on the Via di Ripetta we will come to the Piazza del Popolo. Before us in the plaza, we see an obelisk. This *Piazza del Popolo Obelisk (Obeliscus Augusti in Circo Maximo)* is one of the two Egyptian monoliths that have enjoyed the longest tenure in Rome. The red granite monument dates back to the XIX Dynasty. From the hieroglyphs we have ascertained that the obelisk was quarried and partially inscribed during the reign of the Pharaoh, Seti I (1308-1290) B.C.). After Ramses II (1290-1224 B.C.) came to power in 1290 B.C., he had the inscribing completed and the monument was erected at Heliopolis.

In 10 B.C. Augustus had it brought to Rome and erected near the eastern end of the spina of the Circus Maximus. Latin inscriptions dedicating the monument were affixed to the northern and southern sides of the base. A gilt ball of bronze crowned by a gnomon (pointer) was placed at the top of the monolith.

According to contemporary literature of the 5th Century, the obelisk was still standing at that time. Sometime in the Middle Ages it fell or was knocked down, where it lay buried under a thin layer of soil. A Renaissance scholar by the name of Leone Battista Alberti found the obelisk in 1471, but left it lying without attempting to restore it.

In 1587 it was rediscovered. This time it was raised, as Pope Sixtus V (1588-1590) decided to use it to decorate the Piazza del Popolo. The obelisk was erected at its present site in 1588. A new base was built, but the inscriptions of Augustus were preserved. New ones dedicating the obelisk to the Virgin were also added in 1588.

North of the piazza we can see a gate with a central arch and two smaller side arches. This is the *Porta Flaminia,* the gate that opened onto the Via Flaminia. Although the Via Flaminia was built in 220 B.C., the gate was not then part of it. In reality it was a gate in the Aurelian Walls. Thus, the porta dates back only as far as 272. Originally, there were two semicircular towers on each side of the gate. Pope Sixtus IV (1471-1484) faced the porta with marble in the 15th Century. In 1655 the inner side of the gate was remodeled by Bernini. The towers were pulled down in 1877 and in 1878 the side arched openings were added.

Leaving the Piazza del Popolo, we take a nice long walk southward on the Via del Corso. Eventually we will arrive at the Piazza Colonna on the right hand side of the street. The dominating feature in the plaza is the *Column of Marcus Aurelius (Columna Marci Aurelii Antonini).* It stands 29.77m. (100 Roman feet) high and is made of 26 rings of white marble. The shaft itself is 26.50m. (86.94 ft.) high with a diameter of 3.90m. (12.80 ft.), setting upon a marble base. A spiral staircase within the column, made up of 200 steps, leads us to the top if we have made the proper arrangements. The interior is lighted by 56 rectangular loopholes.

This column, modelled after the column of Trajan (97-117), was begun after the death of Marcus Aurelius (161-180) in 180 and completed in 193. The column is covered with reliefs depicting the wars with the Quadi, Marcomanni, and the Sarmatians that occurred between 172 and 175. Over the centuries it suffered extensive damage, forcing Domenico Fontana to restore it in 1589. At that time a new base was constructed from marble taken from the Septizonium of the Palatine.

Moving west about a half-a-block, we come to the Piazza di Montecitorio, where we see another red granite obelisk. Brought from Egypt in 10 B.C. at the same time as the one we saw in the Piazza del Popolo, this *Obelisk of the Piazza di Montecitorio (Obeliscus Augusti in Campo Martio)* was placed not far from the Altar of Peace by Augustus. It dated from the reign of Pharaoh Psamtik II (595-589 B.C.) of the XXIV Dynasty. Augustus had it inscribed on the north and south sides of the base when he dedicated the monument. Stripes were then painted on the pavement, and for awhile the obelisk was used as a sun dial.

The obelisk was still standing in the 9th Century, and may not have fallen until the Norman sack of 1084. In 1463 the base was uncovered, but the obelisk itself remained hidden until 1502. In 1587 Pope Sixtus V had it partially uncovered at which time a study of the inscriptions was made.

It continued to lie in place, although it was completely excavated in 1748. Toward the latter half of the 18th Century Pope Pius VI (1775-1799) was beginning to rebuild the Piazza di Montecitorio. In 1788 the repair and transfer of the monolith began. Travertine, brick and iron were the new materials needed to renovate the obelisk. It was unveiled at its present site in 1792.

Just south of the Piazza Colonna (walk about two blocks and turn left) is the Piazza di Pietra. Here in this plaza we can see an ancient wall and eleven fluted columns of marble. These are the ruins of the *Hadrianeum* (*Templum Divi Hadriani*). The temple was built and dedicated by Antonius Pius (138-161) in 145 to his divine father Hadrian. The columns stand some 15m. (49.21 ft.) in height. At various times in the 16th, 17th, and 19th Centuries pieces of the marble reliefs have been discovered and are now in various museums in Rome and Naples.

We now take the street leaving the piazza in the middle of the west side (where we entered) and walk about one block to the Vicolo della Spada d'Orlando. Immediately after turning right on this street we see the remains of an ancient wall and the stump of a column. The column is on the right side of the street and the wall is on the left. These are the ruins of the *Temple of Matidia* (*Templum Matidiae*), built by Hadrian around 120 and dedicated to his mother-in-law, Matidia. The ruins were first discovered in 1619.

Now let us retrace our steps to the Piazza di Pietra and over to the Via del Corso, we turn right and walk to the Piazza Venezia and to a bus. If this tour of the ruins of the Campus Martius has been undertaken in one day, then the sightseer is very weary, indeed!!

CHAPTER 8

Aventine, Caelian, and Out The Appian Way

The next area to be covered in our tour is very large. It extends from the Aventine Hill to the Caelian Hill, out the Appian Way, and back to the Caelian. We begin our jaunt at the Met Station located at the southwest end of the Circus Maximus. Next, we walk up the hill on the Viale Aventino, turn right at the first street for one block, and find to our left the Piazza S. Prisca.

Here in the plaza we find ourselves on the *Aventine Hill* (*Mons Aventinus*). The hill has a maximum elevation of about 45.7m. (150 ft.) above sea level, and encompasses an area of about 29 acres. Although lying within the Servian Walls, some scholars feel that in reality it was not within the city limits until the mid-1st Century A.D.

In front of us, on the western side of the piazza, lies the Church of S. Prisca. It is the *Mithraeum* (*Mithraeum Domus Sanctae Priscae*), now lying beneath the church, that receives our immediate attention. The Mithraeum or Temple of Mithras is open only from 10:00 to 11:30 a.m. daily; our state permits hold no value here, we must pay to enter.

Of all the male oriental deities who found their way to Rome over the centuries, Mithras was the most popular. Mithras probably had his origin in India, but it was in Persia that he became important. He became the faithful lieutenant of Ahura-Mazda, the Persian god of goodness and light, aiding Mazda in his struggle against Ahriman. In the Persian religion of Zoroastrianism, Ahriman commanded the forces of darkness and evil. Eventually, a cult developed with Mithras as the central figure, and the new cult contained much secret ritual. Mithraism became popular with the Roman legionnaires, and was brought back to Rome in the 1st Centuries B.C. and A.D. by the veterans returning from the East.

Beneath the church and behind the crypt we enter the Mithraeum. Of all the temples to Mithras in Rome, this one is probably the best preserved of them all. The Mithraeum was built into a house that dates to the end of the 1st Century A.D. In the 4th Century the Christians secured control of the building, and after thoroughly destroying the interior, they built the apse of their church over the temple. There the Mithraeum lay hidden over the centuries until discovered by some Augustinian monks in 1934. These monks slowly began to excavate the temple, but World War II interrupted the procedure. In 1947 the Netherlands Historical Institute resumed the excavations which were finally completed in 1958.

As we enter the temple we conclude that it is a typical Roman Mithraeum — a long narrow room with benches flanking the sides. On each side of the entrance to a Mithraeum there were statues of torchbearers, known by the names of Cautes and Cautopates. At the entrance to this one only the figure of Cautes remains, but minus his head, the result of the uncontrolled fury of the Christians. At the end of the Mithraeum we see a large niche containing the reclining figure of Oceanus-Saturnus. Behind him on the wall we see a figure of Mithras sacrificing a bull. On the right-hand corner, below the niche, is an inscription dedicating the temple of Mithras. On the left wall we see paintings, showing servants leading a sacrificial procession of a bull, a ram, and a pig. These paintings date to about 220. Behind the Mithraeum is a small chapel that also seems to be dedicated to Mithras.

After our visit to the Mithraeum, we exit the piazza by way of the Via del Tempio di Diana on the northwest side of the plaza, entering the Piazza del Tempio di Diana, passing through it and on to the Piazza G. Regina, bear left for a few steps, and then turn right on Via Raimondo da Capua to the *Church of S. Sabina*. This church dating back to ancient Rome, rates a few minutes of our time.

S. Sabina with its twenty-four Corinthian columns is a classical example of a 5th Century Christian basilica. It was built by an Illyrian priest in the 5th Century, during the administration of Pope Celestine I (422-432) and constructed above the site of a temple dedicated to Juno Regina. Pope Sixtus III (432-440) dedicated it to S. Sabina in 432. Sabina was a Christian martyr, supposedly put to death by Hadrian in the 2nd Century. Restorations were carried out in 1222, 1587, and 1938. The repairs of 1936-38 restored the church to its original appearance.

On the north side of the church we see a beautiful public park filled with orange trees. This lovely park is the Parco Savello. At the edge of the park along the slope of the hill are the remains of the *Servian Walls* (*Murus Servii Tulii*). We mentioned these walls briefly when we noted them at the base of the Capitoline Hill. The largest and best preserved section of these walls lie along the slope of the Aventine. At the overlook next to the church, we are afforded a tantalizing glimpse of the walls, down to the right and almost hidden in the vegetation. This particular wall is made of large greyish-yellow blocks of tufa.

According to legend, these walls were built by King Servius Tullius (673-642 B.C.) in the 7th Century B.C. A recent archaeological study, however, indicates that the walls are much younger. By the beginning of the Republic in 509 B.C., the city of Rome had long since outgrown its protective walls. In 387 B.C. the Gauls came down from the Po Valley and sacked the city of Rome. After this disaster Rome built these so-called Servian Walls. Although the city eventually outgrew them, they were kept repaired through the year 87 B.C.

If we walk back through the park and on in front of the church along the Via di S. Sabina, we will exit the Piazza Pietra d'Illiria. We take a left on Via di S. Alessio, walk upon it to the Piazza Albina, exit this square at the far right corner and where Via dei Decii joins Via S. Anselmo, we see another section of the Servian Walls. Continuing down S. Anselmo to its entrance into Piazza Albania, we see on our right some more of these walls.

We next proceed south from the Piazza Albania along the Viale Manlio Gelsomini to the Via della Marmorata, then turn right on this street and proceed to the Tiber River. At the river we find ourselves within the Piazza dell'Emporio in front of the Ponte Sublicio. The plaza gets its name from the *Emporium*, which was the warehouse and harbor area for Rome for about 450 years. This harbor extended from just north of the Ponte Sublicio to about the vicinity of the Ponte Testaccio.

After Rome had defeated Carthage in the 2nd Punic War and her trade and commerce had increased, there was a great need for a harbor area to take care of the goods making the 28.9km. (18 mile) journey up the Tiber from Ostia. In 193 B.C. the docks and warehouses were dedicated. This dock area served Rome until the end of the 3rd Century, when the Aurelian Walls were built over the area. Excavations in 1868-1870 discovered the Emporium, and further work was carried out in 1919 and 1952. Just north of the Ponte Sublicio we can see the remains of piers and warehouses built into the embankment. More remains of ramps and stone rings where the ships moored are covered in the weeds south of the bridge.

We walk along the river to the sixth street on the left which is Via Florio. Turning left on this street we see, before we get to the Church of S. Maria Liberatrice, the ruins of an ancient building. Here are located the remains of the *Porticus Aemilia*. When the emporium was dedicated in 193 B.C., a large market place to handle the trade goods was built in the form of a porticus. It took its name from the two aediles responsible for its construction, L. Aemilius Paullus and L. Aemilius Lepidus. After completion it lay about 90m. (295.28 ft.) from the river and measured 487m. (1,598 ft.) by 60m. (197 ft.), with the long axis paralleling the river. Large scale repairs were conducted to the porticus in 174 B.C. Most of the ruins that we see now, date back to this reconstruction of 174.

The ruins that we are viewing, made of opus incertum and brick, show the remains of two entranceways at the lower level and four openings at the second floor level. More ruins can be seen along the left side of the Via Giovanni Branco between Via Florio and Via Rubattino. Also, along the Via Benjamino Franklin near its intersection with Lungotevere Testaccio more ruins of this large structure can be detected.

Behind the Porticus Aemilia was a large warehouse called the *Horrea Galbae*. If we walk away from the river on Via Rubattino we find it changes its name to Via Nicola Zabaglia after it crosses Via G. Branca. Along the Via N. Zabaglia, on the left after crossing Via Galvani, we detect the foundation ruins of this great warehouse. The Horrea Galbae measured about 200m. (656 ft.) by 155m. (509 ft.). It was probably built around 193 B.C. at the same time as the Emporium and Porticus Aemilia were constructed. The Emperor Galba restored it in 68, thus, the name Horrea Galbae. Between 1885 and 1955 the ruins were excavated.

We now continue down Via Nicola Zabaglia to its intersection with Via Galvani and, there to our right, we see a high hill known as the *Mons Testaceus* (*Monte Testaccio*). This hill, 50m. (164 ft.) in height, is very unique in that it is an artificial mound made up of broken bits of pottery. Broken sherds of pottery from the dock area were discarded here as early as the beginning of the Empire period. If we climb to the top of the hill we see the pottery exposed in most places, yet, it is overgrown with shrubs and brush in other spots.

After our tour of the artificial hill, let us now retrace our steps on the Via Galvani to Via Nicolo Zabaglia, where we turn left and continue along the street until it passes through the *Aurelian Walls* (*Muri Aureliani*). By the mid-3rd Century B.C., Rome had outgrown the Servian Walls, but its officials felt no need to build any more until the middle of the 3rd Century A.D., when the power of Rome had diminished in the political anarchy of the struggles for power among the various generals. These walls were begun in 270 during the rule of Aurelian and completed about 280-281 under Probus. Upon completion the wall measured 18.84km. (11.7 miles) in length.

The wall had 381 towers spaced every 29.6m (97.1 ft. or 100 Roman feet) apart, along with 18 gateways or portae, and several smaller openings or posterulae. It is made up of a concrete core covered with brick. The width of the wall varies from 3.5 to 4.0m. (11.5 to 13 ft.) with the towers projecting out 4 to 5m. (13 to 16.5 ft.) on each side of the walls. An average height is 7.5 to 8m. (24.6 to 26.25 ft.) with an elevation of 10m. (33 ft.) reached in places. Maxentius restored the walls in the early 4th Century, but the greater part of the outer walls date to a restoration by Honorius and Arcadius in 403.

To the right the walls end near the river. They originally made a right angle turn here and ran northwest until they joined the river about where the Via Evangelista Torricelli joins the Lungotevere Testaccio. The fortifications then commenced on the opposite bank of the Tiber, running away from the river up the Janiculum Hill almost to the Porta San Pancrazio. They then turned back to the river crossing at a point between the Ponte Garibaldi and Ponte Sisto bridges. At the two points where the walls had openings at the river, a chain was stretched across to keep ships out. After crossing the river again, the walls paralleled the river to about the junction of Lungotevere Arnaldo da Brescia and Via Luisa di Savoia, then turned right to the Porta Flaminia. Only on the side of the Tiber where we are standing, are the walls preserved. On this, the right bank, they are well preserved except in a few places.

Meanwhile, getting back to our tour, we turn left along the outside of the walls and follow them until we come to a pyramid structure built into the walls, or actually the walls were built against the pyramid. This is the *Pyramid of Cestius* (*Sepulcrum C. Cestii*), built probably between 15 and 12 B.C. C. Cestius, praetor and tribune, had the pyramid built as his tomb. Marcus Agrippa, faithful lieutenant and son-in-law of Augustus (27 B.C. - 14 A.D.), was designated as an heir on the tomb. It reaches a height of about 35m. (115 ft.) and the base is about 30m. square (98.4 ft.). The base is of travertine, while the rest of the tomb is made of marble. Pope Alexander VII (1655-1667) restored the structure in 1663, and while in the process he built a new door on the west side to lead into the burial chamber.

To our right we see a gateway in the wall flanked by two imposing rounded towers. This gate is the *Porta Ostiensis* or, as it is known by its modern name — the *Porta S. Paolo*. On each side of the towers the walls are torn down to allow space for modern traffic to move. The single gate opens into a courtyard which then provides the sightseer access into the city by means of two openings.

After entering the city, we are on the Viale della Piramide Cestia, which becomes the Viale Aventino after passing the Piazza Albania. The street eventually takes us to the Piazza Porta Capena at the southeast end of the Circus Maximus. The plaza and the park take their name from the gateway in the Servian Walls that was located in the area, the *Porta Capena*. Built in 386 or 385 B.C., the Porta Capena gave access to the Via Ostiensis, the road to the port city of Ostia.

As we continue up the street past the Piazza del Circo Massimo to the first winding street to the right, which is the Salita di S. Gregorio that becomes the Clivo di Scauro, we take a right on the street, and there find ourselves upon the *Clivus Scauri* of ancient Rome. It branched off the road connecting the Circus Maximus and Colosseum, built in the 1st Century and connected with the *Vicus Capitis Africae* about where the modern Via S. Paolo della Croce intersects with the Via della Navicella. The Clivus Scauri is followed by the modern Clivo di Scauro and Via S. Paolo della Croce.

Ascending the ancient Clivus Scauri, we are making an ascent to the *Caelian Hill.* Like the Palatine, Capitoline, and Aventine, the Caelian is one of the isolated hills of Rome, not connected to any other hill or tableland. The Caelian covers an area of about 45 acres and has an elevation of approximately 48m. (157.5 ft.) above sea level.

Continuing up the street, we approach the *Church of SS. John and Paul* (*SS. Giovanni et Paolo*) situated on the left side of the street. Here, the street passes under some brick arches that project from a Roman house of the 2nd Century. The church was built over the remains of this house known as the *Domus Johannis et Pauli.* Actually, beneath the church can be found the ruins of three houses. Upon entering the lower level of the church, we see two rooms that are very well preserved, complete with wall paintings. On the northwest side of these two rooms is a well preserved nymphaeum, also with wall paintings.

According to tradition, the Christian brothers, John and Paul, were executed here during the administration of Julian the Apostate (360-363) in 360 or 361. By the end of that century the houses had been converted into a large chapel that served as a memorial for the two brothers. The chapel itself was referred to as the *Titulus Byzantia.* Pope Symmachus (498-514) built the church over the chapel about 499, using the chapel as the crypt for the new church. The building suffered almost complete destruction during the Norman sack of 1084. Cardinal Giovanni Conti rebuilt the church between 1154 and 1159 under direction of Pope Adrian IV (1154-1159).

Beyond the church the street passes under an arch, known as the *Arch of Dolabella (Arcus Dolabellae et Silani).* It was erected in 10 by the Consuls P. Cornelius Dolabella and C. Junius Silanus. Some scholars feel that it was built on the former site of one of the gates in the Servian Walls, either the *Porta Caelemontana* or *Porta Querquetulana.* After 59 the arch supported a branch of the Aqua Claudia.

Immediately after passing under the arch we are on the Via Claudia. We turn left and walk for a way, and before us we see the imposing ruins of a large structure on our left. This is the *Temple of Claudius (Templum Divi Claudii)* or *Claudium.* It was begun by Agrippina, the widow of Claudius, shortly after the death of that emperor in 54. His successor, Nero, converted it into a nymphaeum and a reservoir for the aqueduct (Aqua Claudia) that fed the Palatine Hill. In 70 Vespasian rebuilt and rededicated it to its original purpose. At least two churches were quartered in the Claudium in the Middle Ages. Our permits along with a custodian will allow us to wander through this immense edifice overlooking the Colosseum. Today, we can only look and speculate, since the original function of only a few of the rooms have been identified.

After satisfying our curiosity by wandering around the Temple of Claudius, we now retrace our steps down the Via Claudia, turn left on Via di S. Stefano Rotondo, and take the walkway on our right to the *Church of S. Stefano Rotondo.* This rounded, two-storied building surrounded by a colonnade was originally known as the *Macellum Magnum.* It was built by Nero in the year 59. He probably built it as the central administrative building for the market square that lay within the central portion. It may have been a smaller copy of the Pantheon, however, if this is true, the interior is vastly different. Pope Simplicius (468-483) made it into a church between 470 and 480, dedicating it to Saint Stephen.

The front walls of the grounds of S. Stefano Rotondo and its neighbor, Calvary Hospital, are made up of ruins of the Aqua Claudia. As we move back to the intersection of Via S. Stefano Rotondo and Via della Navicella, we see a pier of this aqueduct located in the middle of the street.

PLATE 27

A. Porta Ostiensis (Outside)

B. Aurelian Walls near Monte Testaccio

PLATE 28

A. Pyramid of Cestius

B. Baths of Caracalla

PLATE 29

A. Baths of Caracalla

B. Palaestra of Baths of Caracalla

PLATE 30

A. Porta Latina

B. Via Appia

PLATE 31

A. Circus Maxentius

B. Tomb of Cecelia Metella

PLATE 32

A. Lateran Obelisk

B. Basilica of S. John Lateran

South of S. Stefano Rotondo church were some military barracks called the *Castra Peregrina*, which housed the peregrini, who acted as a police force for Rome. Today, we can see nothing, but the excavations of 1904-1909 uncovered the site. Five rows of rooms and three streets were uncovered during these excavations.

If we turn left on Navicella and walk a few steps, we come to the entrance of the Villa Celimontana on the right hand side of the street. After entering this lovely park, we turn left on Viale Cardinale Francesco Spellman and there at the end of the street we see an obelisk called the *Obelisk of Celimontana* (*Obeliscus Capitolinus*). This monolith of red granite was inscribed and erected in Heliopolis in Egypt by the Pharaoh Ramses II (1290-1224 B.C.) in the 13th Century B.C. When it arrived in Rome, we have no way of knowing at this time. No classical writer gives us any clue about the matter. After the arrival of the obelisk in Rome it was erected in the Iseum Campense, remaining there until it fell in the Middle Ages.

In the 13th Century as Rome was undergoing a restoration, the upper part of the obelisk was discovered. It was then placed in front of the Church of S. Maria d'Aracoeli with a new bottom portion added. In 1542 it was taken down to build a new convent. The obelisk was presented to Ciriaco Mattei in 1582 for his Villa Mattei. In 1817 it was re-erected on the south side of the villa at its present locality. The Villa Celimontana is the contemporary name for the Villa Mattei.

After emerging from the park of the Villa Celimontana, we turn right on the Via della Navicella and to the right, at the end of the brick wall and behind the iron fence, we see the remains of ancient walls. These are the ruins of the *Cohortium Vigilum Stationes* or *Barracks of the Cohort of Vigiles*. The vigiles were the police and firemen of Rome. From inscriptions it seems that this structure dates to the 2nd Century. It was first uncovered in 1820 and further finds were made in 1931. More remains exist at No. 2 Via Valle delle Camene.

Continuing down Via della Navicella, we arrive at a gate in the Aurelian Walls. Its ancient name is unknown, but in the Middle Ages it became known as the *Porta Metrovia*. Today, it is called *Porta Metroni*. When the wall was first built between 270 and 281 the gate was just a small opening. Then, in the early 4th Century a tower was built above the gate. Later, at some unknown time, the gate was walled up. The original gate lies between the two modern gateways, and we can see where it was walled up.

Passing through the gate we now walk to the right along the Viale Metronia that parallels the wall. As we walk along we continue our study of the Aurelian Walls. After a few minutes, we find ourselves at another gate, the *Porta Latina*. This gate with the semicircular towers on each side, is one of the original portae of the walls, but the upper portion with the windows was added by Honorius (395-423). In 1408 King Ladislaus of Naples walled it shut, but, then it was reopened the next year. Again it was shut from 1565 to

1669. In the early 19th Century, the Via Latina was abandoned, and the gate was walled up in 1808, remaining closed until its final reopening in 1911.

After entering the gateway, we spot to our left a pleasant little park, the Park of the Scipios (Parco di Scipioni). At the edge of the park is the *Tomb of Pomponius Hylas* (*Sepulcrum Pomponii Hylae, Columbaria Pomponii Hylae*). One of our party should cross the park and ring the bell at the gate of the Tomb of the Scipios. The custodian will sell us a ticket to visit the tomb. Pomponius Hylas, a prominent Roman of the 1st Century, built it for he and his wife Pomponia Vitalis. The tomb was discovered by Pietro Campana in 1831. A stairway of 28 steps takes us into the tomb, where we can see above the door the inscription of the tomb owner. The burial chamber has an arched ceiling that is beautifully decorated with paintings. There are many niches in the walls that contained the burial urns that held the ashes of the deceased. Some people not related to the Hylas family were buried here in the 2nd Century.

Let us now continue up the Via di Porta Latina through the Piazzale Numa Pompilio, continuing on the Via delle Terme di Caracalla just beyond the Baths of Caracalla (the imposing ruins on our left) to the Via Antonina. We now turn left on Via Antonina and ascend to the *Church of S. Balbina.* This church, perched on the edge of the Aventine Hill, is built over the ruins of the *Domus Cilonis.* This early home belonged to L. Fabius Cilo, a close friend of the Emperor Septimius Severus (193-211). In the courtyard of the hospital next to the church, we see the remains of the Domus Cilonis. Although the house was given to Cilo in 204 by Severus, it was actually built earlier in the 2nd Century during the rule of Hadrian (117-138).

Now let's retrace our steps to the entrance of the *Baths of Caracalla* (*Thermae Caracallae, Thermae Antoninianae*) located near the center of the structure on the side facing the Via delle Terme di Caracalla. These giant baths, second largest in Rome, were begun in 212 and the main building was dedicated by the Emperor Caracalla (211-217) in 216. Elagabalus (218-222) and Severus Alexander, emperors in the 220's and 230's added the surrounding walls and buildings. The baths were in continuous use until the Goths cut the water supply to them by destroying a portion of the aqueducts in 537. Although some excavations were started in the 16th Century, it was not until 1824 that a thorough study was begun. The final excavations were completed in 1939.

After completion the Baths of Caracalla measured 330m. sq. (1,082.68 ft. sq.), covering an area of approximately 27 acres. Besides the bathing halls, there were galleries, libraries, and exercise rooms. A bath in one of the Roman bath houses was a long drawn out procedure. A potential bather might engage in calisthenics before or after the bath. The facilities were usually either segregated for the sexes, or at certain times of the day were reserved for men and at other times for women. First, the bather entered a small hot room, the sudatoria, which induced perspiration. Then the bather entered a large room called the calidarium, which had a pool of hot water and a very steamy atmosphere. Occasionally, one dipped in the pool, but for the most part the bath was a steambath. The next stage was the stay in the tepidarium, a room of mild temperatures to cool one down. Finally, one plunged into a bath of cold water in the pool of the frigidarium, to be followed by a brisk rub-down. Many freshly bathed Romans then spent several hours in idle chatter and gossip.

Upon entering the Baths of Caracalla, we find that we are in the *Frigidarium*. Most of this area was occupied by the pool. On the sides of the room we see the remains of small cubicles, which were the dressing rooms or *Apodyteria*. The next room or central hall is the *Tepidarium,* flanked on each end by the exercise rooms or *Palaestrae*. As we wander through this great edifice we should note the beautiful pavement that is so well preserved in places. Behind the Tepidarium we see the great circular hall that was the *Calidarium*. Each summer the opera *Aida* is staged here, as evidenced by the stage settings. Across the courtyard and behind the Calidarium we see the remains of the library.

Beneath the pavement there are many corridors and furnace rooms that were used to heat water for the baths. We will need our permit and a custodian to lead us into these subterranean rooms. One of these rooms turns out to be a temple dedicated to Mithras, known as the *Mithraeum of the Baths of Caracalla (Mithraeum Thermarum Antoninianarum)*. This Mithraeum discovered in 1912 was evidently built about the same time as the baths. It is the largest temple or sanctuary to Mithras in Rome, measuring 23 by 9.7m. (75.46 by 31.82 ft.). The greater portion of the roof has been removed.

Now, let us take a right turn to the Piazzale Numa Pompilio, where we move down the middle fork, which is the Via di Porta San Sebastiano. After a short walk we arrive at the entrance of the *Tomb of the Scipios (Sepulcrum Scipionum, Sepolcro degli Scipioni, Hypogaeum Scipionum)*. The custodian who answers the bell here will allow us to wander unchaperoned through this tomb that was built in the early 3rd Century B.C. Inhumation rather than cremation was practiced by the Scipio family so the early burials were in scarcophagi rather than funerary urns. L. Scipio Barbatus, the consul for 298 B.C., was the first to be buried here. Ironically, Scipio Africanus, the great conqueror of Hannibal, is not buried here. Disgusted with the politics of Rome, Scipio spent the last years of his life and died at Liturnium in 183 B.C. There are about five galleries that are open to the public. On the left (as we stand with our backs to the entrance) we see the substructures of a 3rd Century house built above the tomb.

Just past the entrance to the Tomb of the Scipios we see another tomb entrance (both open to the street at No. 9). There are actually three separate tombs here containing niches for funerary urns. Special permission from the Superintendent of Antiquities allows us to enter this tomb called the *Tombs* of the Marcella Family (*Sepulcra Familiae Marcellae et Aliorum, Columbaria Familiae Marcellae*). Filling the walls are hundreds of niches to house urns. The niches resemble dovecotes that house pigeons, therefore, some scholars call these tombs columbaria. In the first century the freedmen (freed slaves) of the family of Marcella, the first wife of Agrippa, were buried here.

Continuing down the street we pass under an arch known as the *Arch of Drusus* (*Arco di Druso*). This name was given to it in the 16th Century. In reality the arch is part of the remains of the *Aqua Antoniniana*, the aqueduct that supplied water to the Baths of Caracalla. To the left another arch of the aqueduct can be detected.

Just past the arch we enter the *Porta Appia* (modern name is *Porta S. Sebastiano*) that leads us outside the imperial walls of the city. This gate, flanked by two circular towers, dates back to the repairs made by Honorius and Arcadius between 401 and 402.

If we walk down the walls to the right as far as the first street intersection, we find ourselves at the site of the *Porta Ardeatina*. This gate has been closed since about 1542. The Porta Ardeatina was never flanked by towers.

Retracing our steps to the Porta Appia, we now find ourselves on the *Via Appia*, or *Appian Way*. Actually, we were on the Appian Way as we walked upon the Via delle Terme di Caracalla. This famous street, the Via Appia, began at the Septizonium at the corner of the Palatine Hill about where the Piazza di Circo Massimo is located, then it continued along the Via Caracalla to the Piazalle Numa Pompilio, then followed the path that is covered today by the Via di Porta S. Sebastiano to the Porta Appia, where we now stand. The portion of the Via Appia from the gate to about 300m. south, was also sometimes referred to as the *Clivus Martius*.

Appius Claudius, the Censor of 312 B.C., built the Via Appia as a military road, to aid in the wars against the Samnites, as Rome tried to take their territory. Beginning just inside the Porta Appia, after the Aurelian Walls were completed, markers or milestones were set up every mile. The road was later lengthened to run on to Tarentum and finally terminated at Brundisium.

Although the Via Appia lies outside Rome, it is well worth the effort to explore a portion of it. We can catch Bus 118 just outside the city walls. Most of the famous catacombs lie along the Via Appia. There are probably more tombs along this road than any other thoroughfare in the vicinity of Rome. The road forks at the Church of Domine Que Vadis, the right fork becoming the Via Ardeatino. Continuing down the Via Appia on the bus, we decide that we can't visit all the catacombs, so we will visit two of the more famous.

The bus will stop near the entrance of the Catacombs of S. Sebastian (S. Sebastiano) and here is where we get off. We must then walk back a few steps to the *Catacombs of S. Calixtus* (*S. Callistio*). Our permits will not give us free admission here, so we have to buy tickets. Here we also have to attach ourselves to a guided tour, since no wandering alone in the catacombs is allowed. These catacombs, consisting of four levels are open from 8:30-12:00 and 3:00-6:30. They are the largest and most complex in Rome. Originally, the burial area comprised five separate cemeteries that were eventually connected by galleries. Miles and miles of these galleries are not open to the public.

Pope Calixtus (219-223) had been in charge of this cemetery, prior to assuming the Chair of S. Peter in 219, thus he gives his name to these catacombs. Burials continued here until near the close of the 5th Century. Beginning in the 6th Century they became a place for Christian pilgrims to visit. The catacombs were despoiled in 756 by the Lombards and again in 846 by the Arab invaders.

One of the most spectacular sections of the tombs is the *Crypt of the Popes,* discovered by G. B. DeRossi, the great Christian archaeologist, in 1854. The tombstones of the following popes were discovered: Pontianus (230-235), Anteros (235-236), Fabianus (236-250), Lucius (253-254), and Eutychianus (275-283). Some scholars, on the basis of an inscription, believe that Pope Sixtus II or Xystus II (257-258) may also be buried here.

Emerging once again into the sunlight, we continue by foot on the very short hike along the Via Appia to the *Catacombs of S. Sebastian (S. Sebastiano).* Again we must buy a ticket and participate in a guided tour through the underground galleries. These burial chambers were opened in the early 3rd Century. They became famous because of the idea that the bodies of Saints Peter and Paul were concealed here from 258 to 298. In the early 4th Century the *Basilica of S. Sebastian* was built although the present name was not given it until the Middle Ages. After its completion it was called *Basilica of the Apostles.* Sebastian, a Christian martyr, was executed during the persecution of Diocletian (284-305) in 303. The location of the catacomb of S. Sebastian was never lost like most of the others, but remained a continuous pilgrimage site for Christians through the centuries.

Across the street and down a bit from S. Sebastian there are remains of a large structure, and to the left of it some smaller ruins, with a modern home built amidst the ruins. The remains of the smaller structure mark the site of the *Temple of Romulus (Templum Romuli, Tempio di Romolo).* Like the one in the Forum, this one is not dedicated to the founder of Rome, but to the son of Maxentius (310-312) who died in 307. The circular part lying within the enclosure is probably the actual tomb of the young Romulus. To visit this site and the circus, permission must be obtained from the landowner.

The much larger structure to the right is the remains of the *Circus Maxentius (Circo di Massenzio).* Built by the Emperor Maxentius at the beginning of the 4th Century, the circus is oriented with the long axis running east to west. It is 482m. (1,581.36 ft.) by 79m. (259.19 ft.) and seated 18,000 spectators. The obelisk that we carefully examined in the Piazza Navona originally stood here on the spina of the Circus Maxentius. On the north side, if we look carefully, the imperial box can be detected. Behind the box was a large porticus that was about 182.88m. (600 ft.) in length. Much of the outer walls and the eastern end of the spina are still well preserved.

This area, called the Campagna, along the Appian Way is very picturesque and peaceful. At the top of the hill, along the Via Appia south of the Circus, we see on the left the ruins of a large circular building. This is the *Tomb of Cecelia Metella (Sepulcrum Ceceliae Metellae)*, wife of the son of M. Licinius Crassus, one of the triumvirs with Caesar and Pompey. The tomb consists of a core of concrete faced with travertine. Two halls, one above the other, lead into the burial chamber. The roof as well as the outer walls are missing. This tomb is architecturally similar to the Tomb of Augustus in the Campus Martius. The diameter of the structure is about 18.29m. (60 ft.), so it is rather large for a lady who was not of the imperial household. Pope Boniface VIII (1294-1303) gave it to his relatives in 1300 who made it into a guardhouse to collect tolls from travellers on their way to and from Rome. This act led to the building of the Via Appia Nuova to the east and the abandonment of the Old Appian Way. Not until the 19th Century was the Appian Way cleared for traffic again.

The second stop past the Tomb of Cecelia Metella is where bus service terminates. For those in excellent shape the journey can be continued on foot, but for others a car should be hired. Down the Via Appia, about 1.37km., we come to the fourth milestone on the right side of the road standing high above the villa walls. Across the Appian Way and down a few meters the *Tomb of Marcus Servilius* can be seen at No. 191. From here southward the road is flanked by tombs for more than three kilometers. This tomb was discovered in 1808. About 46m. (151 ft.) past the Tomb of M. Servilius we come upon the *Tomb of Seneca.* Here the great classical writer was laid to rest after his execution upon the orders of Nero.

On the right hand side of the road about 183m. (200 yds.) further on we find in close proximity the *Tomb of St. Urban,* built in the 2nd Century, the *Tomb of Ilarius Fuscus,* probably from the same century, and the *Tomb of the Freed Claudian Slaves,* dating back to the 1st Centuries B.C. and A.D.

Slightly more than 1.5km. from the Tomb of the Claudian Slaves we can see on the left an aqueduct terminating at a ruined building. This structure was one of the nymphaea of the *Villa Quintili,* a large estate owned by this agricultural family who were prominent in the 2nd and 3rd Centuries. One of the family, Maximus Quintilius, was put to death for crossing the Emperor Commodus. The entire area between here and the New Appian Way was covered by this great estate, and much of the ruins can still be detected by the observant.

Almost a kilometer down the road we see another large circular tomb, the *Casal Rotondo.* A house rests atop the tomb, a remnant of the medieval tower built there. Earlier scholars felt that this was the tomb of Cotta, because of an inscription nearby. Today, however, archaeologists feel that this may or may not be the tomb of C. Aurelius Cotta, the great consul of 75 B.C.

For the weary, a rest is well deserved. After a short rest we take the Via di Casal Rotondo to the left. After a leisurely walk through this beautiful part of the Campagna we come, after about a kilometer, to the Via Appia Nuova (New Appian Way). The two Appian roads converge at the town of Frattocchie about 6.4 kilometers away. On the New Appian Way we turn left and catch a tram back to Rome.

As we approach Rome, it is best to get off the tram at the stop just inside the walls, just after entering the *Porta S. Giovanni.* To the left we see an older gate flanked by circular towers, open to foot traffic only. This gate is the *Porta Asinaria,* built as a small opening in the Aurelian Walls in the period from 270 to 280. The towers were added by Honorius at the start of the 5th Century, at a time he was strengthening the walls. When King Ladislaus of Naples conquered Rome in 1408, he sealed up the gate, however, it was opened during this same year. Pope Pius IV (1559-1565) walled it up again in 1565 and it was replaced by the new Porta S. Giovanni in 1574. Finally, in 1951 the gate was again opened to pedestrian traffic.

After entering the Porta Asinaria let's bear to the left toward the large church. On the northeast side of the church in the Piazza di S. Giovanni in Laterano we see another Egyptian obelisk. This is the *Lateran Obelisk* or *Obeliscus Constantii,* which is one of the oldest obelisks in Rome. Although of great age, it was a late arrival in the "Eternal City." The red granite monolith was hewn, inscribed, and dedicated by Thutmose III of the XVIII Dynasty. At his death, however, it had not been erected. Shortly after Thutmose IV became pharaoh in 1413 B.C., he erected the obelisk at the great temple of Amon-Re at Karnak outside the capitol city of Thebes.

The obelisk remained at Thebes until 337, when Constantine the Great (310-337) brought it down the Nile to Alexandria to ship it to Rome. Before this task could be completed Constantine died. His son, Constantius II (353-360), completed this herculean task in 357, and erected it on the spina of the Circus Maximus. In the middle of the 6th Century it was knocked down by plundering barbarians. Eventually it became covered with silt and debris to a depth of about 7m. (22.97 ft.). In 1587 it was discovered under the silt, broken into three pieces. Pope Sixtus V (1585-1590) had Domenico Fontana repair it and erect it here at its present site in 1588.

At the place where the Via dell'Amba Aradam exits the piazza there is a vaulted brick structure. These are the remains of the *Thermae Lateranenses* (*Lateran Baths*), to be more specific the ruins of the frigidarium. The roof stands about 13.5m. (44.29 ft.) above the pavement, and the frigidarium measures 10m. by 12.5m. (32.81 x 41.01 ft.). This bathing establishment dates to the early 3rd Century.

Moving back toward the church, we see the *Lateran Baptistry* (*S. Giovanni in Fonte*). This small octagonal structure is built over other earlier structures. Constantine built a circular baptistry over the earlier baths. Then in 435 Pope Sixtus III (432-440) built the existing structure. If we look back across the square we can see above a building, two arches of the Aqua Claudia.

The remaining large building houses the *Basilica of S. John Lateran* (*Basilica di S. Giovanni in Laterno*) and the *Lateran Palace* (*Palazzo Pontificio*). This great edifice is built over the ruins of a large Roman house of the 1st Century, the *Domus Lateranorum* or *House of Plautius Lateranus.* Senator Lateranus was involved in the plot of Piso to kill Nero (54-68) in 65, and for this involvement lost his life. Shortly after his tragic death, the house passed into the hands of the family of Marcus Aurelius (161-180). There is some speculation that the future emperor was born at this site. By the beginning of the 4th Century, the property belonged to Fausta, the wife of Constantine the Great. After the death of Fausta in 326, Constantine probably presented the building to Pope Sylvester I (314-335).

When the Vandals under Gaiseric sacked Rome in 455, they carried off all the Lateran treasures to their kingdom in North Africa. In the early 6th Century Justinian defeated the Vandals and took the Lateran valuables back to Constantinople. He decided to ship them to Jerusalem, but the ship sank and the treasures were lost at sea.

At the close of the 8th Century Pope Adrian I (772-795) repaired the building and made it the seat of the Popes. Technically, it is still the official residence of the pope. The building was almost completely destroyed by an earthquake in 896, but it was rebuilt in 904 by Pope Sergius III (904-911). A fire in 1308 severely damaged it, but Urban V (1362-1370) rebuilt it in the mid-14th Century.

More repairs and additions were made to the building in the 15th Century by Popes Martin V (1417-1431) and Alexander VI (1492-1503). An hour or two spent within the basilica (open from 6:30 a.m. until a half hour before sunset) is time well spent. The bronze doors of the main entrance came from the Senate House in the Forum.

Another ancient church worth a visit here on the eastern flank of the Caelian Hill is the *Church of SS. Quattro Coronati.* To get there we exit the Piazza di S. Giovanni in Laterano, take the first street to the left, the Via di S. Stefano Rotondo, then take a right on the first street which is the Via dei SS. Quattro. After a short walk we see the church ahead of us. A small church or chapel was built on this spot as early as 364. Rising above the church today is a great medieval tower. In medieval times the church served as a temporary residence for the pope. By the 7th Century the church had fallen into ruins. In 625 Pope Honorius I (625-638) had it rebuilt. Pope Leo IV (847-855) enlarged the church and added the crypt in the 9th Century. The Norman sack of Rome in 1084 partially destroyed the building, however, Pope Paschal II (1099-1118) had it restored in 1111. Inside, we find that this is another of the many fascinating churches of Rome.

This tour of the Aventine, Caelian, out the Appian Way, and back to the Caelian has taken us about two and a half days. We still have a half day in which to visit *S. Paul Without the Walls* (*S. Paolo fuori le Mura*). Bus 18 or 23 will take us to the church, or we can ride the Metropolitana (the railway train) to the Stazione S. Paolo. The basilica lies about 1.8 kilometers from the Porta Ostiense or Porta S. Paolo along the Via Ostiense. It is open every day from 5:30 a.m. to 7:30 p.m.

St. Paul was supposedly beheaded in this area and his body may have been concealed for awhile at S. Sebastiano, as we noted earlier. Later the saint was buried here, which was evidently used as both a pagan and a Christian burial ground. The Emperors Valentinian II (388-392), Theodosius the Great (394-395), and Honorius enlarged the church in the late 4th and early 5th Centuries. A fire burned the basilica on July 24, 1823. Pope Pius VII (1800-1823) who was dying at the time, was never told of this disaster, because it was his favorite church. Pope Leo XII (1823-1829) began to restore it in 1823. The basilica was completed and dedicated by Pope Pius IX (1846-1878) in 1854. Until the building of the new St. Peter's Basilica, this was the largest church in Rome. As the church was being rebuilt, archaeologists found a large necropolis beneath the building.

In conclusion, it is obvious that this tour of the Aventine, Caelian, Appian Way, and S. Paul Without the Walls has covered a tremendous amount of territory. It has been exhausting for those who walked all the way, but at the same time we have seen the picturesque countryside and visited some of the oldest and most venerated churches of Rome.

CHAPTER 9

Ruins Of The Esquiline

Our next area to be toured is the region that lies on the Esquiline. In reality the Esquiline is a plateau — a continuation of the Northern Heights that extend into Rome. The Romans called the area in the vicinity of the modern train station, or Stazione Termini, the Esquiline. It also was an earlier term used for the Oppian and Cespian Hills. Actually, the Esquiline produces three spurs in this vicinity. The Oppian Hill, dominated by the Park of Trajan, is by far the largest spur. St. Peter in chains occupies most of the Fagutal spur, while S. Mary Major lies on the Cespian spur.

Today's tour will begin on the east side of the Colosseum (opposite the Palatine Hill). As we move east from the Flavian Amphitheater along the Via S. Giovanni in Laterano, we are walking over the remains of the *Castra Misenatium*, buried beneath the pavement. These ruins were uncovered in 1912 as a municipal drain was being constructed and have since been covered again. It was here that the sailors from Misenum who were serving duty at the Colosseum had their barracks. They acted as maintenance men and custodial workers.

On the left side of the street, lying beneath the street level, are located the semi-circular ruins of a structure. This is the remains of the *Ludus Magnus*, which was the training arena for the gladiators. The training ground was a small scale model of the Colosseum, and was evidently built not long after the construction of the Flavian Amphitheater. Excavation first uncovered the Ludus Magnus in 1937. More excavations were carried out at the site between 1960 and 1961.

Continuing down the street for about another block and a half, we arrive at the *Basilica of S. Clemente*, situated on the left side of the street. Upon entering, we find ourselves in a basilica dating back to about 1100, with some of the furnishings possibly dating as early as the 6th Century. A visit through the church and out into the courtyard is time well spent. After this we walk to the back and pay our admission fee (our permits are not valid here) to the Dominican Father with the Irish brogue, and then we descend to the lower level. As we descend the stairs we pass from the 12th Century to the 4th Century.

At the foot of the stairs we take a right turn and descend another half dozen steps, and find ourselves at the eastern end of the 4th Century Basilica. The hall that runs diagonally to the nave is called the *Narthex* and dates to about the year 350. If we turn right at the last of the steps we enter the North Aisle. On the right hand wall, about two-thirds of the way down, we see a pagan sarcophagus that dates to the end of the 1st Century. It was brought up here from the lower level. To the left there is another narrow aisle, but the right hand wall was the extent of the original nave. When construction started on the upper basilica around 1100 the area of the nave was reduced.

The nave is filled with columns that support the upper church. At the west end of the South Aisle there are stairs to descend to the lower level. At the head of the stairs we see the tomb of St. Cyril, who was buried here in 885. After descending the stairs, we now find that we have moved into the 1st Century. If we turn left and then right, we find ourselves in a passageway. The house that we are in dates to the end of the 1st Century. On our left, through a barred door, we can see a temple dedicated to Mithras. This *Mithraeum Domus Clementis,* with the altar at the rear, was added shortly after the beginning of the 3rd Century. The temple was discovered by Father Joseph Mullooly in 1869.

On the right hand side of the aisle there are two rooms. Several archaeologists are of the opinion that the room on the far right may have been a school where aspirants received their training in the mysteries of the Mithraic cult. Past this room is another barred door, and from behind the grating comes the sound of rushing water. This is a drainage tunnel that connects with the Cloaca Maxima.

Between this room and the Mithraeum we find a doorway that takes us out of the building, across an ancient alley and through another door into a home that was built about the middle of the 1st Century. This house is known as the *Domus Clementis* or *House of St. Clement,* who was pope between 91 and 96. The long axis of the other house was oriented north-south, but this one is aligned east-west. This building, lying directly under the 4th Century Church, is 29.6m. (97.1 ft.) by 40.0m. (131.2 ft.). Directly in front of us lies the central courtyard which is still unexcavated.

Turning right we walk all the way to the end of the passage, where we find two rooms that were excavated between 1930 and 1938. Retracing our steps and then walking to the opposite end of the passage we find ourselves in another room, which was cleared between 1940 and 1945. Taking a right turn, we walk through a long, dimly lit passage to a room that was not excavated until 1970. At the end of the room is a staircase leading upward toward another barred door. Behind this door is a small catacomb, discovered in 1938. On either side of the passage there are eight wall tombs. This catacomb probably dates to the 5th or 6th Century. In this room there is also a set of stairs that takes us up to the second level.

Returning to ground level, let us go into the courtyard and recount the history of S. Clemente. About the middle of the 1st Century the Domus Clementis was built and Pope Clement (Clemens) resided here. Toward the close of the century the neighboring house was built. After banishment from

Rome in 96 of Clemens, the ex-pope went to the Black Sea region where he died around the year 97. His house was probably regarded as a Christian monument after this, and evidently served as a meeting place for early Christians. Shortly after 200 a Mithraeum was founded in the house across the alley, and Christians and Mithraic followers held their meetings in close proximity.

Constantine may have dedicated the Domus Clementis to the deceased pope between 313 and 320. Because of the rising level of debris, the courtyard of the Domus Clementis was filled in with rubble to support the new basilica that was built above it toward the middle of the 4th Century. After the suppression of all pagan religions in 395, the church acquired the other house and filled in the Mithraeum. A stairway to connect the two levels was maintained to visit the lower level. The apse of the new basilica extended over the area of the old Mithraeum.

Church documents reveal that Pope Zosimius (417-418) held a meeting in the new church in 417. According to tradition the missionaries to the Slavs, Cyril, and Methodius, brought the body of S. Clement back to Rome in 867, and buried it somewhere in the church. The burial site is still unknown. We have already seen the tomb of Cyril, who was buried there in 885.

Robert Guiscard destroyed much of the basilica in his sack of Rome in 1084. After Pope Paschal II (1099-1118) was elected to the chair of St. Peter in 1099, he began to have the new basilica built above the 4th Century one. It was completed and dedicated in 1128 during the administration of Pope Honorius II (1124-1130). Eventually all knowledge of the lower church was lost.

In 1403 Pope Boniface IX (1389-1404) placed the church in the hands of the Augustinian Order, who kept it until 1643, at which time Pope Urban VIII (1623-1644) reclaimed it for the papacy. Pope Innocent X (1644-1655) handed it over to the Dominicans in 1645. In 1677 the basilica and convent of S. Clemente were put in charge of the Irish Dominicans, who have administered it ever since.

Father Joseph Mullooly of the Irish Dominicans began to excavate beneath the basilica in 1857, discovering the earlier 4th Century basilica. Within a couple of years he had also discovered the 1st Century houses at the lower level. By 1869 Father Mullooly had discovered the Mithraeum, but there was such a drainage of ground water into the area that the excavations were discontinued. Father Louis Nolan took over the excavations in 1912 and promptly drilled a tunnel from S. Clemente to a sewer near the Colosseum. The tunnel, completed in 1914, is 700m. (2,297 ft.) in length, lying 14m. (46 ft.) below the modern pavement. With the completion of the tunnel, the area was drained of all water and the Mithraeum was excavated. Further archaeological work has continued up to the present day.

After leaving the church, we now walk to the front, turn left on Via dei Querciti and walk one block to Via Labicana. Here, we take a right and proceed to the second street on the left which is Via Pietro Verri, turn left and walk one block and there ahead of us on the flank of the Oppian Hill we see the remains of a temple. These ruins are the remnants of the *Oppian Iseum*. This great temple to the Egyptian moon-goddess, Isis, was the second largest in Rome, ranking only behind the Iseum Campense. Not only was there an Iseum, but there was also an adjoining temple dedicated to the Egyptian god Serapis. In fact, in the late empire this region was called the *Region of Isis et Serapis*. Not much of the structure has survived, but numerous artifacts have been found in the vicinity. The Iseum was built in the 1st Century B.C. and survived until the 5th Century.

Leaving the Piazza Iside, we need to walk left along the Via Ludovico Muratori until it merges into the Via Mecenate where it becomes the Viale della Domus Aurea. Making another left on this new street, we continue for a block, and then on the right we see the entrance to the *Domus Aurea* (*Golden House*), lying on the flank of the Oppian Hill.

Before entering this famed palace of Nero, let us briefly review its history. After Nero bacame emperor in 54, he was not content with the Domus Tiberiana on the Palatine. The new emperor had his builders begin construction of the Domus Transitoria that we mentioned in our Palatine and Forum tours. This great palace completed within six or eight years reached from the Palatine across part of the Forum and onto the Esquiline. It was destroyed in the great fire of 64 and Nero then built his famous Golden House that was completed by 66. The grounds surrounding the Domus Aurea includes at least 125 acres that contained the vestibule that is now occupied by the Temple of Venus and Rome, and the area of the Colosseum that was a lake. After Nero's death in 68, the palace was neglected.

Vespasian (69-79) built the Colosseum where the lake had been. Domitian (81-96) had the covered passageways leading from the Forum to the Golden House converted into the Porticus Margaritaria and Horrea Piperataria (see Forum Chapter). The vestibule was covered by the Temple of Venus and Rome in the time of Hadrian (117-138). A great fire in 104 damaged the outside of the structure. Trajan (97-117) then built his baths over the structure and the memory of the location of the Domus Aurea became lost. In the 16th Century the ruins were identified and excavations have continued until the present. Great portions have still not been cleared of earth and rubble.

As we enter the entrance we find ourselves in a large passageway that may have been a porticus. We should make sure we have with us a good flashlight and a pair of binoculars to view the paintings at a high level. After securing an English speaking guide we may begin our tour. We walk about 40m. (131 ft.), turn right and walk to a large peristylum (peristyle). To the left of the peristyle, we see the remains of several rooms. These rooms have ceilings that are approximately 20m. (65.62 ft.) above the level of the floor.

In the center of the peristyle is a room with a vaulted ceiling, containing

FIGURE 9

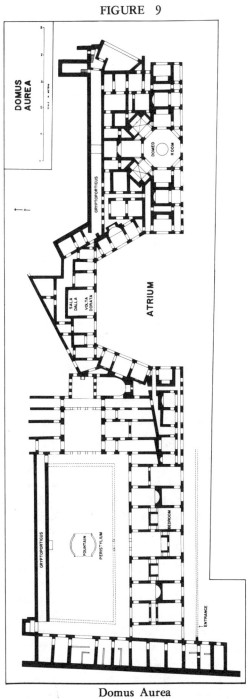

Domus Aurea

a fountain. This was probably the central area of the western wing of the palace. Behind the peristyle, running east-west, is a cryptoporticus. In front of the peristyle there are two rooms we should visit. One is probably a bedroom which may have been a guest room. At the end of the room there is a large alcove. It is flanked by smaller ones, both which have portions of the top bricked-in. Diagonally to the right of this room, there is another chamber that has an exedra at the south end. In the center of the apse or exedra is the pedestal that originally held a statue. Evidently, this room served as a small chapel. At the extreme eastern portion of the back corner of the western wing we can still see the ruins of a small nymphaeum.

Passing from the western to the eastern wing, we come to a large room called the *Sala della Volta Dorata* (*Room with the Gilded Vault*). To the south of this room there is a large, five-sided courtyard or atrium. We can see that it has not been completely excavated. There are some beautiful paintings on the ceiling of this great entrance hall of the palace. Behind this room we find a passageway that connected the central portion with the eastern wing of the palace. Running behind the eastern wing of the palace is another large cryptoporticus. Parts of the vaulted ceiling have collapsed in this long passageway. In the front center of the eastern wing there is a large eight-sided room. A circular opening lets light into the dome-shaped room. Rooms fan out in all directions from this large chamber. The octagonal room may have been the *Triclinium* or *Dining Room.* This large room reminds us somewhat of the Pantheon. There are many other rooms that we are permitted to wander through. Much work still remains to be done before the Domus Aurea will give up all its secrets.

After leaving the Domus Aurea, let us turn right and walk along the street. On the right hand side of the street, across from the Colosseum and nestled against the base of the Oppian Hill are brick ruins. These are the remains of the *Baths of Titus* (*Thermae Titi*). They were built against the southwest corner of the Domus Aurea by Titus, and were probably dedicated in 80 at the same time as the Colosseum. These are the smallest of the Roman baths that are recorded. The Baths of Titus measured about 120m. (393.70 ft.) by 105m. (344.49 ft.). In the 16th Century knowledge of the site was lost, and it was not rediscovered until 1895.

Let us retrace our path to the right of the entrance to the Domus Aurea, then ascend the steps to the *Park of Trajan* (*Parco di Trajano*). This beautiful park is named after the emperor who built a bath that occupied the area now covered by the park. Nero's Golden House burned in 104 and shortly after this destruction, Trajan built his great bath over the ruins. These are called the *Baths of Trajan* (*Thermae Trajani*). On June 22, 109 the Baths were officially dedicated. In the late Middle Ages, the officials of Rome and the popes began using its material for building purposes. By about 1800 most of the great structure had been dismantled. After completion the bath measured

FIGURE 10

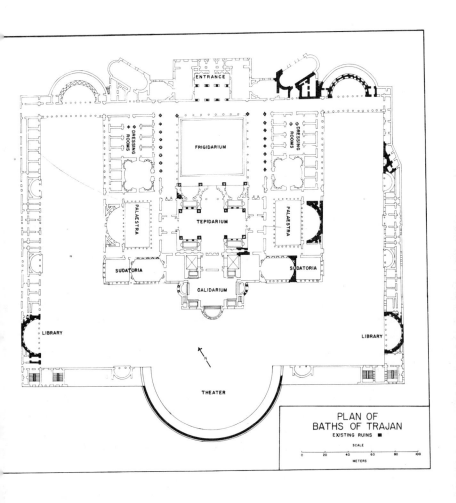

Baths of Trajan

about 340m. (1,115.48 ft.) by 330m. (1,082.68 ft.), with the long axis aligned in a northwesterly-southeasterly direction.

The great apse or exedra built above the Domus Aurea probably served as a theater. Walking right at about a 45° angle from the center of the theater area, we come to a large section of ruins. These are the remains of the east walls of a room that lay to the east of the Calidarium. Behind this chamber we come upon another large stretch of semi-circular wall. This was the exedra or apse of the eastern Palaestra (exercise yard). Beyond this we see fragments of the eastern wall. North of these rooms we see another semi-circular section of wall. This represents the northeast exedra built into the north side of the outside walls. To the left of this are more ruins with the modern street passing under an arched opening. These ruins represent a hall located between the main entrance and the northeast exedra. If we walk diagonally across the baths to the southwest, lying above the baths of Titus, we see imposing ruins that lie very near the Viale del Monte Oppio, but across the street from the main portion of the park. This was the southwest exedra that marked the end of the great library contained within the baths. Remains of the southeast exedra can be seen at the other side of the park.

In the area near the corners of the Via Terme di Trajano there is a large structure known as the *Sette Sale*. This is on the grounds of the Palazzo Brancaccio, therefore, we must secure permission to enter. The Sette Sale is the name given to the water tanks that provided the Baths of Trajan with an adequate water supply. The Sette Sale, composed of nine chambers, received its water from the Aqua Trajani. It measures about 70m. (229.66 ft.) by 53m. (173.88 ft.).

Across the street near the intersection of Viale del Monte Oppio and Via delle Sette Sale are the monastic grounds and buildings of San Tomaso. These grounds are under the direction of the Carmelite Order, who are also in charge of the small church on the corner, *S. Martino ai Monti.* If one of the Carmelite fathers is free, we can get him to carry us below the church to the early Roman house. After descending the stairs, we enter the house at the left side of a hall. Two large piers divide the hall into two aisles. This hall is aligned north-south and measures 18m. (59.06 ft.) by 11m. (36.09 ft.). In the left hand corner we can see the vestibule with doors that opened onto the Roman streets. North of the vestibule is a courtyard or atrium. On the side of the hall (east side) are the remains of three small rooms. At the north end of the hall near the center of the east aisle is a stairway that connects to an upper floor. The stairs are blocked, so, we will be unable to ascend to the upper story, which is made up of nine rooms and chambers.

This house was built either in the late 3rd or early 4th Century. Pope Silvester I (314-335) founded a church in this home in the early 4th Century. It became known as the *Titulus Equitii* or *Titulus Silvestri.* At the beginning of the 6th Century Pope Symmachus (498-514) built a church over the Titulus Equiti, dedicating it to St. Martin of Tours and St. Silvester. Although the

PLATE 33

A. Ludus Magnus

B. Entrance to Domus Aurea

PLATE   34

A.   Baths of Trajan

B.   Calidarium of Baths of Trajan

PLATE 35

A. S. Clemente — 4th Century Level

B. Arch of Gallienus

PLATE 36

A. Nymphaeum Aquae Juliae

B. Nymphaeum Hortorum Licianorum

PLATE 37

A. Porta Praenestina (Maggiore)

B. Tomb of the Baker

PLATE 38

A. Aqua Claudia

B. Amphitheater Castrense

facade of the church is 18th Century architecture, the greatest portion of the building dates to the 9th Century. It was rebuilt by Pope Sergius II (844-847) who started construction and by Pope Leo IV (847-855) who completed the project.

Returning to the street, we walk back to Via Sette Sale, turn down it and walk until we find ourselves at the church of *S. Pietro in Vincoli* (*S. Peter in Chains*). Before entering the basilica, we should pause and reflect upon the history of the church.

Legend relates that Empress Athenais Eudoxia, wife of the Byzantine Emperor Theodosius II (408-450), sent one of the chains that Herod had used to bind St. Peter in Jerusalem to her daughter in Rome. This daughter, Eudoxia, was the wife of the Roman Emperor Valentinian III (425-455). She took the chain and built a basilica to house it, adding a chain that had been used on Peter while he was locked in the Mamertine Prison. In 432 Pope Sixtus III (432-440) dedicated the building as a church, naming it *Basilica Eudoxiana*. Gradually, the name was changed to S. Peter in Chains. The last major repairs made upon the church were made in 1490 by Julius II (1503-1513) before he ascended to the Chair of St. Peter.

Inside the church twenty fluted marble columns divide the interior into three aisles. Everyone looks at the chains (supposedly the originals) that are on display. The other eye catching masterpiece on display in the church is the statue of Moses on the tomb of Pope Julius II, placed there by Michaelangelo in 1544. Michelangelo showed his individuality by substituting the rays of the sun touching the head of Moses with horns. This is Michelangelo's famed "Horned Moses." Further wandering through the church reveals the tombs of several important personages. Some of those worth noting are Cardinal Aldobrandini, Jacopo di Bussi (eminent scholar), Eustachius Ursinus (noted theologian), the Pollaiuolo brothers, Antonia and Pietro (Builders of monuments at S. Peter's Church), and Leonardo Grosso della Rovere (nephew of Pope Julius II).

After leaving the church, we now descend the stairs that pass through a tunnel to the Via Cavour. We then turn right on the Via Cavour, walk to the first street intersecting it from the left, and walk one block upon this street to the Via Urbana. Taking a right on Via Urbana, we find ourselves, after a walk of four or five blocks, at the *Church of S. Pudentiana* (*S. Pudenziana*), located on the left side of the street. This church, lying below street level, is supposedly one of the most ancient churches in Rome.

According to legend, St. Peter lived here in a house owned by Senator Pudens, along with his daughters Pudentiana and Prassede. Archaeological studies, however, have revealed that this building was a bath, dating back to the early 2nd Century. About 145 Pope Pius I (142-157) converted a portion of the building into a church. Pope Siricus (384-399) enlarged the church in 385. Historical documents show that at this time the church was called *Titulus Pudentianae*. Restorations to the building were carried out in the late 8th

Century by Pope Adrian I (792-795). By this time its name had been changed to the Church of S. Pudentiana. Most of the building we see today dates from the restoration of Cardinal Enrico Gaetani in 1597.

Inside the church we can still see traces of the 5th Century decorations. If we walk down the left aisle we can see the ruins of the 2nd Century building, excavated behind the apse. Another place to see more of the ruins of the baths is at the corner of Via Agostino Depretis and Via Cesare Balbo, located northwest of the church.

Walking east on Via A. Depretis, we quickly arrive at the immense structure of the *Church of S. Maria Maggiore (S. Mary Major)*. As we approach the church, we first enter the *Piazza del Esquilino*. Upon entering the plaza, we observe an obelisk. This monolith, the *Esquiline Obelisk (Obelisci Mausolei Augusti-Esquilino)*, does not come from Egypt, but is a Roman copy. Shortly after being given all his powers in 27 B.C., Augustus began to build himself a mausoleum. Two uninscribed obelisks were hewn and placed at the tomb site. During the Middle Ages the two obelisks fell and became covered with detritus. The western obelisk was uncovered in 1519, but it remained lying *in situ* for another sixty-eight years. In 1587 Domenico Fontana erected it at the present site. Its function was to decorate the villa of Pope Sixtus V (1585-1590).

S. Maria Maggiore is one of the seven pilgrimage churches of Rome. Various legends grew up about the builder of the basilica. Archaeologists have now determined that the first church was built by Pope Sixtus III (432-440) in the middle of the 5th Century. Many Roman ladies still secretly worshipped at a shrine of Juno located in the vicinity. Wishing to substitute for the pagan cult, Sixtus built the basilica and dedicated it to the Virgin Mary. An hour spent wandering within this immense church can be both satisfying and fascinating.

If we exit from the east side of the church, we find ourselves in the *Piazza di S. Maria Maggiore*, which is a very busy intersection. Let us leave near the southeast corner of the plazza on the Via di S. Prassede and after a short walk we arrive at the *Church of S. Prassede*, located on the right side of the street. In 64 or 65 Nero had twenty-three Christians killed on this spot. Prassede, the sister of Pudentiana, buried the bodies in a well. According to tradition Prassede was also buried in the well. About 157 Pope Pius I (142-157) erected a small shrine on the spot to honor the sainted girl. The shrine was replaced by the basilica in 822, the work of Pope Paschal I (817-824). This church is worthy of exploration.

After our exploration of the church let us now move over one block to Via Merulana, walk east on it to the first street to the left, which is Via S. Vito. Walking along the Via S. Vito, we pass through an arch. This is the *Arch of Gallienus (Arcus Galleini)*, that was a gate with triple openings in the Servian Walls. In the 1st Century Augustus built it to replace the Porta Esquilina. It was rebuilt in 262 and dedicated to the Emperor Gallienus (253-

268). Today, only the central opening remains. The arch, made of travertine, is 8.80m. (28.87 ft.) high, 7.30m. (23.95 ft.) wide, and 3.50m. (11.48 ft.) deep.

Returning to Via Merulana, we proceed east on the street to the intersection of Via Leopardi. On the left we see a triangular area known as the *Largo Leopardi*. Here we see a building built into the remains of the Servian Walls. These ruins are of the *Auditorium of Maecenas (Auditorium Maecenatis)*. This small theater was built in the *Gardens of Maecenas,* one of the great garden parks of Ancient Rome. The structure was built between 40 and 35 B.C.

With permission we are able to gain access to the auditorium. The floor lies about 7m. (22.97 ft.) below the modern street level. Descending into the building, we find that we are in a rectangular room or hall that is oriented almost in an east-west direction. The auditorium measures about 24.1m. (79.06 ft.) by 10.6m. (34.78 ft.). At the west end we find an apse or exedra with seven semi-circular steps, creating the appearance of a stage. In the wall of the apse there are five niches or alcoves, that probably housed statues. On each side of the hall we can see six alcoves that are deeper than the ones on the stage walls.

After leaving the auditorium we walk along Via Leopardi for one block and find ourselves at the Piazza Vittorio Emanuele II. Here at this end of the plaza we see the large ruins of an ancient structure. These are the remains of the *Nymphaeum Aquae Juliae.* At the top of the ruins we can see the semicircular remains of the central chamber. On the left a portion of the lateral arch can be detected. There was one on the right, but it is now completely missing. Marble statues once stood in these openings until they were removed to the Capitoline Hill in 1590. From the brickwork it has been determined that the nymphaeum was built in the early 3rd Century during the rule of Alexander Severus (222-235).

If we exit at the opposite end of the plaza in the center this puts us on the Via Conte Verde, which we should stay on until we reach Viale Manzoni. Then we turn left on Manzoni to the first street on the right, which is Via Luigi Luzzatti. Here at the intersection of two streets at No. 2B Luzzatti, we find ourselves at the *Sepulcrum Aureliorum,* a Christian tomb dating from the early 3rd Century.

Most of the upper chamber has been destroyed, but the stairs leading to the lower rooms have been preserved. If we take the south stairs we first enter a vestibule only four steps down. Here we can see some wall paintings. In the lower chamber there are some very beautiful paintings on the walls, including peacocks. Climbing back up and then descending the north stairs we enter the other burial chamber, which also has very beautiful wall paintings. At the north end of this room is another set of stairs leading down into a small catacomb. After construction began on the Aurelian Wall in 270, the tomb had to be abandoned. Roman law forbade burial within the walls of the city.

After leaving the tomb, let us continue northward on Via Manzoni to the Via di Porta Maggiore, turn right on this street, then take the first street on the left. As we turn onto the Via Pietro Micca, we see at the end of the street a very large dome-like structure. This structure, located on the north side of the Via Giovanni Giolitti, is known as the *Nymphaeum Hortorum Licianorum.* In ancient times it was situated in the *Horti Liciniani (Licinian Gardens)* that covered this entire area. Many people still refer to it as the *Temple of Minerva (Minerva Medici)*, a name erroneously given it in the 17th Century.

The nymphaeum was built in the middle of the 3rd Century, probably, by the Emperor Licinius Gallenius (253-268). Debate continues among scholars as to whether the structure was a nymphaeum or a great banquet room. The lower part is penetrated by many windows. Brick is the major building material used. Above the lower portion there is a large ten-sided dome. The roof has long since collapsed. As late as the start of the 19th Century, the nymphaeum was still in good shape. The roof collapsed in 1828, and the following year it suffered damage from lightning. In 1942 the building was partially restored.

With our curiosity satisfied about the nymphaeum, we now walk east on the Via Giovanni Giolitti to the Aurelian Walls, and there before us is the *Porta Praenestina.* When Aurelian began the walls in 270 he incorporated these two arches of the Aqua Claudia and the Anio Novus into his walls and made them into a double gateway. This spot was a junction for many of the aqueducts entering Rome. Honorius built guard towers at the gate in 403. The gateway has been called the *Porta Maggiore* since the 10th Century. In the early 19th Century the towers were pulled down. Excavations of 1955 through 1957 revealed the foundations and ancient road level.

This gate is open today, but only to foot traffic. The travertine structure is 32m. (104.99 ft.) high and 24m. (78.74 ft.) wide. In the center, between the main arches, is a smaller opening that is 5.10m. (16.73 ft.) in height and in width measures 1.80m. (5.91 ft.). It is walled up, and probably has been since the 6th Century. The main two openings are 14m. (45.93 ft.) high, 6.35m. (20.83 ft.) wide, and 6.20m. (20.34 ft.) deep.

Just inside the Porta Praenestina we note the remains of a wall. These walls marked the boundaries of the *Vivarium,* the enclosure where the animals slated to be used in the amphitheater were housed. Evidence indicates that the Vivarium was probably built in the 1st Century, at the same time the Colosseum was being constructed.

Turning to the north side of the gate we see the famous *Tomb of the Baker (Sepulcrum Eurysacis).* It is constructed of concrete and faced with travertine. Above the base we see a section composed of piers and columns. At the upper level there are circular openings, made in the tomb to resemble ovens. Evidently, M. Vergileus Eurysacis was one of Rome's better known bakers. At his death in the latter part of the 1st Century B.C., his wife,

Atinia, built the tomb. Friezes on the north and south sides go into all phases of bread making.

When the Aqua Claudia, the Anio Novus, and the Aurelian Walls were built, the tomb was left untouched. But, when Honorius remodeled the Porta Praenestina in 403, he built the central tower over the tomb. In 1838 Pope Gregory XVI (1831-1846) had the tomb cleared. This sepulcher, along with the Pyramid of Cestius, ranks as one of the unique tombs of Rome.

Away from the Porta Maggiore and on the left back side of the Via Prenestina we can see a brick structure jutting out from the railroad embankment. This is the entrance to the *Basilica Sotterranea* (*Basilica di Porta Maggiore*) that was discovered in 1917 by a railroad crew while making repairs to the Rome-to-Naples railway line. The basilica is remarkably well preserved, lying here under the tracks.

Inside the building piers divide the interior into a nave and two aisles, with an apse at the north end of the nave. The ceilings are vaulted and very beautifully decorated. Prior to entering the nave there is a rectangular vestibule that measures 3.50m. (11.48 ft.) by 3.62m. (11.88 ft.). The main portion of the basilica measures 12m. (39.37 ft.) by 9m. (29.53 ft.) and lies approximately 7.25m. (23.79 ft.) below the modern street level. It evidently dates from the 1st Century, and from the ceiling and wall paintings it has been determined that this was the meeting place of a Neo-Pythagorean sect.

Retracing our steps back to the Porta Maggiore, we now continue east on the Via Casilina to where the Aurelian Walls make a right angle turn. Near this point we see the elevated duct of the *Aqua Claudia.* This aqueduct collected spring waters on the slope of Mt. Ripoli over 64.37 km. (40 miles) away. Total length of the aqueduct was 68.75km. (42.72 miles) of which 15km. (9.32 miles) is elevated. Most of this aqueduct is still preserved as it wanders through the Campagna. At its junction with the walls it is then built into the walls all the way to the Porta Maggiore. None of the main channel is preserved in its entirety from the gate into the city. This aqueduct was begun by Caligula in 38 and completed in 52, during the rule of Claudius. At various spots within the city remains of its arches can be seen. Other places where its arches can be seen are on the slope of the Palatine, Via S. Paolo della Croce, Via della Navicella, Via di S. Stefano Rotondo, Via Merulana, Via Domenico Fontana, and Via Statilia.

Walking back through the Porta Maggiore, we see an arch over the Via Eleniana. This is an arch of the *Arcus Neroniani,* another aqueduct that topped the Aqua Claudius here at the Porta Maggiore. The Arcus Neroniani, built in the 1st Century, can still be traced onto the grounds of the Villa Wolkonsky.

Above the Porta Maggiore we see the lower channel of the Aqua Claudia and the upper one which is the *Anio Novus.* This latter aqueduct that collected its water from the Anio River was begun by Caligula in 38 and completed by Claudius in 52. The water from this aqueduct tended to be undrinkable until Trajan extended the aqueduct higher into the mountains to collect pure spring water. The Anio Novus carried the largest volume of any of the Roman aqueducts. It extended for 82.08km. (51 miles), then joined the Aqua Claudia at the 7th milestone. From this point they continued into Rome supported upon the same arches.

Northeast of the Porta Maggiore where the tram rails pass through an opening in the walls, we can see, built into the walls, the channels of three aqueducts. The top duct is the *Aqua Julia*. Under the Aqua Julia we see the channel of the *Aqua Tepula*, and below it the *Aqua Marcia*. The Aqua Marcia was constructed between 144 and 140 B.C. A praetor by the name of Q. Marcius Rex was put in charge of the project. Water was collected from mountain springs and brought into Rome with a channel length of 91.44km. (56.81 miles). From the Porta Maggiore the three aqueducts continued as far as the Baths of Diocletian using the same arches.

The Aqua Tepula was built in 125 B.C., and collected its waters from the springs in the Alban Hills. From its collection point to Rome, the distance was about 17.75km. (11.03 miles). In 33 B.C. Agrippa built the Aqua Julia that collected water from higher up in the Alban Hills, water that was very pure. Total length of its channel was 22.85km. (14.20 miles). Agrippa joined the two channels, mixing the waters between the 10th and 6th milestones, to improve the quality. They continued to Rome on the same arches, then joined with the Aqua Tepula. A branch of the Aqua Julia ran from the Porta Maggiore to the Nymphaeum of the Aqua Julia that we examined in the Piazza Vittorio Emanuele II.

If we walk back down the outside of the walls to the point where the Aqua Claudia joined the walls, we see a modern aqueduct, *Aqua Felice*, built in 1587. Following this aqueduct will bring us to where it makes a right angle turn to the left for a short distance, then continues south-easterly. From this point on, behind No. 19 Via Nuora, we are now looking at the remains of the Aqua Claudia, which is preserved from here to its end. From the city wall to about the intersection of Via Ozieri and Via Mistretta, the aqueduct is built on the north wall of the *Circus Varianus*.

This circus, which was 56.5m. (1,853.67 ft.) long and 125m. (410.10 ft.) wide, was probably built by the Emperor Elagabalus (218-222) early in the 3rd Century. The Aurelian Walls were built across the west end, and for about 150m. (492.13 ft.) extended within the city. If we walk back to the Piazza Lodi, take the southeast exit along Via Alghero, we can see a few stones of the south walls near the southwestern curve of the circus at Number 3 V. Alghero.

We may now retrace our steps to the Piazza Lodi, then exit left on the Via La Spezia to the Piazza Camerino, turn right through the plaza to the Via Caltagirone. Continuing on the Via Caltagirone we come to the Aurelian Walls, where we turn left on the Viale Castrense and walk parallel to the walls. After a short walk we arrive at a semicircular bulge in the walls. This shows the outline of the *Castrense Amphitheater* (*Amphitheatrum Castrense*). As we pass the semicircle we arrive at a gap in the walls, where we can again enter the city and walk around the opposite side of the amphitheater. About two-thirds of the walls within the city are still preserved, only the portions on the northwestern side have been removed.

This elliptical arena was a part of the Sessorium (which we will visit later) and was probably built during the rule of Elagabalus (218-222) in the early 3rd Century. It measures 88.5m. (290.35 ft.) by 78m. (255.91 ft.) and had three stories. We can see only the first level and portions of the second. When the Aurelian Walls were built in the latter part of the 3rd Century, the structure was incorporated. The outer walls of the arena formed this section of the Aurelian Walls. The arched openings or arcades were walled up to make a solid wall. Not much of interest remains within the arena.

To the north and east of the amphitheater and adjacent to it, is the great structure of the *Church of S. Croce in Gerusalemme* (*St. Cross in Jerusalem*). This church was built from an eastern portion of the Sessorium. After her return from the holy land in the early 320's, Helena, mother of Constantine the Great, converted this part of the palace into a chapel. This church has also been called the *Basilica Sessoriana* or *Basilica Heleniana*. According to tradition, Helena placed a portion of the "true cross" in the foundation of the chapel. Toward the close of the 4th Century the building was converted into a true basilica. Pope Gregory I (590-604) converted it into a titular church at the close of the 6th Century. We should spend an hour or two browsing in this beautiful church (open from 6:00 a.m. to 1:30 p.m. and again from 3:00 to 8:00 p.m.).

The *Sessorium* or *Palatium Sessoriuanum* was a large complex that was probably built early in the 3rd Century by Elagabalus. It included a temple, the palace, the Circus Varianus, the Amphitheatrum Castrense, and a bath. Constantine the Great later came into possession of this great palace that was almost a villa. An atrium of the palace, measuring 39.25m. (121.77 ft.) long and 24.8m. (81.37 ft.) wide was converted into the Church of S. Croce in Gerusalemme. When the Aurelian Walls were built, they cut the grounds of the palace in half. North of the church we can see more ruins of the Sessorium.

Now we will exit the Piazza di S. Croce in Gerusalemme on the north side on the Via Eleniana, and continue on this street to the intersection with Via Germano Sommeiller. At the intersection we see the ruins of the reservoir (lying below street level) that supplied water to the *Baths of Helena* (*Thermae Helenae*). These baths belonged to the Sessorium complex. They were built by Elagabalus in the 3rd Century and restored by the Empress Helena. Originally, there were twelve chambers in the reservoir.

Leaving this site we continue up the Via Eleniana, passing under the Aqua Claudia, to the Piazzale di Porta Maggiore. Unfortunately, we can't see it now, but at the intersection of the plaza and the Via di Porta Maggiore, we are standing over the *Sepulcrum Statiliorum*. This tomb, the burial site of the family of Statilius Taurus, was excavated in 1875. It contained many beautiful paintings. The paintings, dating from the 3rd Century were photographed, some of the wall reliefs were taken to museums, and the tomb was covered up again.

Let us now leave the piazza on the southwest corner on the Via Statilia. On the right hand corner of the intersection of the Via Statilia and Via di S. Croce in Gerusalemme there are some ruins of a tomb. These are the remains of the *Sepulcrum Quinctriorum* (*Tomb of P. Quinctius*). The tombs date from the end of the 1st Century B.C. There are several other tombs grouped around this sepulcher. They were discovered in 1916.

We must now get permission to enter the Villa Wolkonsky. On the south side of the A. Neroniani there is another tomb called the *Tomb of Vitalis* (*Sepulcrum T. Claudii Vitalis*). It was built for T. Claudius Vitalis and his family in the middle of the 1st Century. The tomb consisted of three levels, of which two are well preserved. Inside the tomb we see the burial niches.

After leaving the tomb, we admit that another full day has been well spent touring the Esquiline. We can say that this hill was a region of palaces, gardens, aqueducts, and tombs.

CHAPTER 10

Quirinal, Viminal, and Pincian

Today's itinerary provides us with a look at the ruins of the Quirinal, Viminal, and Pincian Hills. In reality, what we are looking at is the northern part of the Esquiline and three of its spurs. The southern spur is called the Viminal; the much larger middle one is the Quirinal; and the large northern one is the Pincian. Our journey will cover a large chunk of territory.

Our tour begins at the train station, where we catch Bus 66 to the *Church of S. Lawrence outside the Walls* (*S. Lorenzo fuori le Mura*). The church is dedicated to St. Lawrence, a deacon serving under Pope Sixtus II (257-258). Sixtus was put to death in 258 during the Christian persecutions of Valerianus (253-260) and Gallienus (253-268). Lawrence begged the authorities to allow him to follow the example of his master — a fate that was arranged for him three days later when he was burned at the stake. Early in the 3rd Century a Christian widow by the name of Cyrica donated land for a catacomb. Lawrence was buried here in the *Catacomb of S. Cyrica.* In the next century Constantine the Great (310-337) built a basilica over the hallowed site.

Pope Pelagius II (579-590) rebuilt the church in 579. More restorations and rebuilding were carried out by various popes throughout the ensuing centuries. Despite all these repairs the church retains the style of the early Christian basilica. At least a half hour should be spent touring the church.

After leaving the church it is best to walk back toward Rome on the ancient *Via Tiburtina*, the road that connected Rome with Tibur (Tivoli). As we approach the Aurelian Walls we see to the right of the modern gate, an opening now closed off by an iron railing. This opening was the original gate in the walls, the *Porta Tiburtina*, constructed when the walls were built between 270 and 280. Conduits of the Aqua Julia, Aqua Marcia, and Aqua Tepula passed along the gate arches. When the walls were built the arches of these aqueducts were incorporated into the walls. Honorius (395-423) added the rectangular towers about 403. The gate remained in use until partially destroyed by Pope Pius IX (1846-1878) in 1869.

Turning right inside the walls, we find ourselves upon the Via Marsala, which takes us along the side of the train station (to our left). Upon reaching the front of the station, we see more of the *Servian Walls* that were described in Chapter 8. A long stretch of them is also preserved across the street in the Piazza Cinquecento.

The rounded structure sitting away from the walls is part of the distribution chamber of the Aqua Marcia. This aqueduct was also discussed in Chapter 8. Just past the Aqua Marcia chamber we see a section of tufa that resembles the Servian Walls. That is what it is, and it contains the *Porta Viminalis,* one of the original gates, built in 387 B.C.

If we cross the street to the Piazza Cinquecento, and then walk left, we arrive at the *Obelisk of the Piazza Cinquecento (Obeliscus Isei Campensis).* This monolith of red granite was transported from Egypt. It was inscribed and erected at Heliopolis by Ramses II (1290-1224 B.C.) in the 13th Century B.C. Who brought it to Rome or when it was brought is not known. The best guess is that it arrived in the imperial city in the 1st Century, where it was placed in the courtyard of the Iseum Campense (see Chapter 7).

It fell in the Middle Ages, but did not break. In 1719 the obelisk was discovered, but the find was kept secret. Workers excavating for the foundation of a library in the Dominican monastery made the find. Some scholars feel that if the obelisk had been reported, construction would be delayed, thus the need for secrecy was justified. It was discovered again in 1883, and this time the monolith was uncovered. In 1887 it was erected at the front of the train station to honor those Italian soldiers killed in the Ethiopian War. The area was renovated and the obelisk was moved to its present position in 1924.

Moving across the street from the obelisk, we find ourselves at the giant building that marks the remains of the *Baths of Diocletian (Thermae Diocletiani).* These baths were the largest in Rome, even larger than the Baths of Caracalla. Maximian (286-305), the co-emperor with Diocletian (284-305), began this giant bath house in 298. The structure was completed and dedicated in the spring of 305 in the name of both emperors. After completion the Baths of Diocletian were approximately 475 by 430m. (1,558.4 by 1,410.8 ft.), encompassing an area of about 50 acres (twice the size of the Palatine Hill). The central building was 280 by 160m. (918.6 by 524.9 ft.), covering an area of approximately 11 acres. A great portion of the site is covered by the Piazza della Repubblica and the buildings south of it.

Our knowledge of the history of these baths during ancient times is very scanty. There is some evidence to indicate that the baths continued to function until the early part of the 6th Century. In the 16th and 17th Centuries the baths suffered a great deal, when material was removed from them for building purposes. Michelangelo converted the Tepidarium into the *Church of S. Maria degli Angeli* between 1563 and 1566. The state converted a portion of the west side into a museum in 1898.

If we move to our left into Republican Square (Piazza della Repubblica), we are standing in the area of the *Calidarium.* In front of us the Church of S. Maria degli Angeli occupies the *Tepidarium.* Let us walk completely around the building, looking at the ruins behind the church. We keep walking until we arrive back at the corner opposite the obelisk, which is the entrance to the

FIGURE 11

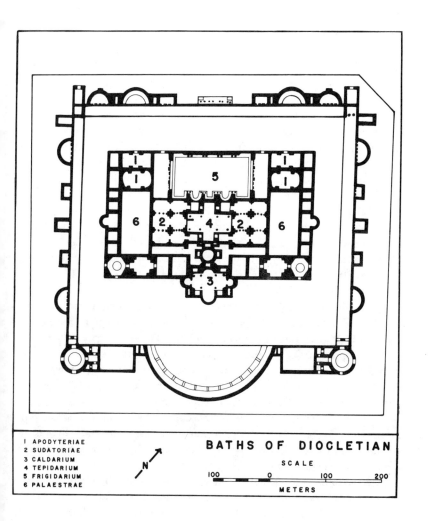

Baths of Diocletian

Museo Nazionale Romano (see plan of the Baths). This museum is built in the *Frigidarium* and part of the *Palaestra.* We should spend at least two hours visiting this very large and very splendid museum. A 200 page book can be purchased at the door that describes the contents of the museum, a very large museum collection, indeed!

After leaving the museum let us take two left turns and walk north in front of the train station with the museum to our left. We quickly pass through the Piazza dell' Indipendenza and shortly the street deadends into the Viale Castro Pretorio. In front of us is an Italian military base and the National Library. They are occupying the grounds of the *Castra Praetoria* (*Barracks of the Praetorian Guard*). The Praetorian bodyguard began as the personal bodyguard of Augustus (27 B.C. - 14 A.D.) when he became Rome's first emperor in 27 B.C. Later their numbers grew until they reached a figure of about 9,000. They acted not only as the bodyguard of the emperor, but became a police force for Italy. In the middle of the 1st Century they became so powerful, that from time to time they appointed and removed emperors, many times by assassination.

This camp patterned after the typical Roman camp was built by Tiberius (14-37) about 23. It was rectangular with rounded corners, containing gates on all four sides. The camp measured about 440 by 380m. (1,443.6 by 1,246.7 ft.) with walls that were 4.75m. (15.6 ft.) in height. When Aurelian (270-275) built his walls in the 270's he incorporated the camp so that the walls made a U-shape at the camp. He also raised the height of the walls to about 7.75m. (25 ft.).

We walk to the right until we come to the Via Monzamboso and turn left. Behind the houses at Nos. 4, 5, and 6 is the walled up arch of the *Porta Chiusa* which was a gate in the Aurelian Wall. To see this gate we turn left on Via Osoppo and walk to the walls and turn left on the deadend street Via della Sforzesca. Then we retrace our steps back and continue on down Viale dell' Universita to the first street to the left which is Viale del Policlinico. After turning left on Via Policlinico we find that we are walking along the walls which form the back side of the Castra Praetoria. The street will eventually make a left turn and continue along the walls until there is an opening to let a street pass through. At this point we have completely walked around about eight-tenths of the camp.

Let us continue to walk along the outside of the Aurelian Walls until we see a rounded tower built into the fortifications. Just before getting to the tower we see a bulge in the wall with pieces of travertine inbedded. This is the site of the *Tomb of Q. Haterius* (*Sepulcrum A. Haterii*). The celebrated Roman orator was buried here in 26.

When the Aurelian Walls were built in the late 3rd Century, the south tower of the *Porta Nomentana* was built over the tomb. The tower was rounded like the one to the north. Between the two towers was the gate that opened onto the *Via Nomentana.* In 1826 the tomb was discovered under the

PLATE 39

A. Servian Walls (near Train Station)

B. Porta Salaria

PLATE 40

A. Baths of Diocletian

B. Milvian Bridge

tower and the tower was torn down. Pope Pius IV (1559-1565) had walled up the gate in 1564 and replaced it with the modern Porta Pia which lies about 75m. (246 ft.) farther along the walls from the Porta Nomentana.

Next, we continue along the walls to the second opening through which the Via Salaria passes. For those who want to see an interesting tomb, they should turn right and walk on the left side of the Via Salaria for about 1 km. (.6 mile) to No. 125. Lying behind an iron fence, we can see the front part of a circular tomb, jutting out from the mound of earth. This is the *Tomb of M. Lucilius Paetus* (*Sepulcrum Lucilli Paeti*) built by this former tribune and praefect for himself and his sister Lucilia Polla. He patterned it after the circular Etruscan tombs, building it toward the close of the 1st Century B.C. The height of the tomb was 16m. (52.2 ft.) and had a diameter of 34.9m. (114.5 ft.). A corridor led into a burial chamber that measured 1.7 by 1.55m. (5.6 x 5.1 ft.). In the early 2nd Century it was covered with earth but it was reopened for Christian burials in the 4th Century.

Retracing our steps down the Via Salaria we arrive back at the opening in the walls. At this spot the *Porta Salaria* once stood. It was one of the original openings in the Aurelian Walls flanked by two semicircular towers. In 1870 the gate was so badly damaged by artillery fire that it was torn down and replaced by a new one in 1873. To relieve traffic congestion in 1921 the modern gate was also demolished.

If we step over the iron fence and walk farther along the walls, after about 30.4m. (100 ft.) we arrive at a semicircular facade of a travertine tomb. These are the remains of the *Tomb of Cornelia,* daughter of L. Scipio. The tomb was built in the 2nd Century B.C., and was later covered by the west tower of the Porta Salaria. When the tower was torn down in 1871 the tomb was moved slightly, and then moved again to this site in 1950.

Walking back and entering through the opening, we see on our left another tomb. This is the *Tomb of Q. Sulpicius Maximus* (*Sepulcrum A. Sulpicii Maximi*), an eleven year old boy, that dates to the end of the 1st Century. The eastern tower of the Porta Salaria was constructed over it and was rediscovered when the tower was torn down in 1871. It was moved slightly to preserve it, and then when the modern gate was torn down in 1921, it was placed at its present position. The rectangular tomb, measuring about 6 by 4m. (20 x 13 ft.), is built of tufa and marble.

After entering the city, we see that the street intersection makes a W. We take the middle one, which is Via Calabria and then left as it deadends into Via Collina. The first street to the right from Collina brings us into the Piazza Sallustio. Walking on to the right we see at No. 21 P. Sallustio some brick remains lying about 14m. (46 ft.) below the modern street level. These are some of the ruins of buildings of the *Gardens of Sallust* (*Horti Sallustiani*). Named after their designer, the historian C. Sallustius Crispus, the gardens occupied a large area on the Viminal, Quirinal, and Pincian, and the valleys between. They were built about the year 40 B.C.

Looking down, we see the remains of a four storied brick building that was the large central palace of the gardens. Other ruins from the gardens can be seen several streets away on Via Lucullo and on Via Friuli on the grounds of the American Embassy.

Now we keep to the right to Via Nerva where we take a right, exiting the piazza at the northwest corner. After Via Nerva ends at the next street we must take a left and then immediately a right on Via Puglie all the way to the Aurelian Walls. We turn left at the walls and walk along them for six or seven blocks until we come to the *Porta Pinciana* which has openings for traffic on each side, but the gate itself is open only to pedestrian traffic. It was only a small gate in the Aurelian Walls at their inception, but was turned into a major gateway by Honorius around 403. If we step outside we are able to see the round towers on each side of the gateway.

Moving back into the city we find we are on the Via Vittorio Veneto, better known simply as Via Veneto. We stay on Via Veneto until it ends in the Piazza Barberini. After entering the piazza we turn right and then almost immediately take a left on Via Quattro Fontane. On the left are the grounds of the Villa Barberini, which we enter and walk through the Palazzo Barberini and up a ramp. This puts us in the gardens behind the palace and to our right we see the remains of the *Barberini Mithraeum* (*Mithraeum Domus Barbarinorum*). It is protected from the elements by a greenhouse-type structure. It measures 11.85 by 6.25m. (38.9 by 20.5 ft.) and was probably built in the latter part of the 1st Century. It was discovered in 1936, and some of its wall paintings are still preserved.

Walking back to the street we turn left and then right on the first street which is Via del Quirinale. At No. 30 on the left side of the street there is an interesting monument beneath the building. If we can get one of the policemen to take us down, we can see the *Ara Incendii Neronis.* It is a travertine altar with some marble, built by Domitian (81-96) in the 1st Century to remember the great fire of 64 under Nero. The altar was discovered in 1888.

After our return to the street, we now continue down Via del Quirinale. In the piazza there is an obelisk. This *Quirinale Obelisk* (*Obeliscus Mausolei Augusti*) was one of the two obelisks placed in front of the Tomb of Augustus in the 1st Century. It is not a genuine Egyptian obelisk but only a Roman copy. It was discovered lying under silt in 1527 but left where it lay. Pope Pius VI (1775-1799) began renovating the Piazza del Quirinale in 1782 and the following year the obelisk was erected here.

Under the pavement of the Piazza and in the gardens of the Palazzo Quirinale are the ruins of a *Temple of Serapis* (*Quirinale Serapeum*). The temple was built by Caracalla (218-222) in the 3rd Century. Today, very little remains to be seen.

We can take the steps down beside the palace and find ourselves upon Via della Dataria. On the left side of the street at No. 21 there is a tomb beneath the building. It may be very difficult to get someone to take us down, but, if we can, we will be able to view the *Tomb of Sempronius (Sepulcrum Semproniorum)*. It was built in the 1st Century B.C. for Cn. Sempronius, his mother Larcia, and his sister Sempronia. The tomb was discovered in 1863.

After reaching Via dei Lucchesi, we cross it and here Via Dataria becomes Via dell Umilta. We continue down Via Umilta for one block then turn left on Via Archeto until it deadends into a building. If we walk to the right we find ourselves in front of the building, which is the *Church of SS. Apostoli.* This interesting church, open from 6:30 a.m. - 12 a.m. and 4-7 p.m., is worth at least a half hour of our time. It was built by Pope Julius I (337-352) and completed in 340. He dedicated it to the Saints Philip and James. Pope Pelagius (555-561) added on to the structure in 560. In the early 15th Century Pope Martin V (1417-1431) rebuilt and made many changes in the church. Then in the early 18th Century the early church was completely rebuilt. Very little of the classical structure remains today.

After visiting the church, we retrace our path to Via Lucchesi, take a left on it, passing by the famous Trevi Fountain, and walk to Via del Tritone. We then walk right for a few steps and then take a left on Via del Nazareno. On the left side of the street behind an iron fence we see the ruins of the *Aqua Virgo.* This aqueduct was built by Agrippa in 19 B.C., and was underground for most of its course. It collected its waters from springs north of Rome, sending them through a channel of 20.7km. (12.9 miles), emerging here on the slope of the Pincian Hill, as it took water to the Baths of Agrippa in the Campus Martius.

We return to Tritone, turn left on it for one block, then take the middle fork which is Via Francesco Crispi. After walking on Crispi for a couple of blocks we take a left on Via Sistina which leads us to the Church of Trinita dei Monti, located above the famous Spanish Steps. Here in front of the church we see an Egyptian obelisk made of red granite. This is the *Trinita dei Monti Obelisk (Obeliscus Hortorum Sallustianorum)*.

It came from Egypt, probably in the early 3rd Century, and was inscribed and erected in the Gardens of Sallust. It probably fell and broke into two pieces sometime in the 8th Century. The obelisk, minus its base was moved to the Piazza di S. Giovanni in Laterano by Pope Clement XII (1730-1740) in 1743. Due to the ill health of Clement the obelisk was never erected in the piazza. However, it was erected at its present site by Pope Pius VI (1775-1799) in 1789. The base was moved to the gardens near S. Maria d'Aracoeli on the Capitoline in 1843.

This place where we are standing, including the area behind the church and extending north of the Aurelian Walls, was once covered by the *Acilian Gardens (Horti Aciliorum)*. The Acilian family probably built these gardens in the 1st Century B.C. As we walk in front of the church along the Viale della Trinita dei Monti, we are walking in these ancient gardens. We walk up the steps and take a right on the Viale Villa Medici to the Aurelian Walls to a stop where we are actually on top of them. At the walls we turn left in this beautiful park and walk one block to the Viale dell' Obelisco. This Pincian Park and the beautiful park, the Villa Borghese north of the walls, are remnants of the Acilian Gardens.

If we turn left on Viale dell' Obelisco we arrive at an obelisk in the middle of the street. This is the *Pincian Obelisk* (*Obeliscus Antinoi*) and is a Roman copy of an Egyptian obelisk. It was inscribed with Egyptian hieroglyphics and erected in front of the tomb of Antinous in 130. The tomb was located on the Via Labicana outside the city walls. Antinous was a favorite of the Emperor Hadrian (117-138). After Antinous drowned in the Nile in 130, Hadrian named a city after him in Egypt (Antinoopolis) and built the tomb for him outside Rome, complete with the obelisk.

In the early 3rd Century the obelisk was moved to the Circus Varianus where it remained and fell during the Middle Ages. The owner of the property erected it in 1570, but it fell shortly after this. Cardinal Francesco Barberini removed it to his gardens in 1642. In 1769 Pope Clement XIV (1769-1774) put the broken obelisk in the Pigna Gardens in the Vatican. Finally, Pope Pius VII (1800-1823) had it erected at its present site in 1822.

If we walk past the obelisk on a diagonal path to the right we find ourselves at a beautiful overlook at the edge of the park. Here we have an excellent view of the Piazza del Popolo. We can bear to the right and walk down the steps to the piazza. After walking through the Porta Flaminia we continue on the Via Flaminia to the first bus stop. Here we can catch Bus 1 to the river, getting off in the Piazzale Cardinal Consalvi. In front of us is the *Milvian Bridge* (*Pons Mulvius*), the site of one of Constantine the Great's (310-337) significant battles.

As the year 310 began there were five Roman emperors including Constantine. The senior emperor, Galerius (305-311) died in 311 shortly after ending the persecution of Christians. Then in 312 Constantine and Maxentius (310-312) declared war upon each other. The forces of Constantine met those of Maxentius here near the Milvian Bridge, which at that time was still a pontoon bridge. There is some debate, but several scholars feel that before the battle got underway Constantine had his soldiers paint the sign of the cross on their shields. He supposedly had a vision the night before urging him to fight under the sign of the Christians. After the battle got underway the army of Constantine forced the troops of Maxentius back upon the bridge, which collapsed under their weight, drowning many and causing mass confusion. Constantine quickly won the battle and Maxentius was killed. By 324 Constantine had put down all opposition and was sole emperor of the Roman Empire until his death in 337.

The bridge was probably built in 220 B.C. when the Via Flaminia was completed. Some scholars maintain that the bridge has been made of stone since its inception and was never a pontoon bridge. Perhaps the causeway was wooden, but the arches and piers were of stone. Certain scholars have made a good case for the stone arches that we see today as dating back to 109 B.C.

If we walk across the river to the bus stop, we can catch Bus 1 back to Rome. On our return trip, we can truthfully say that we covered a lot of territory on today's tour.

CHAPTER 11

The Transtiberim

Our journey today takes us across the Tiber River. We will be looking at the area of the Vatican and Janiculum Hills. This region was referred to by the ancient Romans as the Transtiberim. The local natives break the area up into districts. Along the river and east of the Janiculum, the district is referred to as the Trastevere. The Janiculum and its slopes are called the Giancolo. Around St. Peter's the area is referred to as the Vatican. To the east of the Vatican the district around the Tomb of Hadrian is called the Borgo. Of the two hills the Vatican is the higher since it reaches a height of 146m. (479 ft.) above sea level. In Rome, however, the Janiculum reaches a height of 89m. (292 ft.), while the Vatican only attains 75m. (246 ft.) within the Vatican City. Of all the hills in Rome, the Janiculum has the coolest temperatures in August.

Today's tour should begin near the *Tomb of Hadrian (Mausoleum Hadriani)*. If we take Bus 64 from the Train Station or Piazza Venezia, we should get off just before we get to the river. This way we can cross the river on the Ponte San Angelo and drink in the majesty of this great tomb.

When Hadrian (117-138) became emperor in 117 the Tomb of Augustus was filled with urns containing ashes of the deceased. Nerva (96-98) was the last emperor to have his ashes interred in the Mausoleum of Augustus. The ashes of Trajan (97-117) had been buried at the base of his column. Using the Tomb of Augustus as a model, Hadrian had his builders begin his mausoleum in the *Gardens of Domitian.* The structure was not completed until 139, about a year after the death of Hadrian. His adopted son and the new emperor, Antoninus Pius (138-161), dedicated the tomb and placed the ashes of Hadrian in here, dedicating the monument to his step-father's memory.

The circular tomb sits upon a square base, made of a concrete and tufa core with walls of travertine and a facing of white marble. It is 84m. sq. (275.6 ft.), covering an area of almost 2 acres, and has a height of 10m. (32.8 ft.). The drum has a diameter of 64m. (210 ft.). It is built of concrete and tufa, faced with travertine and then with marble. The tomb itself rose 21m. (68.9 ft.). Access to the tomb was provided by three archways facing the bridge. The central opening is 2.4m. (7.9 ft.) wide and the lateral ones have a width of 2.1m. (6.9 ft.). An inclined ramp, 16m. (52.5 ft.) in length leads down to a vestibule. Then, a spiral passage, 9m. (29.5 ft.) high and 3m. (9.8 ft.) wide, leads to a point above the vestibule where the burial chamber is located. The sepulchral room measures 9m. by 8m. (29.5 x 26.2 ft.), and is 12m. (39.4 ft.) high.

Earth was placed on top of the tomb, just like the Tomb of Augustus, and a beautiful garden was laid out. Within the garden was a statue of Hadrian, and probably of other emperors as well. Emperors and their families from Hadrian through Marcus Aurelius (161-180) had their ashes interred in this magnificent tomb.

Aurelian (270-275) incorporated the tomb into his walls in the late 3rd Century. In 537 the Goths besieged Rome, and many of the defenders hurled the statues from the gardens down upon the heads of the besiegers. The popes of medieval times sought refuge here from time to time and gradually the tomb was converted into a fortress. Shortly after Gregory I (590-604), also known as the Great, became pope in 590, Rome began suffering a great and devastating plague. One day Gregory saw a vision of the Archangel Michael hovering over the tomb of Hadrian. The angel was in the act of sheathing his sword. After this the plague ceased, and the tomb became known as the *Castel S. Angelo* (*Castle of the Angel*).

Hadrian's Tomb is open every day from 9:00 A.M. to 1:00 P.M. We enter through the original entrance and walk down the ramp to the vestibule. Here in the vestibule we can see models showing how the mausoleum looked at different periods of history. Then we climb the winding ramp to the burial chamber. In the late 15th Century the flooring was removed and to cross the burial chamber one crossed a wooden drawbridge. This isolated the papal apartment during the many sieges of Rome. The floor was restored in 1822. At least two hours can be spent in the rest of the castle, looking at the beautiful rooms, the museum of military arms and uniforms, and the fortifications of the structure. From the top of the castle a beautiful view of S. Peter's Square is afforded.

After leaving the Castel S. Angelo, we turn right and walk along the river to the first street on our right, which takes us into the Piazza Pia. Passing through the Piazza Pia, we turn right for one block and find to our left the street called Borgo S. Angelo. We turn left on this street and find that the street parallels a wall that connects with the Tomb of Hadrian. There is much dispute as to the identity of the builder of these walls, generally referred to as the *Walls of Leo IV*. The walls enclose a fortified corridor connecting the Tomb of Hadrian with the Vatican City. On top of the walls there is also a walkway protected by battlements on each side.

Some scholars contend that Pope Leo IV (847-855) built the wall in 847 after becoming pope. He did this because Arab conquerors had destroyed large portions of the churches of S. Paul and S. Peter in 846. Other scholars contend that Pope Nicholas III (1277-1280) had the wall constructed in 1277. Still others credit Pope John XXIII (1410-1415), the anti-Pope, with being the builder. From time to time various popes have used it as an escape route during sieges of the Vatican City.

By following the walls we find ourselves moving into the Piazza S. Pietro, which occupies a portion of the *Circus of Gaius and Nero* (*Circus Gai et Neronis*), also called the *Circus Vaticanus*. From some substructures discovered in the 16th Century it appears that the circus was approximately 323m. (1,060 ft.) long and 74m. (243 ft.) wide. It was begun by Caligula (37-41) and completed by Nero (54-68) in the middle of the 1st Century. The circus occupied a portion of a large garden that covered the slope of the Vatican, called the *Horti Agrippinae*. This garden was built a few years before the circus was created by Agrippina, the mother of Caligula.

Here in the plaza we can see an obelisk, the *Vatican Obelisk* (*Obeliscus Vaticanus*). This red granite obelisk probably came from Egypt. It was hewn in the 4th Century B.C. upon orders from the Pharaoh Nectanebos (361-343 B.C.) of the XXX Dynasty. Evidently, the obelisk was erected at Heliopolis in the 4th Century B.C., but it was never inscribed. Ptolemy II (283-246 B.C.) probably moved it to Alexandria and placed it in front of a temple in the 3rd Century B.C. In 29 B.C. Octavianus (before he became Emperor Augustus) had it moved to the Forum Julium in Alexandria. After Caligula became emperor in 37 he brought the monolith from Egypt to Rome and had it erected on the spine of the Circus Vaticanus. The original site was just south of the Church of S. Peter.

In the Middle Ages a bronze ball was placed on top of the obelisk, and a legend developed indicating that the ashes of Julius Caesar were buried in this ball. After the renovations of the Vatican City began Pope Sixtus V (1585-1590) had his architect Domencia Fontana move it to its present location in 1586.

Now we turn our attention to the largest church in the world, the *Basilica of S. Peter.* According to theologians, this great edifice is built over the Tomb of St. Peter. Peter was put to death here on the lower slope of the Vatican Hill on June 29 in the year of 67. From archeological studies it has been deduced that this was also used as a pagan burial ground. Such a practice was legal since this portion of the hill lay outside the city limits of ancient Rome. After his death Peter was buried here by his loyal followers. Shortly after he became pope in 78, Cletus I, or Anencletus (78-91) as he is sometimes called, placed a monument over the grave of Peter, calling it the *Memoira.*

Between 315 and 320 Constantine (310-337) took steps to honor the martyred saint. He and Pope Sylvester I (314-335) exhumed the body and placed it in a silver casket along with a golden cross. They placed the casket within a bronze sarcophagus and buried the saint in the original grave. Constantine and the pope built a small chapel over the site, and, at the same time erected an altar directly over the grave. This chapel, called the *Confessio Petri,* now lies beneath the High Altar. In 323 Constantine built a basilica to enclose the chapel and grave.

The basilica probably retained its original form until the late 6th Century. After 590 Pope Gregory the Great began to make alterations. Pope

Nicholas V (1447-1455) made some changes in the structure in 1450. Shortly after becoming pope in 1503, Julius II (1503-1513) decided to build a new basilica, and ordered his architect, Donato Bramante, to begin tearing down the old structure. This unwarranted destruction was completed in 1506 and the foundation of the new basilica was laid. Julius died in 1513, followed by Bramante the next year, two events that brought the building project to a temporary halt. Over the next few years not much was accomplished. Pope Paul III (1534-1549) appointed Antonio Sangallo chief architect in 1539. In 1546, before a great deal of progress had been made, Sangallo died. Paul then appointed Michelangelo who completed the planning. The new basilica was formally dedicated on November 18, 1626 by Pope Urban VIII (1634-1644). In this century more external construction was carried out around the basilica.

This book is no place to go into the detailed description of the interior of the basilica. There are many books and monographs that do this admirably. One should spend at least two hours wandering through this most famous of churches.

A visit to the *Crypt of S. Peter* is certainly in order. Here lie many of the popes and other important people out of Rome's long and turbulent past. To get to the entrance to the crypt we go out the front of the basilica and make two right turns that bring us to a gate guarded by the famous Swiss Guards dressed in their colorful uniforms. They will allow us to enter to visit the crypt. We go to the right of the Sacristy and at the wall of the basilica we find the entrance to the crypt. After entering we discover that there are actually six museum rooms through which we should walk.

After touring these rooms we return to the third room and descend into the crypt or *Sacre Grotte.* This is divided into two grottoes. The first one we enter is the *Grotte Vecchie.* It is divided into three aisles: North Aisle, Central Aisle, and South Aisle. At least fourteen popes and cardinals are buried in the *North Aisle.* The earliest pope buried here is the English Pope Adrian IV (1154-1159) who was interred in the Egyptian granite sarcophagus.

Otto II, the German emperor who died in 983, is buried in the *Central Aisle.* These are not original burials as the Grotte Vecchie was not opened until 1606. Most of the tombs of the South Aisle are burials that date from the 10th to 20th Centuries.

Moving into the *Grotte Nuove* we find ourselves in a semicircular passage. This crypt, opened in the 1530's, is older than the Grotte Vecchie. The term "New Grotto" is misleading. It is called this because it was decorated later than the other crypt. As we go back we see another passage that leads to the *Preconstantinian Necropolis,* excavated in the 1940's and 1950's. Here we find the early pagan and Christian burials. To enter this we must have a permit granted by the office of the Reverenda Fabbrica, located not far from the entrance to the crypt. It usually takes a week at least to get this permission. It is well worth the trouble, however, as this crypt is of great interest to the archaeologist.

PLATE 41

A. Tomb of Hadrian

B. Base of Hadrian's Tomb

PLATE 42

A. S. Peter's Square

B. Walls of Leo IV

There are two ways to reach our next destination. For those who love to walk it is recommended that they exit the Piazza S. Pietro on the south side near the middle, walk through the Piazza del S. Uffizio, cross the street, and walk along the outside of the walls. These are the *Walls of Urban VIII*, who was pope from 1623 to 1644. He had these walls built in 1642 to connect the Vatican City with the rest of the Transtiberim region. The walls run along the west slope of the Janiculum until they reach the corner of the hill, then continue along the southern slope to the Tiber River. At one spot along the south slope the walls have collapsed. However, the most picturesque route is to exit the Square of S. Peter on the southeast corner and walk along Borgo S. Spirito toward the river. As we reach the street that parallels the river (Lungotevere in Sassia), we turn right and walk to the bus stop where we catch Bus 41. After the bus begins its winding climb up the Janiculum Hill, we get off at the first stop, and walk the rest of the way.

As we climb the hill there are many beautiful panoramic views of Rome on the other side of the Tiber. One has many chances to take pictures of the Pantheon and other landmarks that can be identified. The first excellent overlook is at the Piazzale del Faro, where a model of a lighthouse is located. Another beautiful view is afforded as one ascends the hill at the Piazzale Anita Garibaldi, a square dedicated to the wife of one of Italy's great 19th Century soldiers. We are now above the Walls of Urban VIII and a view of the countryside to the west is unfolded for us. Our third panoramic view is found next to the Piazzale Garibaldi. Here in the beautiful park setting we catch beautiful views both to the east and to the west.

A short walk brings us quickly to the *Porta S. Pancrazio*, the only original gate in the Walls of Urban VIII. Today it stands isolated, with streets encircling it on all sides. Although used as an apartment building today, it was the site of a heroic battle in 1849. Here the French attempted to enter Rome, but the heroic defenses of Giuseppe Garibaldi and his forces successfully defended the Roman Republic. Schoolboys volunteered and participated in this great battle.

This gate stands at the site of the ancient *Porta Aurelia*. The Porta Aurelia was one of the original gates in the Aurelian Walls, built in the late 3rd Century. Here at the gate the walls made the base portion of a flat-bottomed U. The *Via Aurelia Antica* passed through this porta, leading to Cerveteri, or the ancient Etruscan city of Caere. It had double gates with a courtyard in between, and it also had rectangular towers on the outside. The Porta Aurelia survived until 1642 when Urban VIII had it torn down to make way for his new walls. It was replaced by the Porta S. Pancrazio, which was badly damaged in the battle of 1849. The new gate we see now was built by Pope Pius IX (1846-1878) in 1854.

Now, let us walk outside the walls and take a short stroll on the ancient Aurelian Way (Via Aurelia Antica). On the left we see the beautiful grounds of the Villa Doria Pamphili. One of the houses beside the road is built over some ancient ruins. These remains are part of the *Aqua Trajana*, an aqueduct built by the Emperor Trajan. He built the conduit in 109 to supply water to his baths on the Oppian Hill. Several channels collected spring water from the hills west of Lago di Bracciano and funneled it into a reservoir near the town of Vicarello. The true aqueduct began here and ran a distance of 57.7km. (35.9 miles). As it neared the top of the Janiculum it became subterranean for most of the remainder of its journey.

After viewing the ruins of the aqueduct, we retrace our path to the Porta Aurelia (P. S. Pancrazio) and enter the walls. We branch off to the right and walk down Via Angelo Masina. About a half block down the street at No. 5 we see the entrance of the American Academy in Rome. As construction was being carried out in 1912, a 45m. (148 ft.) section of the Aqua Trajana was discovered running beneath the main building.

The first street to cross A. Masina is Via Giacomo Medici, upon which we take a right, cross the street, and stop at No. 11. Under this building in 1926 a section of the *Aqua Alsietina* was discovered. This aqueduct was built by Augustus (27 B.C.-14 A.D.) in the 1st Century to supply water to the *Naumachia* which was a great storage reservoir on the slope of the Janiculum further down. As the water was unpalatable, it was used to provide water for mock naval battles. It was also used to irrigate orchards in the Transtiberim region. The length of its channel was 32.8km. (20.4 miles).

It is time to walk back to Via Angelo Masina and turn right. Here the street becomes Viale Trenta Aprile. This street makes a horseshoe bend, crosses Via Nicola Fabrizi, and becomes Via Dandolo. We follow Dandolo on its winding course, and stop on the right hand side of the street at No. 47. Behind the fence we see the ruins of the *Temple of Jupiter Heliopolitanus*. It was dedicated to the Romanized Syrian god. A sign on the gate calls it the *Santuario Siriaco (Syrian Sanctuary)*.

This temple is administered by the Superintendent of Antiquities and a caretaker lives in the house at the site. It was built and dedicated to the deity by an unknown builder in the 1st Century. About 178 a builder by the name of M. Antonius Gaionas constructed another temple on the site. Then in the late 4th Century Emperor Julian the Apostate (361-363) built a new temple. Julian was trying to restore paganism to Rome during his administration. The ruins that we now see date to the 4th Century. If we ring the bell the caretaker will let us in to look around. At the far end of the structure we can see several niches in the wall. Next door at No. 45 a few remains of the walls can be detected.

Leaving the temple we continue down the hill on Via Dandolo to where it curves and crosses Via Glorioso. We turn right on Glorioso and walk to Viale di Trastevere, cross it, and walk through the gap in the walls. These are the Walls of Urban VIII. We turn left outside the walls and walk parallel to them until we reach a gate which is the *Porta Portese.* Here we make a right turn along the *Via Portuense.* About .5km. (.3 mile) down the street we come to the *Porta Portuensis,* which is one of the gates in the Aurelian Walls that once crossed the street here. It is on the right all covered by signs. Actually, what we see is a portion of the right side of the gate. The porta was destroyed in 1643 when the Walls of Urban VIII were built.

Now it is time to retrace our steps to the Porta Portese and continue up the street within the walls which is known as Via di S. Michele. After the first street intersection our thoroughfare becomes Via S. Cecelia. A short walk brings us into the Piazza di S. Cecelia and there to the right is the *Church of S. Cecelia in Trastevere.* The church is open from 9 to 12 a.m. and from 4 to 6 p.m. daily. After entering the gate we find ourselves in a beautiful garden.

Here we should sit down for a few minutes and reflect upon the history of the church. It was built over the ruins of several houses, including the *Domus Caeciliorum* or *House of Cecelia.* According to tradition Cecelia, a prominent Roman matron, was put to death for practicing Christianity in the early 3rd Century. A church then was built in the house where she and her husband, Valerianus, lived. This was carried out between 223 and 225 by Pope Urban I (223-230). Some theologians maintain she lived later and was martyred in 303. The present church was built above the earlier structures by Pope Paschal I (817-824) in the 9th Century. Extensive alterations were carried out on the structure in 1725.

In 1599 Cardinal Sfondrati had the tomb of St. Cecelia opened. She was found wrapped in a golden robe, lying upon her side. The three sword marks of the executioner were still visible upon her neck. Pope Clement VIII (1592-1605) came and viewed the body of the martyred saint and had an artist sketch her.

We should first wander through the church looking at the chapels and tombs. After we have accomplished this, we pay our fee and enter the crypt located to the left of the door as one enters. Descending the stairs we find ourselves in a long room. To our left beyond the railing we can see the original tile of the House of Cecelia. Following the passage to the left brings us into a room with beautiful mosaic tiles on the floor. To the right of this room we find a room with large circular holes in the floor. These holes are taning vats, and this building, called the *Coraria Septimiana,* was a tannery. Past the tannery we arrive at an older set of rooms that seems to date to the late 1st Century B.C. The tannery dates to the 2nd Century A.D. and the rooms near the front may not have been built until the 3rd Century. At the end of the crypt is a modern, but beautiful and small Byzantine Chapel.

Upon leaving the garden at the front of the church, we turn left and walk to the first street which is Via dei Genovesi and turn left on it. After crossing Via della Luce the next street we encounter is Viale di Trastevere. We turn right upon this street and immediately find ourselves in the Piazza S. Sonnino. There to our right we see a wall. Behind this are the ruins of the *VII Cohortium Vigilum Stationes (Station of the VII Cohort)* which was the fire station for the Transtiberim region. It is usually open to the public on Saturday morning, otherwise we have to get special permission to enter. The *Atrium* of the barracks along with the impluvium to catch rainwater is still in fairly good shape. This building that housed the firemen dates to the early 1st Century.

If we walk north to the first street, which is Via della Lungaretta, turn right on it, and then left on Via della Luce, we find ourselves at the river. Looking to our right we see a bridge leading to an island. This bridge, known by the modern name of *Ponte Cestio,* was called the *Pons Cestius* in ancient times. It was built by a Roman official by the name of Cestius in the 1st Century B.C. In 152 Antoninus Pius rebuilt the bridge, using travertine from the Theater of Marcellus. Evidently, the structure was destroyed by a flood in the middle of the 4th Century. It was rebuilt in 370, using more building material from the Theater of Marcellus, and dedicated as the *Pons Gratiani.* In the late 19th Century the channel was widened and the bridge was taken down and rebuilt. More than half of the building material consists of the original travertine blocks.

If we cross the bridge we arrive at *Tiber Island* or *Insula Tiberina* (*Isola Tiberina*). The length of the island is about 270m. (886 ft.) long and 70m. (230 ft.) wide. Today the dominant structure of the island is the hospital, but in ancient Rome several temples were built here. One temple was dedicated to Aesculapius, the god of healing. The symbol of this god was the snake which can still be seen down by the river to the left of the Church of S. Bartolomeo. It is inscribed in the travertine wall that is shaped like the prow of a ship.

There was also an obelisk on the island. About 292 the *Temple of Aesculapius* was completed and an obelisk was placed in front of it. The site of the obelisk was in front of where the Church of S. Bartolomeo now stands. It was made of red granite and probably came from Egypt. The hieroglyphic inscriptions were put on the monolith in Rome. This obelisk remained standing until well into the 16th Century. Today, fragments of the monolith can be seen in museums in Naples, Paris, and Munich.

After our tour of the island, we now retrace our path across the Pons Cestius and take a right along the river. Our next objective is the second bridge from the island, the *Ponte Sisto.* It is built over the foundation of the *Pons Aurelius.* Perhaps, the Pons Aurelius was built as early as the 1st Century B.C. Undoubtedly, one of the forks of the Via Aurelia crossed the river here at that time. It was rebuilt in 367 and was known variously as *Pons Antoninus, P. Janicularis,* and *P. Valentinianus,* to name only three of its titles. During periods of low water the original ruins can be seen beneath the new bridge.

Turning from the river, let us walk right on Via Ponte Sisto until it empties into Via di S. Dorotea which in turn terminates at Via Porta Settimiana. If we turn right on this street we will quickly come to an arch across the street which is the remains of the *Porta Septimiana.* This was one of the original gates in the Aurelian Walls. What we see is the result of the restoration by Pope Pius VI (1775-1799) in 1798.

Leaving the arch we walk south on the street passing Via Dorotea and after about several blocks of walking on Via della Scala we arrive at the *Church of S. Maria in Trastevere.* This church, one of the oldest in Rome, certainly deserves a half hour or more of our time. It was probably built in 222 or 223 by Pope Callistus I (219-223) with permission of Emperor Severus Alexander (222-235). The church was very small in 337. Pope Julius I (337-352) built a larger basilica. Most of the building that we now see dates to the restorations of Pope Innocent II (1130-1143) in the 12th Century, and a large number of the mosaics in the church portray the Virgin Mary.

CHAPTER 12

Hadrian's Villa

Today's tour will take us away from the city of Rome. We will travel to the *Villa of Hadrian* (*Villa Adriano*) located near the town of Tivoli. The ancient Roman name for Tivoli was Tibur, and near the town itself many villas of prominent Romans were situated. Hadrian's Villa is the largest and most spectacular of them all.

We start our journey by going to the train station, cross to the Piazza Cinquecento, and when we arrive behind the Baths of Diocletian we will catch a bus to Tivoli. After boarding the bus we settle back for the half-hour journey. Hadrian (117-138) was a nephew of the Emperor Trajan (97-117). He was formally adopted and designated as his successor by Trajan, so, at the death of his step-father in 117, Hadrian was recognized as the new emperor by the Senate, the Army, and the Praetorian Guard.

The new emperor was a great believer and admirer of the Greek culture. Under Hadrian Greek culture became vogue in Rome once again. He also started a new fashion: the wearing of a beard. Beards had been popular among rulers until the time of Alexander the Great (336-323 B.C.). Alexander had been clean shaven and ordered his troops to shave with regularity. This was to make it difficult for the enemy to have a convenient handhold. This beardless trend had lasted until the days of Hadrian. As the new emperor now sported a beard, the new trend in fashion had been established.

Hadrian spent a great deal of his time touring the provinces. Construction on the villa began in 118, and after Hadrian returned from the East in 125 the villa began to take on more Greek and Egyptian characteristics. The villa was probably not completed until about 135, which was only three years before his death. It is built on the slope of the Sabine Hills on a plateau between two small valleys.

As the bus starts up the long slope to Tivoli, we should watch for the sign advertising the villa. When we see it we ask the driver to stop. After leaving the bus we will have a walk of slightly over a kilometer, although a bus does run from the main road (the Via Tiburtina) to the villa.

The new entrance to the villa brings us in on the western side. Today, the exact location of the ancient entrance is unknown. A maximum length for the villa, measuring from the Palaestra to the Academy, is about 1,175m. (1,285 yds.). At its widest part, from the west end of the Poikile to the Piazza d'Oro, it is about 525m. (574 yds.). Hadrian evidently built this villa over the ruins of an earlier one. At the northeast corner there are ruins that date to the early 1st Century B.C.

After entering the villa the first structure we encounter is the *Poikile* (*Pecile*). It inherited its name from the Poikile of Athens, although it was much larger than its Greek ancestor. The building is a rectangular porticus that measures 232m. (761 ft.) by 97m. (318 ft.). Its colonnaded roof, covering all but the center portion, stood about 9m. (30 ft.) above the pavement. Near the top of the wall the holes that held the beams that supported the roof can still be seen.

In the middle there was an opening to the sky above the fish tank or pond. The fishpond measures 106.8m. (350 ft.) long and 26.0m. (85 ft.) wide, and is 1.5m. (5 ft.) deep. Gardens were built around the pond. These ancient ponds have been repaired and have functioned since 1953.

As we entered the Poikile we were on the north side. The long axis runs east-west. On the west and south sides of the Poikile there are many small rooms, called the *Hundred Small Rooms* (*Le Cento Camerelle*). We walk outside the walls to visit some of these rooms. The rooms, built on four levels, were the quarters of servants and members of the imperial bodyguard. From here we have a beautiful view of the valley below.

At the northeast end of the Poikile we climb a short set of steps and find ourselves in the *Library* (*Hall of the Philosopher, Temple of the Stairs*). This room measures about 20.6m. (68 ft.) by 14.4m. (47 ft.), and to the right we see an apse or exedra. Most scholars believe that this was probably a reading room.

Walking on through the Library, we find ourselves in a circular building called the *Maritime Theater* (*Teatro Marritimo*) or *Circular Porticus.* It has a diameter of 42.6m. (140 ft.). The roof of the porticus is supported by 40 un-fluted columns. In the middle of the porticus is a pond, and in the middle of the pond is an island.

This island was supposedly Hadrian's studio where he could isolate himself. Originally, there were two small marble bridges that connected the island to the porticus. The concrete bridge that we use today is a recent restoration.

We retrace our steps back to the Poikile and arriving there we im-mediately turn left and walk up the slope. Here we see a structure known as the *Thermal Building.* The first room we enter is a circular one called the *Sun-Bath* or *Heliocaminus.* Toward the southwest are large openings that allowed the sun to shine into the room. Air from the furnaces was forced in beneath the floor of the pool.

Next to the sun-bath is another room called the *Frigidarium.* This was built as an open air bath where the Ancient Romans cooled themselves in the waters after bathing in the sun-bath room.

FIGURE 12

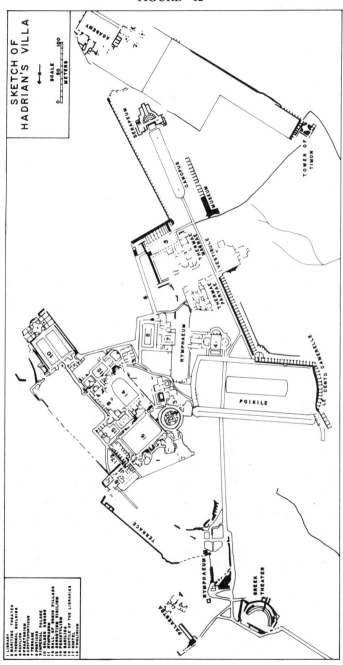

Plan of Hadrian's Villa (Tivoli)

Again we return to the Poikile, walk across the short end, turn right, and almost immediately, take a left, where we find ourselves in a structure called the *Pavilion*. Upon entering the building we find a rectangular fountain. Behind the fountain we can see the main room, surrounded on three sides by exedrae. This has been identified as a banquet room.

If we walk to the left through a room we come to a large *Nymphaeum*. Because of its large rectangular size, 127m. (417 ft.) by 22m. (72 ft.), it was previously called the *Stadium*. The structure was evidently a nymphaeum for the large banquet hall.

We now retrace our steps to where we entered the banquet hall and turn left briefly and then slightly left again, and we find ourselves on a roadway. After walking about 100m. (328 ft.) we see some large ruins on our left. We continue to a point where a path runs between two structures. Here, we turn left on the path and to our left are the ruins of a *Therma* or bath. This one is known as the *Small Baths* (*Thermae Parvae, Piccole Terme*). When we enter the structure the first major room we approach is elliptical shaped with apses or exedrae at each end. In each exedra there is a basin. Behind this room we find a circular room that may have been the *Calidarium*. There are several other rooms, their function which is not fully understood.

Across the path to the south we see the *Large Baths* (*Thermae Magnae, Grandi Terme*). The first room we enter has an apse or exedra on the north end. To the left of this room is a large swimming or bathing pool. A low wall with two columns separates the two halls. To the right of the largest room there is a large circular room. South of this there are three large rooms whose functions have not been ascertained. To the east of these are the ruins of at least three more chambers.

On the other side of the street from the baths is a platform known as the *Vestibule* which was evidently built for a scenic view. It overlooks the shallow valley on the west side of the villa.

Continuing down the street we come to an enclosure called the *Canopus*. On the left side there is a wall that is 240m. (787 ft.) long. The boundary to the right is the two storied building which still contains the remains of twenty rooms. This building was probably as long as the west wall, however only about 105m. (345 ft.) remain today. Canopus was an honored town in the Egyptian delta, as well as a god. Hadrian spent time in Egypt, so he probably named his artificial valley from the town and the god. Beautiful paintings remain on the ceiling of some of these rooms.

The dominant feature of the Canopus is the large rectangular pool in the center. It is about 125m. (410 ft.) in length and 22m. (72 ft.) wide. This end where we are standing is semicircular, while the south end is straight. At the far end (south) we see a temple, which we will examine later. There are statues around the pond.

At the beginning of the rooms on the west side is the *Museum*. In fact it occupies six of the rooms of the Canopus. Material excavated from the

PLATE 43

A. Entrance to Poikile (Hadrian's Villa)

B. Poikile Fishpond (Hadrian's Villa)

PLATE 44

A. Maritime Theater (Hadrian's Villa)

B. Timon's Tower (Hadrian's Villa)

PLATE 45

A. Canopus & Serapeum (Hadrian's Villa)

B. Canopus & Lake (Hadrian's Villa)

PLATE 46

A. Tile Floor Near Canopus (Hadrian's Villa)

B. Baths (Hadrian's Villa)

Canopus and other parts of the villa are exhibited in the museum. It has been in existence since 1958. Now is a good time to spend at least a half hour browsing in the museum.

When we finish in the museum we should come out and turn left and then turn left again along a path that runs east from the road. After walking approximately 230m. (755 ft.) we reach a towerlike structure known as the *Tower of Timon* or the *Tower of Roccabrauna* (brown rock). On the ground floor there is a large octagonal room and some smaller ones. After checking out these rooms we move to the eastern side of the tower and climb to the top. From the top of the tower we are afforded an excellent view of the surrounding countryside. Perhaps sentinels watched from here to spot messengers on their way to the villa.

Leaving the tower we follow the path across the olive grove in a southeasterly direction. After a walk of about 325m. (355 yds.) we arrive at some more ruins. These are the remains of the *Academy* (*Accademia*). Since the area is open to the breezes blowing in from the sea many archaeologists feel that this was the home of the emperor in the summer. The complex of buildings received its name from Plato's Academy in Athens.

To the left of the large rectangular room there is a rounded one that is supposedly the *Temple of Apollo.* It has two levels and is one of the few rooms that a function has been assigned.

As we walk back north from the academy, we take the right hand fork of the path which carries us to the top of the *Serapeum.* We are now at the temple dedicated to the Egyptian god Serapis, that we saw at the end of the pond in the Canopus. We can walk above and in the rooms of this great semicircular building. In front of the building is a small rectangular pond which overflowed into the long rectangular pond that we have already examined. There are two levels to this great temple.

If we walk back down the valley of the Canopus we pick up a path on the right just as we reach the *Large Baths.* After turning right and walking up the slope we arrive at the *Praetorium.* This three tiered building is called the Praetorium because it was thought that the members of the Praetorian Guard resided here. If we examine these dark, uncomfortable rooms we quickly determine that it is doubtful if the elite members of the emperor's bodyguard ever lived here. These were probably no more than storage rooms.

At the edge of the Praetorium there is a *Cryptoporticus* that we enter and follow to the north. It must have been much larger in its original form, connecting various parts of the villa. After a short walk we come out into the opening again and find ourselves at the upper end of the path between the Small and Large Baths. We walk down the slope a few steps, take the path to the right, walk along the slope, and then follow the path to the right as it moves up the slope. On our left we see a structure that overlooks the Nymphaeum that we have already visited. This *Terrace* gives a view down into the Nymphaeum. Behind the terrace, to the east, is a *Porticus.* In the center of this structure is a large fish pond. The porticus measures 59m. (194 ft.) by 33.5m. (110 ft.). Below the terrace there is a Cryptoporticus running around all four sides.

Following the path on to the east we come to the *Imperial Palace* which covers almost four acres. If we walk to the right hand corner of the palace we are in what is known as the *Piazza d'Oro (Golden Square)*. This name was given it because of the golden artifacts found here. The Golden Square is one of the four great peristylia belonging to the palace. Behind the *Main Hall* we see a room with four apses or exedrae. Actually, it is in the form of a Greek cross with the ends rounded.

If we walk northeast through the *Octagonal Vestibule*, we arrive at the *Nymphaeum* of the Palace. Southwest of the nymphaeum we enter the *Hall of the Doric Pillars (Sala dei Pilastri Dorici)*. This room measuring 32 by 23m. (105 x 76 ft.) has 30 pillars. Southwest of this room lies the *Cohortium Vigilum (Barracks of the Firemen)*. In case of a fire in the palace they were on the spot.

Turning back to the north we enter the great *Peristylium* of the Palace. On the northwestern and northeastern sides of the peristyle there are various rooms to explore. The room in the northeast corner is a *Basilica.* This room overlooks the valley below. Behind the basilica there is a cryptoporticus with three branches. None of the branches extend for any great distance.

From the peristyle we move into the *Courtyard of the Libraries (Cortile delle Biblioteche)*. This structure lies next to the Maritime Theater that we visited earlier. It is another of the peristyles of the palace. Behind the courtyard are two libraries. The smaller one on the right is the *Biblioteca Latina (Latin Library)* and the larger one on the left is the *Biblioteca Greca (Greek Library)*.

Northwest of the courtyard of the Libraries there is a building that was evidently a *Guest House* or *Hostel.* As we enter the corridor we note that there are five rooms on each side of the passage. At the end of the corridor there is a room that contains many niches. These were probably constructed to hold statues of the deities.

Walking out of the corridor, turning right, and descending some stairs, we arrive in another *Triclinium.* In places we can see beautiful mosaics on the pavement of the floor. On the right wall there is a long corridor lighted by large windows.

Passing through the corridor and walking down the slope we come to a large hall jutting out over the valley. From this *Terrace* or *Pavilion* we look out over the beautiful valley that is drained by the flowing waters of the stream known as the Acqua Ferrata.

After drinking in the majestic beauty of the *Valley* or *Vale of Tempe* we move downslope and follow the path in a westerly direction. We quickly come to a large *Nymphaeum* that originally contained a large fountain. The small summer house known as the *Casino Fede* was built by Count Fede in

1704. This Centini nobleman collected many beautiful sculptures and displayed them on the top floor of the building.

If we take the path to the northeast we will quickly reach a group of ruins known as the *Paleastra*. There are no clues today to hint of the building's function, but 16th Century writers tell us that it was a gymnasium or exercise yard where athletes trained.

Now, let's retrace our steps toward the Nymphaeum and take the right fork in the path. To the right we see a semicircular structure that is the *Greek Theater*. Several rows of seats can be seen, although the stone facing is now missing. Most of the stage has been torn away by builders seeking stone. In this theater Hadrian enjoyed Greek drama productions.

Walking down the road bordered by cypresses, we quickly arrive at the entrance near the Poikile. A walk or a bus takes us back to the Via Tiburtina where we catch the bus back to Rome. As we make the 27.4km. (17 miles) journey to Rome, we can truthfully state that Hadrian's Villa was perhaps the most magnificent villa in the ancient world.

CHAPTER 13

Ostia

Our tour today will again take us outside the city of Rome, this time to the ancient port city of Ostia. This city lies about 23km. (14.3 miles) from the Porta Ostiensis (porta S. Paolo) in the Aurelian Walls. The Via Ostiensis connected Ostia with Rome, and the modern Via Ostiense follows almost literally the path of the old road. Only in a few places can the remains of the ancient roadbed be detected.

According to Roman tradition, Ancus Marcius (642-616 B.C.), the fourth king of Rome, established a settlement at Ostia. Some scholars support the theory that Ancus Marcius did expand Roman territory to the coast, and thereby established a settlement at Ostia in the 7th Century B.C. in order to protect the salt supply that was available in the vicinity.

As the 5th Century B.C. came to a close Rome had been successful in her wars against the Etruscans. It then became imperative to protect the coastal areas of Latium from further Etruscan attacks and at the same time to keep the expanding Greek colonists out of Roman territory. Between 400 and 340 B.C. the Romans built up the area of Ostia by constructing a fortified colony. This fort was surrounded by tufa walls and enclosed about 5.5 acres. The function of the colony was to protect the sea coast and the river mouth. Reliable estimates set the population of the fort at about 300.

After Rome had defeated the Carthaginians in the Punic Wars in the 3rd Century B.C. Ostia became very important now that a river harbor had been built. Large vessels docked at this harbor and shifted their loads to lighter ships, which then went on to Rome with all kinds of trade goods. Ostia began to grow and expand at the beginning of the 2nd Century B.C., and her population became cosmopolitan as foreign merchants began to settle in the city.

In the early 1st Century B.C. the dictator Sulla built new walls around the city of Ostia. A large portion of these walls remains today. They enclose an area of about 160 acres, vastly larger than the 5.5 acres of the 4th Century B.C. Julius Caesar made plans to build a newer and much more adequate harbor, but his death stopped the project in 44 B.C. It was the Emperor Claudius (41-54) who finally built the first great Ostian harbor in the middle of the 1st Century. Trajan (97-117) built a new harbor during his administration in the 2nd Century. Ostia probably reached her peak in the middle of the 2nd Century with a population of about 50,000. After this the city began a slow decline.

To get to Ostia we go to the train station and catch the Met at the lower level. We must get off at the station that says "Ostia Antica." After disembarking, we walk across the tracks and a sign directs us to the ancient city. When we pass through the entrance we are on the *Via Ostiensis* (the same road we stood upon in Rome). Paralleling this road into the city is another road known as the *Via Sepolcro* (*Road of Tombs*). Many tombs are located between the two roads leading up to the city walls.

After entering the excavation area, we need to turn left and walk over to the Via Sepolcro where we then turn right. As we stroll along this street we can look at a few of the more outstanding tombs. This ancient burial ground dates from the 3rd Century B.C. to the 4th Century A.D. At first the only type of burial allowed was cremation. From the time of the Emperor Hadrian (117-138) the custom changed and inhumation was practiced. On the right side of the street past the first large structure is a tomb worth noting. It sits behind two smaller tombs and is made of tufa. This is the best preserved tomb we have seen here in this area.

Two tombs down the street we find also in the middle area between the streets another interesting burial chamber. A lady by the name of Julia Veneria, aged 24, and her baby were buried here. She and the infant probably died in childbirth. It is interesting to read the inscriptions on these sepulchers. On the left side of the street we see a large two-storied tomb. As we reach the wall built by Sulla we have arrived at one of the gates on this side of Ostia known as the *Porta Secondaria*. It was built a century after the walls were constructed. We turn to the right and walk over to the Via Ostiensis. For those who so desire, a walk upon it back to the entrance area to observe the tombs on this street is certainly in order.

Next, we can enter the city through the major gate the *Porta Romana*. A comprehensive tour of the city is not possible in a work of this scope. To do this another book would be required. It would also take a minimum of a week using eight to ten hours per day to accomplish this herculean task. What we will do is to point out selected monuments that can be observed leisurely in one day.

After entering the city, we find to our left an open square known as the *Square of Victory* (*Piazza della Vittorio*). This plaza was built in the 3rd Century. If we look closely we can see that buildings were torn down to get the necessary space for this square. It received its name from a statue of Minerva Victory found in the plaza. To the left we see the remains of a *Nymphaeum* with the fountain. The fountain measures 21m. (68.9 ft.) by 3.6m. (11.8 ft.). In the pavement we see a beautiful mosaic.

The Via Ostiensis becomes the *Decumanus Maximus* after entering the city. It divides the city in half for about 830m. (908 yds.) then turns to the southwest for approximately 310m. (339 yds.) before exiting the city. Over 125m. (134 yds.) have been excavated outside the walls. The Porta Marina is

FIGURE 13

Plan of Ostia

the gate that the Decumanus Maximus passes through in the southwest walls.

Across the street from the Square of Victory we take note of a large building. These ruins are the remains of a *Horrea* or *Warehouse*. It measures about 42m. by 24m. (137.8 ft. by 78.7 ft.). From the type of building material used the warehouse can be dated to about the 1st Century B.C. Because Ostia was a port city it contained many warehouses.

Behind the warehouse and connected to it, we see the *Baths of the Drivers (Thermae Raedariorum)*. There are several mosaics picturing carts being driven, thus the name given to the baths. A study of the structure indicates that the baths were probably built in the 3rd Century in a portion of the warehouse we have already examined. Evidently the warehouse originally occupied all of this space.

The right hand corner of the building on the Decumanus Maximus past the Warehouse is a *Mithraeum,* or Temple to the god Mithras. Owing to its nearness to the gate it is referred to as the *Mithraeum Portae Romanae*. It is one of the fourteen Mithraea to be found in Ostia, and it is typical of the temples to Mithras that we examined in Rome.

Past the building that houses the Mithraeum is another warehouse. This one is called the *Warehouse of Antoninus (Horrea Antoniniani)* and is much larger than the one we looked at earlier. Here, however, very little of the building is left standing. In front of the warehouse and extending in front of the building that housed the Mithraeum, we can see the remains of a porticus. This *Porticus Antoniniani* contained shops that opened on to the Decumanus Maximus.

Continuing down the Decumanus, we see on the right some ruins of *Private Houses.* It appears that in front of these homes there was another porticus paralleling the street. More shops lined this porticus.

Just past these houses is a street running to the right or north at a right angle to the Decumanus Maximus. It is known as the *Via Vigili,* and runs to the river. It took its name from the barracks of the firemen located along the street. The street was probably built at the beginning of the 2nd Century.

Here on the corner of the Decumanus Maximus and Via Vigili a large structure catches our eye. This building is part of the ruins of the *Baths of Neptune (Thermae Neptunis)*. They measure about 75m. (246 ft.) in length by almost 70m. (230 ft.) in width and date to the 2nd Century. Hadrian probably began construction in the 130's and Antoninus Pius (138-161) completed the Baths in the 140's. Many beautiful mosaics can be found on the pavement. Several of the scenes depict the ocean god Neptune, thus, the reason his name is given to the bathing establishment. At the northeast corner (right rear of the building with our backs to the Decumanus Maximus) there is a large cistern, elevated to give water pressure for the baths.

Immediately behind the baths we see the *Cohortium Vigilum Stationes* or *Barracks of the Cohort of Vigiles (Barracks of the Firemen)*. In the middle

PLATE 47

A. Via Ostia Outside Ostia

B. Theater at Ostia

A. Sanctuary of Romulus & Remus at Ostia

B. Capitolium at Ostia

of the building is a large courtyard or atrium. A porticus once ran around the outer walls of the courtyard. Rooms opened to the courtyard at the ground level. At the four corners there are stairs to the upper levels. It appears that there were at least three levels to the building. The main entrance was from the Via Vigili. On each side of the entrance there were rooms that were used as bars where the men off duty could do their drinking. There is no mistaking the function of the room at the southeast corner, it was a latrine. This building was probably constructed in the early 2nd Century. The firemen from Rome served detached duty at Ostia for a period of four months. New troops arrived on the 15th of the months of April, August, and December.

If we turn left and walk east along the side of the barracks we arrive at a street known as the *Via Fontana.* We turn left on this street and to our right we see several private homes. One of these, located about midway of the Baths of Neptune along the street is worth a few minutes of our time. This is the *House of the Painted Ceilings* which contained ten rooms at ground level. We can't be certain how many rooms there were at the upper levels. The room at the right corner on the street is the main room containing the paintings. Originally, these rooms were much larger.

We continue down the Via Fontana to the Decumanus Maximus and across it we see the *Warehouse of Hortensius (Horrea Hortensii).* This building dates from the 1st Century A.D. Although not perfectly rectangular, the structure measures about 105m. (345 ft.) by 62m. (203 ft.). It is another of the large warehouses in which grain was stored.

There is another warehouse on the west side of the Hortensian Warehouse, but it is not quite as large as its counterpart. This new building is known as the *Warehouse of Artemis (Horrea Artemii)* and also probably dates from the 1st Century. Like its neighbor, the Warehouse of Artemis is not rectangular, its east wall keeps it from being so. Roughly speaking, its dimensions are about 60m. (197 ft.) in length and 34m. (112 ft.) in width.

Crossing the Decumanus Maximus from the Warehouse of Artemis will bring us to the structure with the rounded front which is the *Theater of Ostia (Theatrum Ostiensis).* The theater is built in the shape of a semi-circle. At the back the theater is about 86m. (282 ft.) wide and its radius is almost 42m. (138 ft.). The stage is about 36m. (118 ft.) wide and almost 3m. (10 ft.) in depth.

A smaller theater was built here early in the 1st Century. Commodus (180-192) began enlarging it in the late 2nd Century, but Septimius Severus (193-211) completed the task in 196. Most of the structure that we see today dates from this reconstruction. The spaces along the front of the theater were filled with *Shops* or *Tabernae.* On each side of the central entrance two of the rooms were converted into cisterns. These cisterns provided water for aquatic shows. The Department of Antiquities has restored much of the original form of the theater.

Directly behind the theater and abutting it is a large plaza called the

Square of the Guilds (Piazza delle Corporazioni). This large square measuring 84m. by 50m. (276 ft. x 164 ft.) was surrounded by a porticus on all four sides. Under the porticus the remains of 61 rooms can be detected. We can see some of the columns of the porticus, particularly, those located behind the theater. On the pavements mosaics representing the signs or symbols of the foreign guilds can still be seen. Most of these guilds dealt with the grain trade. The square was constructed early in the 1st Century. In the center of the square there is the podium of a temple, complete with two columns and a set of steps leading up to the podium. At the present it is not known to which deity or deities the temple was dedicated.

West of the theater is a structure known as the *Four Republican Temples.* Scholars are not certain when or to whom these temples were dedicated. Statues found in the area indicated that two of them may have been dedicated to Jupiter and to Venus. On the front they opened onto the Decumanus Maximus and were surrounded on the remaining three sides by a porticus. The temples built between 80 and 78 B.C. share a common podium.

Behind the temples and against the square of the guilds we see the *House of Apuleius.* This beautiful private home belonged to a man by the name of Apuleius, according to an inscription. The house which has a long entrance hall leading into an atrium is not typical of the private homes of Ostia. It resembles the houses at the city of Pompeii, and perhaps Apuleius originally came from that city. The house dates from the early 2nd Century.

To the left (west) of the House of Apuleius we see another Mithraeum. Although not belonging to the house, it is usually referred to as the *Mithraeum of Apuleius.* This Mithraeum is one of the best preserved of all the Mithraic temples in Ostia. There are beautiful mosaics on the wall and floor of the temple. This building probably dates to the early 1st Century.

We walk back to the Decumanus Maximus, take a right turn, and walk to the second street on the left. Next we take this street, *Via del Mitreo dei Serpenti,* and the second structure to our right is the *Mithraeum of the Serpents.* Two large serpents with crests on their heads give the name to this Mithraic temple.

If we retrace our steps to the Decumanus Maximus and cross it, we find ourselves on the *Via dei Grandi Horrea.* On the left side of this street we note the *Great Warehouse* or *Horrea Magna.* This great structure, built in 50 to store grain, measures about 114m. (374 ft.) long and 80m. (263 ft.) wide. On the east side there are 20 rooms that were added in the 190's. Behind these rooms there are 11 more and on the opposite side there are located 11 more. On the back or north side, which was originally the front, there are 12 rooms and 11 more are located on the front. Behind these front rooms there is a porticus running across the entire front of the structure. There is then an atrium or courtyard surrounded on three sides by another porticus. In the center there is a double row of rooms, with the east side containing seven and the west side eight. At least 85 rooms are discernable in this great warehouse, the largest one found in Ostia.

The west side of the warehouse borders on the *Via dei Molini*. We turn left upon this street moving to the Decumanus Maximus, jog left slightly as we cross it and we are on the street called the *Semita dei Cippi*. We continue down this street until we pass two streets to our left and then to the right we see the *Baths of the Forum* (*Thermae Fororum*). First we enter the large Palaestra or exercise yard. The symmetry of this structure is strange, being rectangular on the north and east sides, but having roughly a triangular shape on the south and west sides. In the southwest corner of the Palaestra lie the remains of an unidentified temple. Several of the other rooms as well can be identified. The first room to the right on the north side of the Palaestra is the *Calidarium*. If we walk west we pass through two *Tepidaria*, then the *Sudatorium*, and finally a room that may be the *Heliocaminos* or sun room. North of these rooms is the large *Frigidarium*. These sumptuous baths were probably built in the 140's by Antoninus Pius (138-161).

Leaving the baths we return to the Semita dei Cippi and continue south on the thoroughfare until it joins the street known as the *Cardo Maximus*. To the right we see an open area called the *Campus Magnae Matris* (*Field of the Great Mother*). This field or plaza is triangular in shape. By walking southwest to the far corner of the triangle we find ourselves at the *Temple of Cybele* (*Templum Magnae Matris*). This structure, dedicated to the Earth Mother from Asia Minor, was probably built in the middle of the 2nd Century. Two flights of eight stairs lead up to the top of the podium.

Returning to the Cardo Maximus, we make a short walk to the city walls. In front of us is one of the original gates, the *Porta Laurentina*. It was originally flanked by two square towers. The pavement level was raised considerably from the 1st Century B.C. to the 4th Century A.D.

Walking back through the gate, we now head north on the Cardo Maximus. Eventually the street empties into the *Forum*. It is a large and narrow rectangular area, measuring about 140m. by 25m. (459 ft. x 82 ft.), with the long axis running in a north-south line. The forum was probably laid out between 80 and 78 B.C., but altered several times throughout the centuries. Upon entering the Forum we see before us the *Temple of Rome and Augustus* (*Templum Romae et Augusti*). It was built in the Forum shortly after the death of Augustus in 14.

We continue to walk north and cross the Decumanus Maximus which bisects the Forum. At the north end of the Forum there are the remains of two temples that constitute the remains of the *Capitolium*. This structure was built toward the close of the 1st Century B.C., but almost completely replaced by Hadrian in the 2nd Century.

If we walk out of the Forum on the northwest corner we find ourselves upon the *Via Testa*. On the left side of this street there is a large structure that is humorously called the *Little Market* (*Mercatus Parvus*). It is actually a warehouse with 27 large rooms opening onto a courtyard. All of these rooms were used for the storage of trade goods. The building is about 90m. (295 ft.) by 46m. (151 ft.). Its neighbor to the north and built against it was probably constructed for grain storage. The Little Market was built in the 120's or 130's and repaired in the 190's.

Retracing our footsteps back down the Via Testa, we find that we are again in the Forum. We walk along the west side of the Forum to the spot where the Decumanus Maximus makes its exit, and there on the right is the *Curia* or *Senate House*. It is a square building, measuring 11.7m. by 11.7 m. (38 ft. by 38 ft.). It was probably built at the close of the 1st Century as a meeting place for the city council. Some scholars dispute this function, maintaining that it is too small for meetings of such magnitude. The Curia opens onto the Decumanus Maximus and originally it had a pronaos along the front.

Across the street and flanked also by the Forum is a *Basilica*. The Basilica like the Curia was evidently built by Domitian (81-96) toward the close of the 1st Century. Very little besides the foundation remains of this structure which was used as a source of building material by later generations. Still, we can identify the floor plan. The Basilica measures about 40m. (131 ft.) long and 26m. (85 ft.) wide.

Next to the Basilica is another ruined structure that makes up part of the complex of the *Round Temple* (*Templum Rotundum*). The Round Temple is part of the south end of this building. Excavations at the beginning of the 19th Century destroyed much of the temple, as most of the building material was carted away. Some archaeologists have even suggested it might be a *Pantheon.* It was probably built in the middle of the 3rd Century. We can still see remains of the spiral staircase that led to the dome. Its diameter is approximately 24m. (79 ft.).

Let us now return to the Decumanus Maximus, turn left upon it and walk a few paces to where there is a fork in the road. The left fork is the Decumanus Maximus and the one to the right is the *Via della Foce.* We will follow the Via della Foce to its intersection with the first street to the right, the *Via del Tempio d'Ercole.* If we turn right on this street the first building to the right is the *Temple of Hercules.* This temple dedicated to Hercules Invictus is about 30m. (98 ft.) in length and 16m. (53 ft.) in width, with the long axis oriented east-west. The temple was built at the close of the 2nd Century B.C. It was restored by Trajan in the early 2nd Century and fell into disrepair toward the middle of the 4th Century. After Eugenius (392-394) became emperor of the West in 392 he rebuilt the temple. Then, when Theodosius the Great (394-395) united the two empires in 394, he closed the temple forever. Under Theodosius only Christianity was tolerated.

Returning to the Via della Foce we take a right turn and walk upon it for about 80m. (88 yds.) and then to the right we see another large warehouse or horrea. This large structure is the *Warehouse of the Measurers* which was built in the early part of the 2nd Century by Trajan. The building is about 90m. (295 ft.) long and 50m. (164) wide. By now we get the impression that Ostia contained a large number of warehouses to store trade goods bound for Rome, as indeed it did.

When our inspection of the warehouse is completed we continue down the Via della Foce to the next street on the left. We then turn on this street, the *Via dei Serapide,* and the second structure on the right is the *Temple of Serapis* or *Serapeum.* This temple, dedicated to one of the gods of the Nile, was built in the year 127. It is not a very large temple, but we are able to see some pretty mosaics in the structure.

If we continue to walk down the Via dei Serapide and pass through the ruins of a building where the street ends, we will find ourselves upon the street called the *Cardo degli Aurighi,* which we turn left upon. We continue upon this street until the first street intersects it from the right. At the intersection we turn right on the *Via delle Volte Sapente* and the second structure on the right is the *House of Mars.* This house, measuring about 25m. by 25m. (82 ft. by 82 ft.), was probably built and dedicated to Mars, the god of war, in the early 2nd Century. The outline of many of the rooms can still be detected.

As we retrace our steps back to the Cardo degli Aurighi, we take a right and walk down it to its juncture with the Decumanus Maximus. After reaching the Decumanus Maximus we take a right and follow the street all the way to the walls. Here the street passes through the walls by way of the *Porta Marina.* This is one of the original gates, built when the walls were constructed in the early 1st Century B.C.

We walk through the gate and turn left and there in front of us is the *Forum of the Porta Marina,* lying outside the city walls. At the present there is not much information pertaining to the date or the function of this Forum. It is about 44m. (144 ft.) in length and is almost 40m. (131 ft.) in width. At the end there is a large apse or exedra.

At the northwest corner of the Forum is the *Temple of Bona Dea.* This temple, dedicated to the Good Goddess who was worshipped by Roman women, was built about the middle of the 1st Century. Unlike most Roman temples, this one is not raised on a podium. By the start of the 3rd Century this temple was already falling into a state of disrepair. The cult of Bona Dea was losing her popularity, probably being replaced by the Egyptian goddess Isis.

We can now take the Decumanus Maximus and return to the place where we entered the excavations. Then we return to the station and catch a train to Rome. For those who have three or four days to spend in Ostia, it is suggested they buy guidebooks so they can identify all of the magnificent structures. In one day we have been able to look at only a few of the antiquities of this great port city.

APPENDICES

APPENDIX I

Chronological List Of Monuments

Here is a list of the major monuments of Rome, appearing in chronological order, at least those that can be dated with some degree of accuracy. In cases where there is question about the date, a question mark is placed after the monument. The number appearing within parentheses indicates the chapter in which the structure is discussed. Monuments for Hadrian's Villa and Ostia are not included.

850 B.C.....................Forum Sepolcretum (4)

753 B.C.....................Founding of Rome (1, 2)
House of Romulus (2)
Comitium? (4)
Steps of Cacus (2)
Vulcanal? (4)
Murus Romuli (2)
Auguratorium (2)

715 B.C.....................Regia (4)
Temple of Vesta (4)

675 B.C.....................Sacra Via (4)

673 B.C.....................Senate House? (4)

642 B.C.....................Mamertine Prison (3)

600 B.C.....................Cloaca Maxima (4)

575 B.C.....................Temple of Fortune? (6)
Temple of Mater Matuta? (6)

509 B.C.....................Founding of the Republic
Capitoline Temple of Jupiter Maximus (3)

500 B.C.....................Lapis Niger (4)

497 B.C.....................Temple of Saturn (4)

496 B.C.....................Fountain of Juturna (4)

493 B.C.....................Temple of Ceres, Liber, and Libera (6)

484 B.C.....................Temple of Castor and Pollux (4)

450 B.C.....................Old Rostra (4)

445 B.C.....................Lacus Curtius? (4)

431 B.C. . . . . Temple of Apollo (6)

387 B.C. . . . . Servian Walls (8)
Porta Viminalis (10)
Altar of Genius Loci (2)

386 B.C. . . . . Porta Capena (8)

375 B.C. . . . . Navalia (7)

367 B.C. . . . . Temple of Concord (4)

329 B.C. . . . . Circus Maximus (6)

312 B.C. . . . . Via Appia (8)

298 B.C. . . . . Tomb of the Scipios (8)

294 B.C. . . . . Temple of Jupiter Stator (2)

290 B.C. . . . . Temple of Bellona (7)

260 B.C. . . . . Temple of Janus (6)

254 B.C. . . . . Temple of Spes (6)

240 B.C. . . . . Shrine of Juturna? (4)

221 B.C. . . . . Circus Flaminius (7)

220 B.C. . . . . Via Flaminia (10)
Pons Mulvius (10)

201 B.C. . . . . Portico of the Twelve Gods? (3)

194 B.C. . . . . Temple of Juno Sospita (6)

193 B.C. . . . . Emporium (8)
Horrea Galbae (8)
Porticus Aemilia (8)

192 B.C. . . . . Temple of Vejovis (3)

191 B.C. . . . . Temple of Cybele (2)

181 B.C. . . . . Temple of Pietas (6)

179 B.C. . . . . Basilica Aemilia (4)
Pons Aemilianus (6)

150 B.C. . . . . Shrine of Venus Cloacina? (4)

147 B.C. . . . . Porticus Octavia (7)

142 B.C. . . . . Aqua Marcia (9)

125 B.C. . . . . Aqua Tepula (9)

110 B.C. . . . . Porticus Minucia (3)
Iseum Campense? (7)

78 B.C. . . . . Tabularium (3)

75 B.C. . . . . Tribunal Aurelium (4)

Tribunal Praetorium (4)

62 B.C. . . . . Pons Fabricius (6)

55 B.C. . . . . Theater of Pompey (7)

50 B.C. . . . . House of Livia (2)

Domus Caeciliorum (11)

46 B.C. . . . . Basilica Julia (4)

Forum of Caesar (5)

Fountain of Appiades (5)

Pons Cestius (11)

Temple of Venus Genetrix (5)

43 B.C. . . . . Tomb of Hirtius (7)

40 B.C. . . . . Gardens of Sallust (10)

37 B.C. . . . . Auditorium of Maecenas (9)

33 B.C. . . . . Aqua Julia (9)

29 B.C. . . . . Temple of Caesar (4)

Porticus Julia (4)

Arch of Augustus-Actium (4)

28 B.C. . . . . Temple of Apollo (2)

26 B.C. . . . . Tomb of Augustus (7)

Saepta Julia (7)

25 B.C. . . . . Pantheon (7)

Basilica Neptuni (7)

24 B.C. . . . . New Rostra (4)

20 B.C. . . . . Golden Milestone (4)

Tomb of the Baker? (9)

19 B.C. . . . . Aqua Virgo (10)

Arch of Augustus-Parthian (4)

Baths of Agrippa (7)

18 B.C. . . . . Horrea Agrippiana? (4)

13 B.C. . . . . Crypta Balbi (7)

Theater of Balbus (7)

Pyramid of Cestius (8)

11 B.C. . . . . Theater of Marcellus (7)

214

APPENDIX II

List Of Kings And Emperors

A. Kings

Romulus   753-716 B.C.
Numa Pompilius   715-673 B.C.
Tullus Hostilius   673-642 B.C.
Ancus Marcius   642-616 B.C.
Tarquinius Priscus   616-579 B.C.
Servius Tullius   578-535 B.C.
Tarquinius Superbus   535-509 B.C.

B. Emperors

Augustus   27 B.C. - 14 A.D.
Tiberius   14-37
Caligula   37-41
Claudius   41-54
Nero   54-68
Galba   68-69
Otho   69 (Jan.—April)
Vitellius   69 (April—Dec.)
Vespasian   69-79
Titus   79-81
Domitian   81-96
Nerva   96-98
Trajan   97-117
Hadrian   117-138
Antoninus Pius   138-161
Lucius Verus   161-169
Marcus Aurelius   161-180
Commodus   180-192
Pertinax   193 (3 mos.)
Julianus   193 (2 mos.)
Septimius Severus   193-211
Caracalla   211-217
Geta   211-212
Macrinus   217-218
Diadumenianus   217-218

Elagabulus   218-222
Severus Alexander   222-235
Maximinius   235-238
Balbinius   238
Maximus   238
Gordian III   238-244
Philippus   244-249
Decius Trajanus   249-251
Gallus   251-253
Volusianus   251-253
Aemilianus   253
Valerianus   253-260
Gallienus   253-268
Gothicus   268-270
Claudius Quintillus   270
Aurelianus   270-275
Tacitus   275-276
Florianus   276
Probus   276-282
Carus   282-283
Carinus   283-284
Diocletian   284-305
Maximian   286-305
Constantius   305-306
Galerius   305-311
Valerius Severus   306-307
Maxentius   310-312
Maximinius   310-313
Licinius   308-324
Constantine   310-337
After 337 we are concerned only with the western part of the empire.
Constantine II   337-340
Constans   340-350
Magnentius   350-353
Constantius II (both empires)   353-360
Julian (both empires)   360-363
Jovian (both empires)   363-364
Valentinian   364-375
Gratian   375-383
Magnus Maximus   383-388
Valentinian II   388-392
Eugenius   392-394
Theodosius (both empires)   394-395
Honorius   395-423

Valentinian III   425-455
Petronius Maximus   455
Avitus   455-456
Ricimer (did not assume title)   456-472
Majorian   457-461
Severus   461-465
Anthemius   467-472
Olybius   472
Glycerius   473-474
Nepos   474-475
Romulus   475-476

APPENDIX III

List Of Popes

Petrus (Peter) ?-67
Linus 67-78
Anencletus (Cletus) I 78-91
Clemens I 91-96
Evarestus 96-109
Alexander I 109-119
Xystus I 119-127
Telesphorus 127-139
Hyginus 139-142
Pius I 142-157
Anicetus 157-168
Soter 168-177
Eleutherus 177-193
Victor I 193-202
Zephyrinus 202-219
Callistus I 219-223
Urban I 223-230
Pontianus 230-235
Anteros 235-236
Fabianus 236-250
Cornelius 251-253
Lucius 253-254
Stephen I 254-257
Xystus II 257-258
Dionysius 259-268
Felix 269-274
Eutychianus 275-283
Gaius 283-296
Marcellinus 296-304
Marcellus 308-309
Eusebius 309-310
Miltiades 311-314
Sylvester I 314-335
Mark 336
Julius I 337-352

Liberius 352-366
Felix II (anti-pope) 355-365
Damasus I 366-384
Siricius 384-399
Anastasius I 399-401
Innocent I 401-417
Zosimus 417-418
Boniface I 418-422
Celestine I 422-432
Sixtus III 432-440
Leo I (the Great) 440-461
Hilary 461-468
Simplicius 468-483
Felix III 483-492
Gelasius I 492-496
Anastasius II 496-498
Symmachus 498-514
Hormisdas 514-523
John I 523-526
Felix IV 526-530
Boniface II 530-532
John II 533-535
Agopitus I 535-536
Silverius 536-537
Vigilius 537-555
Pelagius I 555-561
John III 561-574
Benedict I 575-579
Pelagius II 579-590
Gregory I (the Great) 590-604
Sabinianus 604-606
Boniface III 607
Boniface IV 608-615
Deusdedit 615-618
Boniface V 619-625
Honorius I 625-638
Severinus 640
John IV 640-642
Theodore I 642-649
Martin I 649-655
Eugenius I 654-657
Vitalian 657-672
Adeodatus 672-676
Donus 676-678

Agatho   678-681
Leo II   682-683
Benedict II   684-685
John V   685-686
Conan   686-687
Sergius I   687-701
John VI   701-705
John VII   705-707
Sisinnius   708
Constantine   708-715
Gregory II   715-731
Gregory III   731-741
Zacharias   741-752
Stephen II   752-757
Paul I   757-767
Constantine (a-p)   767-768
Philip (a-p)   768
Stephen III   768-772
Adrian I   772-795
Leo III   795-816
Stephen IV   816-817
Paschal I   817-824
Eugenius II   824-827
Valentine   827
Gregory IV   827-844
John VIII (a-p)   844
Sergius II   844-847
Leo IV   847-855
Benedict III   855-858
Nicholas I (the Great)   858-867
Adrian II   867-872
John VIII   872-882
Marinus I   882-884
Adrian III   884-885
Stephen V   885-891
Formosus   891-896
Boniface VI   896
Stephen VI   896-897
Romanus (Theodore II)   897
John IX   898-900
Benedict IV   900-903
Leo V   903
Christopher (a-p)   903-904
Sergius III   904-911

Anastasius III   911-913
Lando   913-914
John X   914-928
Leo VI   928
Stephen VII   928-931
John XI   931-935
Leo VII   936-939
Stephen VIII   939-942
Marinus II   942-946
Agapitus II   946-955
John XII   955-964
Leo VIII   963-965
Benedict V   964-966
John XIII   965-972
Benedict VI   973-974
Boniface VII (a-p)   974
Benedict VII   974-983
John XIV   983-984
Boniface VII (a-p)   984-985
John XV   985-996
Gregory V   996-999
John XVI   997-998
Sylvester II   999-1003
John XVII   1003
John XVIII   1004-1009
Sergius IV   1009-1012
Benedict VIII   1012-1024
Gregory VI (a-p)   1012
John XIX   1024-1032
Benedict IX   1032-1044
Sylvester III   1045
Benedict IX   1045
Gregory VI   1045-1046
Clement II   1046-1047
Benedict IX   1047-1048
Damasus II   1048
Leo IX   1049-1054
Victor II   1055-1057
Stephen IX   1057-1058
Benedict X (a-p)   1058-1059
Nicholas II   1059-1061
Alexander II   1061-1073
Honorius II (a-p)   1061-1064
Gregory VII   1073-1085

Clement III (a-p)   1080-1100
Victor III   1086-1087
Urban II   1088-1099
Paschal II   1099-1118
Theodoric (a-p)   1100
Albert (a-p)   1102
Sylvester IV   1105-1111
Gelasius II   1118-1119
Gregory VIII (a-p)   1118-1121
Calixtus II   1119-1124
Honorius II   1124-1130
Innocent II   1130-1143
Anacletus II (a-p)   1130-1138
Celestine II   1143-1144
Lucius II   1144-1145
Eugenius III   1145-1153
Anastastius IV   1153-1154
Adrian IV   1154-1159
Alexander III   1159-1181
Victor IV (a-p)   1159-1164
Paschal III (a-p)   1164-1168
Calixtus III (a-p)   1168-1178
Innocent III (a-p)   1179-1180
Lucius III   1181-1185
Urban III   1185-1187
Gregory VIII   1187
Clement III   1187-1191
Celestine III   1191-1198
Innocent III   1198-1216
Honorius III   1216-1227
Gregory IX   1227-1241
Celestine IV   1241
Innocent IV   1243-1254
Alexander IV   1254-1261
Urban IV   1261-1264
Clement IV   1265-1268
Gregory X   1271-1276
Innocent V   1276
Adrian V   1276
John XXI   1276-1277
Nicholas III   1277-1280
Martin IV   1281-1285
Honorius IV   1285-1287
Nicholas IV   1288-1292

Celestine V   1294
Boniface VIII   1294-1303
Benedict XI   1303-1304
Clement V   1305-1314
John XXII   1316-1334
Nicholas V (a-p)   1328-1330
Benedict XII   1334-1342
Clement VI   1342-1352
Innocent VI   1352-1362
Urban V   1362-1370
Gregory XI   1370-1378
Urban VI   1378-1389
Clement VII (Avignon)   1378-1394
Boniface IX   1389-1404
Benedict XIII (Avig.)   1394-1423
Innocent VII   1404-1406
Gregory XII   1406-1415
Alexander V (a-p)   1409-1410
John XXIII (a-p)   1410-1415
Martin V   1417-1431
Clement VIII (a-p, Avig.)   1423-1429
Benedict XIV (a-p, Avig.)   1425-1430
Eugenius IV   1431-1447
Felix V (a-p)   1439-1449
Nicholas V   1447-1455
Calixtus III   1455-1458
Pius II   1458-1464
Paul II   1464-1471
Sixtus IV   1471-1484
Innocent VIII   1484-1492
Alexander VI   1492-1503
Pius III   1503
Julius II   1503-1513
Leo X   1513-1521
Adrian VI   1522-1523
Clement VII   1523-1534
Paul III   1534-1549
Julius III   1550-1555
Marcellus II   1555
Paul IV   1555-1559
Pius IV   1559-1565
Pius V   1566-1572
Gregory XIII   1572-1585
Sixtus V   1585-1590

Urban VII   1590
Gregory XIV   1590-1591
Innocent IX   1591
Clement VIII   1592-1605
Leo XI   1605
Paul V   1605-1621
Gregory XV   1621-1623
Urban VIII   1623-1644
Innocent X   1644-1655
Alexander VII   1655-1667
Clement IX   1667-1669
Clement X   1670-1676
Innocent XI   1676-1689
Alexander VIII   1689-1691
Innocent XII   1691-1700
Clement XI   1700-1721
Innocent XIII   1721-1724
Benedict XIII   1724-1730
Clement XII   1730-1740
Benedict XIV   1740-1758
Clement XIII   1758-1769
Clement XIV   1769-1774
Pius VI   1775-1799
Pius VII   1800-1823
Leo XII   1823-1829
Pius VIII   1829-1830
Gregory XVI   1831-1846
Pius IX   1846-1878
Leo XIII   1879-1903
Pius X   1903-1914
Benedict XV   1914-1922
Pius XI   1922-1939
Pius XII   1939-1958
John XXIII   1958-1963
Paul VI   1963-1978
John Paul I   1978
John Paul II   1978-

APPENDIX IV

List Of Major Museums

1. Antiquarium del Foro
   Roman Forum
   Open: 9:00 a.m. to 1:00 p.m. daily
   Closed: Tuesday

2. Antiquarium del Palatino
   Palatine Hill
   Open: 9:00 a.m. to 1:00 p.m. daily
   Closed: Tuesday

3. Barracco Museum
   Corso Vittorio Emanuele 168
   Open: 9:00 a.m. to 2:00 p.m. Tu.-Sat.
         also 5:00 to 8:00 p.m. Tu. & Th.
         9:00 a.m. to 1:00 p.m. Sunday
   Closed: Monday

4. Capitoline Museum
   Capitoline Hill (Piazza del Campidoglio)
   Open: 9:00 a.m. to 2:00 p.m. Tu.-Sat.
         also 9:00 to 11:30 p.m. on Sat. in summer
         9:00 a.m. to 1:00 p.m. Sunday
   Closed: Monday

5. Palazzo dei Conservatori
   Capitoline Hill (P. del Campidoglio)
   Open and closed the same hours as the Capitoline Museum.

6. Lateran Museum
   Piazza S. Giovanni in Laterano
   Open: 9:00 a.m. to 2:00 p.m. MWF
   Closed: Tu., Th., Sat., & Sun.

7. Museum of the Castel S. Angelo
   Hadrian's Tomb
   Open: 9:00 a.m. to 1:00 p.m. Tu.-Sun.
   Closed: Monday

8. Museum of Hadrian's Villa
   Villa Adriano, Tivoli
   Open: 9:00 a.m. to 1:00 p.m. daily

9. Museum at Ostia Antica
   Ostia Antica
   Open: 9:00 a.m. to one hour before sunset
   Closed: Monday

10. Museum of Prehistory and Ethnography
    Piazza Marconi, EUR
    Open: 9:00 a.m. to 2:00 p.m. Tu.-Sat.
          9:00 a.m. to 1:00 p.m. Sun.
    Closed: Monday

11. Museum of Roman Civilization
    Piazza G. Angeli, EUR
    Open: 9:00 a.m. to 2:00 p.m. Tu.-Sat.
          also 5:00 to 8:00 p.m. Tu. & Th.
          9:00 to 11:30 p.m. Sat.
          9:00 a.m. to 1:00 p.m. Sun.
    Closed: Monday

12. Museum of the Villa Giulia
    Piazzale di Villa Giulia 9
    Open: 9:00 a.m. to 3:00 p.m. Tu.-Sat.
          9:00 a.m. to 1:00 p.m. Sun.
    Closed: Monday

13. National Museum
    Baths of Diocletian
    Open: 9:30 a.m. to 3:00 p.m. Tu.-Sat.
          9:00 a.m. to 1:00 p.m. Sun.
    Closed: Monday

14. National Museum of Oriental Art
    Via Merulana 248
    Open: 9:00 a.m. to 1:00 p.m. daily
          10:00 a.m. to 1:00 p.m. Sun.
    Closed: Tuesday

15. Vatican Museums
    Vatican City
    Open: 9:00 a.m. to 2:00 p.m. daily
    Closed: Sunday

GLOSSARY

Glossary

Aedes — A small and unprentious temple.

Aedicula — Small chapel or room, usually dedicated for religious purposes.

Amphitheatrum — A circular or oval arena or theater where the rows of seats rise in tiers for better viewing.

Appiades — Water nymphs.

Apse — A semicircular recess in a wall or the semicircular end of a building. Many times the apse is vaulted.

Aqueduct — Conduit that carries water. It may be elevated or subterranean.

Ara— An altar or resting place for a deity.

Arcus — Arch.

Atrium — The entrance room or forecourt in a home. It is sometimes uncovered.

Basilica — A rectangular building, usually with aisles on each side and sometimes down the center (nave). The roof is usually supported by many columns.

Calidarium — The room in a Roman Bath that contains a pool or pools of hot water.

Carcer — Prison.

Castra — Military camp.

Cella — That part of a temple where the statues of deities are housed.

Circus — Stadium or arena used mainly for horse and chariot racing.

Clivus — An inclined roadway.

Cloaca — Sewer or drain.

Colonnade — A row of columns, usually supporting a roof.

Cryptoporticus — A covered passage.

Domus — House.

Equus — Latin term for horse; but, used in archaeology and architecture as a term for a statue with the human figure astride a horse.

Exedra — See apse.

Forum — A square that was originally a market place, but gradually the term was reserved for the area of political and religious functions. Corresponds to the Greek agora.

Frigidarium — The room in a Roman Bath that contained a pool or pools of cold water.

Horrea — Warehouse.

Horti — Plural term for garden (hortus).

Insula — An island; also, a tenement house.

Iseum — Temple dedicated to the Egyptian goddess Isis.

Lacus — Lake or pond.

Lapis — Stone.

Mercatus — Market.

Mithraeum — Temple dedicated to the god Mithras.

Mons — Hill or mound.

Murus — Wall.

Nave — A long central aisle of a basilica.

Nymphaeum — Chamber that contains plants and running water.

Obelisk — A tall slender structure hewn from rock. They originated in Egypt.

Palaestra — An exercise yard.

Peperino — Volcanic rock used as a building stone.

Peristylium — Usually an inner court of a building surrounded by a colonnade.

Podium — Raised structure upon which the Roman temple rested.

Pons — Bridge.

Porta — Gate or door.

Porticus — A covered colonnaded area running along the side or sides of a building.

Pronaos — Porch, usually in front of a temple.

Puteal — Stone curb around the mouth of a well.

Rostra — Speaker's platform.

Sacellum — Small sanctuary or chapel.

Scala — Steps or stairs.

Sepulcrum — Tomb or grave.

Serapeum — Temple dedicated to the Egyptian god Serapis.

Sudatorium — A steamy room for sweating in a Roman Bath.

Tablinum — Reception room.

Templum — Temple.

Tepidarium — Cooling down room in a Roman Bath.

Thermae — Baths.

Triclinium — Dining room.

Tufa — Volcanic rock used by the early Romans as building stone.

Via — Road or way.

Vicus — Street.

SELECT
BIBLIOGRAPHY

Select Bibliography

Amelung, Walther & Heinrich Holtzinger. *The Museums and Ruins of Rome*. London: Duckworth & Co., 1906. 2 vols.

Ashby, Thomas. *The Roman Campagna in Classical Times*. London: E. Benn, 1927.

_____. *Aqueducts of Ancient Rome*, ed. by I. A. Richmond. London: Oxford University Press, 1935.

Aurigemma, Salvatore. *Villa Adriana*. Rome: Libreria Dello Stato, 1961.

Baddeley, Welbore St. Clair. *Recent Discoveries in the Roman Forum*. New York: Macmillan, 1904.

Bagnani, Gilbert. *The Roman Campagna and its Treasures*. London: Methuen, 1929.

Banti, Luisa. *The Etruscan Cities and Their Culture*, tr. Erika Bizzarri. Berkeley: University of California Press, 1973.

Blake, Marion Elizabeth. *Ancient Roman Construction in Italy from the Prehistoric Period to Augustus, Carnegie Inst. Publ. 570*. Washington, DC: Carnegie Institution, 1947.

_____. *Roman Construction in Italy from Tiberius through the Flavians*. Washington, DC: Carnegie Institution, 1959.

_____. *Roman Construction in Italy from Nerva through the Antonines*, edited and completed by Doris Taylor Bishop, Vol. 96 of *Memoirs of the American Philosophical Society*. Philadelphia: American Philosophical Society, 1973.

Bloch, Raymond. *The Origins of Rome*. New York: F. A. Praeger, 1960.

_____. *The Etruscans*. New York: Cowles Book Co., 1969.

Boethius, Axel. *The Golden House of Nero: Some Aspects of Roman Architecture*. Ann Arbor: University of Michigan Press, 1960.

_____ & Others. *Etruscan Culture: Land and People*. New York: Columbia University Press, 1962.

Burn, Robert. *Rome and the Campagna: An Historical and Topographical Description of the Site, Buildings, and Neighborhood of Ancient Rome*. London: Bell & Daldy, 1871.

Burton-Brown, Mrs. E. *Recent Excavations in the Roman Forum, 1894-1904: A Handbook.* New York: C. Scribner's Sons, 1904.

Calza, Guido. *Ostia: Historical Guide to the Monuments,* tr. R. Weeden-Cooke. Rome: Bestetti & Tumminelli, 1926.

Coarelli, Filippo. *Rome.* New York: Madison Square Press, 1972.

_____. *Guida Archeologica di Roma.* Rome: Arnoldo Mondadori, 1974.

Cecchelli, Carlo, *Il Campidoglio.* Milan: Casa Editrice D'Arte Bestetti & Tumminelli, 1925.

Cole, J. P. *Italy: An Introductory Geography.* New York; F. A. Praeger, 1966.

Dennis, George. *Cities and Cemeteries of Etruria,* 3d ed. London: John Murray, 1883. 2 vols.

D'Onofrio, Cesare. *Castel S. Angelo.* Rome: Cassa di Risparmio di Roma, 1971.

Dudley, Donald R. *Urbs Roma: A Source Book of Classical Texts on the City & its Monuments, Selected and Translated with a Commentary.* New York: Phaidon Press, 1967.

Dyer, Thomas H. *The City of Rome: Its Vicissitudes and Monuments from its Foundation to the End of the Middle Ages, With Remarks on the Recent Excavations,* 2nd ed. London: George Bell & Sons, 1883.

Edwards, George Wharton. *Rome.* Philadelphia: Penn. Publishing Co., 1928.

Frank, Tenney. *Roman Buildings of the Republic: An Attempt to Date Them from their Materials,* Vol. III of *Papers and Monographs of the American Academy in Rome.* Rome: American Academy in Rome, 1924.

Frothingham, Arthur L. *The Monuments of Christian Rome from Constantine to the Renaissance.* New York: Macmillan, 1908.

Gjerstad, Einar. *Stratigraphical Researches in the Forum Romanum and along the Sacra Via,* Vol. I of *Early Rome.* Lund: C. W. K. Gleerup, 1953.

_____. *The Tombs,* Vol. II of *Early Rome.* Lund: C. W. K. Gleerup, 1956.

Grant, Michael. *The Roman Forum.* New York: Macmillan, 1970.

Gray, Mrs. Hamilton. *Tour to the Sepulchres of Etruria in 1839,* 2nd ed. London: J. Hatchard & Sons, 1841.

Guarducci, Margherita. *The Tomb of St. Peter,* tr. Joseph McLellan. New York: Hawthorn Books, 1960.

Hanson, John Arthur. *Roman Theatre-Temples.* Princeton, NJ: Princeton University Press, 1959.

Harrel-Courtes, Henry. *Etruscan Italy,* tr. James Hogarth. New York: Orion Press, 1964.

Hencken, Hugh. *Tarquinia, Villanovans and Early Etruscans.* Cambridge, MA: Peabody Museum of Harvard, 1968. 2 vols.

Heurgon, Jacques. *Daily Life of the Etruscans,* tr. James Kirkup. London: Weidenfeld & Nicoloson, 1964.

Hill, Ida Carleton T. *Rome of the Kings: An Archaeological Setting for Livy and Vergil.* New York: E. P. Dutton, 1925.

Homo, Leon. *Lexique de Topographie Romaine.* Paris: Libraire C. Klincksieck, 1900.

Huelsen, Christian C. F. *The Roman Forum, Its History and its Monuments,* 2d ed., tr. Jesse Benedict Carter. New York: G. E. Stechert, 1906.

——————. *The Forum and the Palatine,* tr. Helen H. Tanzer. New York: A. Bruderhausen, 1928.

Iversen, Erik. *The Obelisks of Rome,* Vol. I of *Obelisks in Exile.* Copenhagen: G. E. C. Gad, 1968.

Kirschbaum, Englebert. *The Tombs of St. Peter and St. Paul,* tr. John Murray. New York: St. Martin's Press, 1959.

Lanciani, Rodolfo. *Ancient Rome in the Light of Recent Discoveries.* Boston: Houghton Mifflin, 1882.

——————. *The Ruins and Excavations of Ancient Rome.* Boston: Houghton Mifflin, 1897.

——————. *The Destruction of Ancient Rome.* London: Macmillan, 1899.

——————. *New Tales of Old Rome.* Boston: Houghton Mifflin, 1901.

——————. *Wanderings in the Roman Campagna.* Boston: Houghton Mifflin, 1909.

——————. *The Roman Forum: A Photographic Description of its Monuments.* Rome: Frank & Co., 1910.

——————. *Wanderings Through Ancient Roman Churches.* Boston: Houghton Mifflin, 1924.

——————. *Ancient and Modern Rome.* New York: Longmans, Green, & Co., 1925.

Licht, Kjeld de Fine. *The Rotunda in Rome: A Study of Hadrian's Pantheon.* Copenhagen: Jutland Archaeological Society, 1968.

Lovell, Isabell. *Stories in Stone from the Roman Forum.* New York: Macmillan, 1902.

Lugli, Giuseppe. *I Monumenti Antichi di Roma e Suburio.* Rome: G. Bardi, 1930-38. 3 vols.

_____. *Roma Antica: Il Centro Monumentale.* Rome: G. Bardi, 1946.

_____. *The Roman Forum and the Palatine,* 4th ed., revised. Rome: G. Bardi, 1956.

_____. *Itinerario di Roma Antica.* Milan: Periodici Scientifici, 1970.

MacDonald, William L. *An Introductory Study,* Vol. I of *The Architecture of the Roman Empire,* Vol. XVII of *Yale Publications in the History of Art.* New Haven, CT: Yale University Press, 1965.

MacKendrick, Paul. *The Mute Stones Speak.* New York: St. Martin's Press, 1960.

Masson, Georgina. *The Companion Guide to Rome.* New York: Harper & Row, 1965.

Meade, C. Wade. *A Manual of Egyptian Archaeology for Students of Louisiana Tech-Rome.* Ruston: Louisiana Tech University, 1973.

Meiggs, Russell. *Roman Ostia,* 2nd ed. London: Oxford University Press, 1973.

Middleton, J. Henry. *Ancient Rome in 1888.* Edinburgh: Adam & Charles Black, 1888.

_____. *The Remains of Ancient Rome.* London: Adam & Charles Black, 1892.

Moretti, Giuseppe. *L'Ara Pacis Augustae.* Rome: La Libreria dello Stato, 1948.

Nash, Ernest. *Pictorial Dictionary of Ancient Rome,* 2nd ed. New York: F. A. Praeger, 1968. 2 vols.

Nibby, Antonio. *Roma Antica.* Rome: Tipografia delle Belle Arti, 1838-39. 2 vols.

Nichols, Francis Morgan. *The Roman Forum: A Topographical Study.* London: Longmans & Co., 1877.

_____. *The Marvels of Rome: Or a Picture of the Golden City.* London: Ellis & Elvey, 1889.

Paget, R. F. *Central Italy: An Archaeological Guide.* Park Ridge, NJ: Noyes Press, 1973.

Pallottino, Massimo. *The Etruscans,* rev. ed., tr. J. Cremona. Bloomington: Indiana University Press, 1974.

Parker, John Henry. *The Forum Romanum and Via Sacra,* Vol. II of *The Archaeology of Rome.* London: John Murray, 1876.

_____. *The Flavian Amphitheatre*, Vol. VII of *The Archaeology of Rome*. London: John Murray, 1876.

_____. *The Aqueducts of Ancient Rome*, Vol. VIII of *The Archaeology of Rome*. London: John Murray, 1876.

_____. *The Primitive Fortifications of the City of Rome*, 2nd ed., Vol. I of *The Archaeology of Rome*. London: John Murray, 1878.

_____. *The Twelve Egyptian Obelisks*, 2nd ed., Vol. IV of *The Archaeology of Rome*. London: John Murray, 1878.

_____. *Excavations in Rome, From 1438 to 1862*, Vol. VI of *The Archaeology of Rome*. London: Parker & Co., 1883.

_____. *The Via Sacra*, 2nd ed., Vol. VI of *The Archaeology of Rome*. London: Parker & Co., 1883.

Peet, Thomas E. *The Stone and Bronze Ages in Italy*. London: Oxford University Press, 1909.

Pignatorre, Theodore. *The Ancient Monuments of Rome*. London: Trefoil Publishing Co., 1932.

Platner, Samuel Bell. *A Topographical Dictionary of Ancient Rome*, rev. by Thomas Ashby. London: Oxford University Press, 1929.

Preller, Ludwig. *Die Regionen der Stadt Rom*. Jena: Carl Hochhausen, 1846.

Ramsay, William. *A Manual of Roman Antiquities*, 15th ed., rev. by R. Lanciani. New York: Charles Scribner's Sons, 1895.

Randall-MacIver, David. *The Etruscans*. London: Oxford University Press, 1927.

_____. *Italy Before the Romans*. London: Oxford University Press, 1928.

_____. *Greek Cities in Italy and Sicily*. London: Oxford University Press, 1931.

Richardson, Emeline. *The Etruscans: Their Art and Civilization*. Chicago: University of Chicago Press, 1964.

Richmond, Ian A. *The City Walls of Imperial Rome*. London: Oxford University Press, 1930.

Robathan, Dorothy M. *The Monuments of Ancient Rome*. Rome: "L'Erma" di Bretschneider, 1950.

Rodocanachi, E. *The Roman Capitol in Ancient and Modern Times*, tr. F. Lawton. London: William Heinemann, 1906.

Roullet, Anne. *The Egyptian and Egyptianizing Monuments of Imperial Rome*. Leiden: E. J. Brill, 1972.

Scherer, Margaret R. *The Marvels of Ancient Rome*. London: Phaidon, 1955.

Scullard, H. H. *The Etruscan Cities and Rome.* Ithaca, NY: Cornell University Press, 1967.

Stannard, Harold. *Rome and Her Monuments.* London: T. Fisher Unwin, 1923.

Thynne, Roger. *The Churches of Rome.* New York: E. P. Dutton, 1924.

Toynbee, Jocelyn M. C. & John Ward Perkins. *The Shrine of St. Peter and the Vatican Excavations.* London: Longmans, Green, 1956.

Valentini, Roberto & Giuseppe Zucchetti. *Codice Topografico Citta di Roma.* Rome: Tipografia del Senato, 1940-53. 4 vols.

Van Buren, Albert W. *Ancient Rome: As Revealed by Recent Discoveries.* London: Lovat Dickson, 1936.

Van Deman, Esther B. *The Building of the Roman Aqueducts, Carnegie Inst. Publ. No. 423.* Washington, DC: Carnegie Institution, 1934.

Vermaseren, M. J. & C. C. van Essen. *The Excavations of the Church of Santa Prisca in Rome.* Leiden: E. J. Brill, 1965.

Walker, Donald Smith. *A Geography of Italy.* New York: E. P. Dutton, 1958.

Wey, Francis. *Rome: Its Churches, Monuments, Art, and Antiquities.* London: William Glaisher, 1903.

INDEX

INDEX

250